A.J. CRONIN

The Man
Who Created Dr Finlay

ALAN DAVIES

ALMA BOOKS

ALMA BOOKS LTD
London House
243–253 Lower Mortlake Road
Richmond
Surrey TW9 2LL
United Kingdom
www.almabooks.com

First published by Alma Books Limited in 2011
Copyright © Alan Davies, 2011

Alan Davies asserts his moral right to be identified as the author of this work in
accordance with the Copyright, Designs and Patents Act 1988

Printed in England by MPG Books Group, Cornwall

ISBN: 978-1-84688-112-1

Contents

A.J. Cronin

*"Bright is the ring of words
when the right man rings them."*

Robert Louis Stevenson

WORKS BY A.J. CRONIN

Hatter's Castle (1931)
Three Loves (1932)
Grand Canary (1933)
The Stars Look Down (1935)
The Citadel (1937)
'Vigil in the Night' (1939)
'The Valorous Years' (1940)
Jupiter Laughs (1940)
The Keys of the Kingdom (1941)
The Green Years (1944)
Adventures of a Black Bag (1947)
Shannon's Way (1948)
The Spanish Gardener (1950)
Adventures in Two Worlds (1952)
Beyond This Place (1953)
A Thing of Beauty/Crusader's Tomb (1956)
The Northern Light (1958)
The Innkeeper's Wife (1958)
The Judas Tree (1961)
A Song of Sixpence (1964)
A Pocketful of Rye (1969)
The Minstrel Boy/Desmonde (1975)
The Lady with Carnations (1976)
Gracie Lindsay (1978)
Dr Finlay of Tannochbrae (1978)
Dr Finlay's Casebook (2010)

FICTIONAL PLACE NAMES

Cronin used fictional names in his novels which can easily be traced to real-life equivalents to help readers place towns with geographical accuracy.

Ardbeg	equals	Rhu
Ardencaple		Cardross
Ardfillan		Helensburgh
Darroch		Alexandria
Levenford		Dumbarton
Overton		Clydebank
Portdoran		Greenock
Ralston		Paisley
Winton		Glasgow

Introduction

My regard for A.J. Cronin's writing evolved haphazardly, almost subconsciously, with no outside stimulus. Nowadays I read only what appeals to me, and my appreciation and judgement of a book is free from any extraneous influences. I rate Cronin as an author alongside most of the great names in English literature, even though he is largely ignored in Britain. This biography, however, arose only partially from my appreciation of his work. The overwhelming impulse was to learn more about the man behind the stories, to discover what sort of man, by the simple use of words, could strike such chords deep within me, honing my senses to razor sharpness and expertly exposing the full range of my emotions: in turn, anger, despair and joy.

I was surprised to discover that only one biography existed, a 1985 American publication, *A.J. Cronin*, written by Dale Salwak, a professor of English literature in southern California's Citrus College. That, however, turned out to be heavily weighted towards a literary critique of Cronin's work rather than an account of the man and his times. Professor Salwak himself, in fact, recognized the need for further investigation: "There remain to be studied, however... the relationship between his life and his works... his devotion to Catholicism and social justice..."[1]

Cronin, sometimes referred to as "Rufus" by members of his family because of his hair colour, was just over six feet tall, with an athletic build. His wife, on seeing him for the first time, described him as lanky. He had greenish eyes, and was softly spoken with, surprisingly, little trace of a Scottish accent, though he could "put on" the brogue when it suited him, and he did so in the many speeches he was called upon to deliver in his illustrious career. He was a quiet, shy man, though a touch of innocent Irish devilry, inherited from his father, was always engaging in close company. It was the Irishness in his character that his wife loved best. Alexandra

Cronin, his granddaughter – recalling conversations with her father Andrew, Cronin's youngest son, and her mother Anne – recalls that he was spoken of as a "charmer and very social", the kind of person people were naturally drawn to at parties. According to her parents, she said, he was quite a ham who easily could have become an actor.

He was, also, a keen all-round sportsman who particularly loved football – described by an old schoolfriend as the best left-winger Dumbarton Academy ever had. As a lad he was a Dumbarton supporter, and later, when he moved south, followed Chelsea, always refusing VIP treatment and preferring to watch from the terraces, mixing easily with other fans. He played cricket for the local team when he lived in Storrington in Sussex and turned out regularly for charity matches in the Richmond area when he lived in London. Also a keen salmon fisherman, he enjoyed fishing holidays (especially in Ireland), as well as using every opportunity in his extensive travels around the world to pursue that passion. He and his wife were also avid golfers. In Switzerland both belonged to the Lucerne Golf Club. His handicap of three suggests he was either naturally gifted or spent more time on the fairways than at his desk.

Unlike many in his profession, his life was free of scandal, and it was only his fame and fortune that prevented the description "ordinary". After a few unsatisfactory skirmishes early in his writing career, he developed an almost phobic dread of the press, resulting in a near-monastic silence. He neither sought nor encouraged celebrity status, unless it was to his obvious advantage. Significantly, he neither denied the easy narrative of an underprivileged boy's fairy-tale rise to fame and fortune, nor allowed too close an examination. He was purposely secretive, jealously guarding details of his life, his family and his personality from an inquisitive world audience. In interviews and books, it suited him to peddle half-truths, allowing the natural enthusiasm of reporters and critics to fill in the blanks, usually with exaggerated invention. Thus, from *The Citadel* and *Adventures in Two Worlds*, which both tell the story of a young doctor practising in the valleys of South Wales, critics and readers alike have wrongly assumed that the narrative relates to real events, and have concluded that Cronin himself performed heroically as single-handedly he contained a cholera epidemic, brought babies back from the dead, witnessed mine disasters and rockfalls, performed amputations and tracheotomies *in extremis* and, most famously, joined a thriving west Highlands country practice as an assistant to a cranky old GP.

Of course it is possible that Cronin did not want to be remembered after his death. For a man who enjoyed such a high profile during his lifetime there is precious little original material to help a biographer. There is a full collection of manuscripts of his published works and a quantity of unpublished material, mostly short stories, notes and schemes for work that came to nothing, but few personal insights into his private world. He was a man without vanity who tended to shun publicity, which might account for the paucity of archived material, such as private letters, articles or newspaper cuttings. It is even possible that, unlike other famous personalities who assiduously hoard for posterity's sake, he deliberately destroyed personal papers. His fame (and fortune) is a matter of record, so he and his family, during his life and after his death, cannot have been unaware of the public interest in him, yet the silence surrounding him still frustrates those who are interested in him and his work. During the later stages of his writing career, he may have harboured resentment, even bitterness, at his exclusion from the literary canon of his time. He was unquestionably disillusioned with post-war society, and there is every reason to believe that he felt alienated from Britain after his move to America in 1939. Wherever the truth lies, the fact remains that the lack of data, his natural reserve, his deep suspicion of the press and his incessant wanderings abroad have not helped the biographer's cause.

However, the lack of information about's Cronin's life has not prevented – indeed, may even have encouraged – much supposition and invention about the man, which transmitted from one observer to the next have led to many apocryphal stories. Passing references and thumbnail biographical sketches from newspapers and magazines abound with inconsistencies and exaggerations, further exacerbated by his publishers, who consistently proclaimed that *Adventures in Two Worlds*, published in 1952, was either an autobiography or an autobiographical novel. Other books, particularly *The Citadel*, *The Green Years* and *A Song of Sixpence*, were also described as "strongly autobiographical". It is surely not pedantry to resist the implication behind the term "autobio-graphical" in any novel, when a more accurate description might be "fictional reminiscence".

Writers, of course, draw inspiration from their own experiences of life. These are then moulded, through inventiveness and creativity, into characters and plot. In this regard, Cronin used factual "coat hangers" – people and places – more openly than most writers, especially in some of his later novels. It is vital, therefore, that all claims about Cronin's life are examined to establish whether they derive from evidence, from the balance of probability in relation to human behaviour, or whether they have simply been taken uncritically from the text of his books.

Right up to his death Cronin was well aware of his failure to pro-vide a full-blown, properly documented autobiography. But one summer's day in June 1976, in his lovely mountain home, Champ-Riond, in Baugy Sur Clarens near Montreux, Switzerland, he was particularly sad because "that bloody reporter yesterday" reminded him that he would be eighty the following month. Clearly in a re-flective mood, possibly even a little maudlin, the omens were not good. His secretary and lifelong companion, Nan, told him that she had already bought his birthday present, to which he replied: "It's the last you'll ever give me." She retorted: "Then why did Dr Keller say you were good for another ten years?" She further upbraided him for his ill humour as he reflected too morbidly on old age and the passing of time. The remedy for his melancholy, she suggested, was some good hard work, and she felt that an autobiography would fit the bill. He countered with the amazing assertion that it would be "a sad and sordid story" and that she might be upset to type it. She protested that she knew him well enough not to be, but he insisted that even she did not know the whole truth of his life. She persisted: "Then let's have the whole truth and nothing but the truth… that would be a real book! Better than those little magazine stories you've been doing lately." Nan's coaxing supplied the motivation he had previously lacked, and the work went ahead, but she was never called upon to type it and it is not known if she ever saw the finished article – which probably turned out to be very different from her expectations – or if he ever had any intention of publishing it.

This particular narrative occupies one of nine cheap notebooks, all purchased in Montreux, almost certainly at the same time, and presumably after he moved to Switzerland in 1955. Because of the reference to his eightieth birthday, it must have been written in 1976, and therefore, throughout this book, it will be referred to as the "1976 autobiography" in order to distinguish it from references to unpublished data or documents which are often quoted from the other eight notebooks.

The 1976 autobiography opens with the word "Preface" at the top of the first page, followed by a short introduction:

> I am reclining on the terrace of my Swiss country house, surrounded by new-mown lawns, great masses of roses and peonies in bloom, tall magnificent trees that screen three sides, leaving only the incomparable view of the lake of Geneva far below...

Such a conventionally lyrical opening may seem to promise a fairy tale, possibly the story of a relatively poor and underprivileged lad who, against all the odds, reaches the dizzy heights of literary fame and fortune. In fact, it turns out to be a barren account of one aspect of his life – his courtship and marriage to May Gibson and part of their subsequent life together – which, if published and authenticated, would have had a shattering impact on his faithful readership. It deals with specific times and issues in his life of a very private nature in relation to his marriage, women and Nan herself, and this may explain why he was not prepared to entrust his memories to his son Vincent – himself an accomplished biographer. For a writer who sought earnestly to represent truth in his novels, it is a shame that his own life should be anything but crystal-clear.

There is no doubt that the trail to understanding Cronin has gone cold, and the longer the path remains untrodden the greater the mystery will become. He was in many ways his own executioner. His self-effacing nature discouraged a biography during his lifetime, and without an autobiography – with the exception of the unpublished fragment described above – many of the details of his life and personality have already been lost for ever. Unfortunately, much of what has been written collapses under close scrutiny, revealing that the ordinary has consistently been exaggerated, presumably to make up for the lack of substance, while that which needed thorough investigation has been ignored. Throughout this book, for those very reasons, readers will find numerous challenges to accepted opinion.

It is an altogether unsatisfactory situation compared to other British writers of arguably no greater literary ability. Choosing at random, there are, for example, two recent D.H. Lawrence biographies, as well as a D.H. Lawrence Research Centre at the University of Nottingham. Evelyn Waugh boasts three biographies, in addition to his own published diaries. Frank Swinnerton's *Arnold Bennett 1867–1931*, as well as the existence of an Arnold Bennett Society, assures that writer of immortality. Graham Greene even appointed his own official biographer, Norman Sherry, and to assist his perpetuity there is the Graham Greene Birthplace Trust complete with a Treasurer, a Trust Office and a Newsletter Editor. Many of the books by the writers mentioned above were adapted for the screen, which can only have helped to popularize them, but so were Cronin's. Who did not watch *Dr Finlay's Casebook* in the 1960s? That television series became so popular that when, after his own stories were used up, he threatened to end it rather than use scriptwriters, there was what amounted to a national outcry. Though he had never seen the serial, he was astonished by the affection that the public felt for it, and so he relented, allowing its continuation. However, if you try to buy a Cronin title from any leading British bookseller today, you will fail, while the books of his aforementioned contemporaries are readily available. Except by special arrangement, the same is true of the average provincial British library. Cronin has disappeared from the British psyche. Yet in an ordinary library in Greenwich, Maine, there are Cronin titles to be found on the shelves. Professor Salwak recognized the problem:

> Throughout Cronin's career there has been a wide divergence of opinion about the man and his work – ranging from praise to derision. Few readers on either side of the Atlantic reacted to his work with indifference... and yet though his novels have sold in the millions and were handsomely adapted to the cinema, they are a topic strangely neglected by academic criticism...[2]

Salwak was not alone in his view. Preceding him by some thirty years, Alexander Reid, in a 1953 article, 'The Story of a Best-Seller', commented: "In surveys of Scottish writing over the last forty years the name of A.J. Cronin is often omitted. One reason for the omission is the fact that Dr Cronin severed his connection with Scotland early in life... another is that critical snobbery... writes off all best-selling novels as outside the field of serious criticism..."[3] In the Thirties and Forties Cronin straddled the world of popular fiction like a colossus, outselling most of his contemporaries with ease, yet his popularity earned him few plaudits among the upper echelons of critical reviewers. The *Times* obituary of January 1981, though applauding much of his work, insisted that "his was middle-brow fiction of the most adroit and telling kind..." Too often reviews implied a lack of literary gravitas, reserving profounder recognition for others.

Nor could Cronin look to his lifestyle to augment his literary reputation. As has been discussed, throughout his long career he shunned the limelight, evaded notoriety and, despite the manifold opportunities provided by his great wealth, his seclusive nature became the determining factor in a somewhat ordinary, uneventful life. In September 1931 he confided to Rev. McClelland, the minister of Trinity Church in Glasgow – who was, at the time, arranging a lecture to the Trinity Literary Society and who later became a close acquaintance – that "to be provincial and bourgeois in these days of complexes and cocktail parties is a crime which is hard to live down. But I shall gang my ain gate..." Clearly, it was nature, not polite society, that stirred Cronin's soul. His wife once explained to an American audience the shared beauties of the South Wales valleys, away from the dirt and degradation of the mines:

Many sunny days came that winter, and there was a wild beauty on the high bare heath which stretched far and away above The Glen. A breeze always blew there, intoxicating as wine, which made my husband quote Walt Whitman – "there's a wind on the heath when I feel it on my cheek I want to live for ever". For miles under the racing clouds we would be lost in the exhilarating vastness in this primitive moorland, cut only by a few sheep tracks...[4]

Graham Greene, a contemporary of Cronin, is but one example of a writer whose background and connections have had a considerable, and possibly disproportionate, impact on his reputation. Privileged by birth, worldly, influential and self-absorbed, he had, throughout his lifetime, an eye to posterity. The weight of tributes accorded him was considerable. The *New York Times* obituary protested that the fact "that Mr Greene never received the Nobel Prize in Literature was a source of regret and astonishment to many readers and professionals". Public recognition was equally unbounded with two awards: the prestigious Companion of Honour and the Order of Merit.

The argument could be widened to include the modernist movement of the early twentieth century, which owed its acceptance in serious literary circles as much to its connections in wider society and its outrageous, hell-raising behaviour as to its literary value, while in the world of modern art, outrageousness seemed to have been a prime requirement. Outside its artistic boundaries, the wider movement simply grew too big to ignore, yet its appeal was marginal. Cronin once commented that "the modern tendency towards deliberate obscurity and abstraction is surely an affectation which must pass..."[5] Except as prescribed reading for students, how many people would reach for a Gertrude Stein novel to curl up with for a fireside read on a cold winter's evening? Conversely, the conventional structure and easy style of Cronin's books never hid the message within. That was not accidental. He steadfastly maintained that "in most ages great art has been simple and intelligible".[6]

As a traditionalist in the mould of writers such as Dickens, Bennett and Hardy, he deplored the modernist movement, made up of writers who went out of their way to reject the writing conventions of the great nineteenth-century authors. Cronin was vocal in his criticism of writers like T.S. Eliot, James Joyce and Virginia Woolf – the darling of the Bloomsbury Group, a coterie of well-heeled, unconventional thinkers encompassing many of London's avant-garde literary circles in the first few decades of the twentieth century. Their writing style purposely avoided the traditional requirement to tell a story in which true-to-life characters represent reality as it is, choosing instead to replace conventional narrative with radical new techniques such as "stream of consciousness", wherein the conscious mind is suspended, allowing the unconscious free rein to follow wherever it leads – more often than not producing obscure language and personal fantasies that to many were unintelligible.

In a speech to a literary gathering before the Second World War, Cronin chose to highlight this tendency by quoting at random from one of Gertrude Stein's books: "Tails, cold pails, cold with joy, no joy. A tiny seat that means meadows and a lapse of cuddles with cheese and nearly bats all messed. The post placed a loud loose sprain. A rest is no better. It is better yet. All the time..." Modernism found inspiration in the teachings of the new science of psychoanalysis, expounded by William James, Sigmund Freud and others: a science not in itself unhelpful to the problems of humanity, but in Cronin's judgement it had "a pernicious effect on fiction because it offers easy cuts to psychological profundity... to stress all the moments in life which are hectic and abnormal... but the novel is not a psychopathic ward, nor should the novelist draw from the casebook of the neurologist... his field is the normal... surely, literature is the mouthpiece of the humanities, not the insanities. It is to me, at least, a matter of amazement that such writing is tolerated, let alone revered. There always has been, of course, respect for the unintelligible in every art. To a certain mentality what cannot be understood must be fine: obscurity is the synonym for genius. But to others, myself amongst them, this thing is intricate, pitch-dark rigmarole..."

Proponents of the modernist school would probably have argued that Cronin was almost congenitally predisposed against them, considering the relative disparity in their backgrounds. Most of the modernists, whether in London or Paris, came from affluent families, never had to struggle for anything and almost naturally turned to experimenting with extreme forms of artistic expression and behaviour to avoid the boredom of conformity. Cronin was the opposite – once a struggling Scottish lad on the wrong side of a religious divide, with only a grandfather, a fanatically devoted mother and his own native wit and intelligence to help him.

Cronin suggested that writers of the modern school would always fail because they wrote only "clever little novels... the cocktails and sandwiches of fiction", whereas the major novelist succeeds "because, for the purpose of his art at least, he is taken in at every turn of life, by the hopes and fears, the joy and sorrow of all manner of fellow creatures" and has the power to convey a sense of passionate reality. He ardently praised those writers he admired: Arnold Bennett, John Galsworthy, Somerset Maugham, Francis Brett Young and H.G. Wells – all of whom had reached the pinnacle of their profession, and never "ceased to lay hands on life" – at the same time suggesting, with all due humility, that there was perhaps another ("modesty forbids me to mention") who might be included in their ranks. His speech clearly demonstrated his awareness not only of the pecking order in the world of letters, but also his undoubted aspirations to join those who had already achieved literary greatness. At that point in his life, just before his move to America, Cronin's ambition for greatness seems indisputable.

It is to be expected that the fortunes of most writers fade after death, but Cronin's demise, particularly in Britain, was swifter and longer-lasting than those of contemporaries of no greater ability. Towards the end of his writing career Cronin struggled to find fresh inspiration for his work, and his reputation suffered accordingly. A few critics scorned his efforts, but most, sympathetically, damned him with faint praise. The *Times Literary Supplement* of 23rd October 1948, in a review of *Shannon's Way*, commented: "Dr Cronin's new novel is reminiscent of nothing so much as the act of a once-promising variety artist whose performance has staled with repetition." Nevertheless, failing to hit the heights with every new book over such a long career does not explain the disregard of his greatest works. It seems that once the popular readership waned, there was no secondary source of interest – like prescribed reading in academic institutions – to support the publication of his books. Yet, in researching this book, my visits to his homeland strongly suggested to me that there was no shortage of interest in the man and his books, making it even more difficult to understand why aspiring biographers, during his lifetime, chose to ignore him. The field was empty for them to occupy, and the grass was fresh. Perhaps they did not dig deeply enough to discover that the quiet, conventional Cronin was not all he was considered to be. His relationship with his publishers was often stormy, and his marriage, outwardly normal, was unusual by any standards.

When Cronin finally turned his back on medicine, his introduction to the world of letters had a fairy-tale quality. His books sold in millions across the globe, and many were made into films. If one adopts a commercial, free-market principle, you would conclude that nobody is interested in reading his books, nor in reading about him. While such an explanation might satisfy a conference of economists, it is simply not good enough to explain the indifference surrounding A.J. Cronin.

Sadly, there is worse to follow. Visit his birthplace, and it is as if he never existed. Move four miles east to Dumbarton, where he lived and excelled in his secondary school, and which he used as background for many of his novels, and the only trace of his existence is to be found in the most unlikely setting. In the boardroom of the Dumbarton Football Club, framed and displayed on the wall, is a copy of this letter from Cronin to the secretary of the Club, written on 18th April 1972:

> ...may I say that I should be very pleased if you would care to use my few remarks on Dumbarton Football Club in your Centenary Brochure.
>
> I can assure you that there is no more fervent supporter of the Dumbarton FC than myself, since as a small boy, living down the road from Boghead Park, I spent my Saturday three pennies, not in sweets, for which I was always hungry, but as the entrance fee to the football ground – a real sacrifice in these days when a threepenny bit meant something! Sometimes, on a very wet day, when I went early to the ground, and took part in pailing off the various puddles thereon, I was allowed to stay for the game without payment. I remember many of the players, in particular the great Finlay Speedie, and also many of the games, particularly a Cup Tie with Celtic, which then had the famous Jimmie Quinn at centre forward and "Sonny Jim" at centre half. Celtic scored first, but Dumbarton equalized, to the wild elation of the crowd, which included myself... Unfortunately, Celtic scored another goal later on, to which we all agree they were not entitled. If ever I should be in Dumbarton again I shall certainly pay a visit to Boghead Park. Even here in Switzerland I tune in every Saturday evening to get Dumbarton's score on the BBC Sports programme.

I cannot help feeling that it is a sad day when part of the cultural heritage of the town is only safe in the hands of the local football team. It is also perplexing, because Scotland itself – a small, proud country – is well known for revering its famous sons and daughters. It has been said that, not having an over-abundance of natural resources, the one commodity it had plenty of was talent, and that it exported it to all corners of the earth. Yet Cronin is steadfastly ignored. Other writers – Burns, Scott and Stevenson – are now part of Scottish folklore. There is never a shortage of anecdotes about the charismatic Burns. Ironically, in his meanderings, he visited Cronin's home town of Dumbarton, as a passage from a letter to his friend John Richmond explains: "I have lately been rambling over by Dumbarton and Inverary, and running a drunken race on the side of Loch Lomond with a wild Highlandman…" The upshot of the race was that they collided, fell off their horses, and Burns "got such a skinful of bruises and wounds that I shall be at least four weeks before I dare venture on my journey to Edinburgh".[7] But the drunken, bruised and womanizing Burns eventually made it to Dumbarton, though one can only guess at the state he was in when he arrived. Nevertheless, the elders of the town made him a freeman of the burgh. Doubtless it is impossible for the sober, conventional Cronin to match the romantic, swashbuckling activities of the charismatic poet. All he can offer is a ride on a borrowed motorcycle along the banks of the loch, on a beautiful, blue-skied summer's day, with his greatest and only love astride the pillion, her arms tightly enclosing his body and her auburn hair flowing in the wind. It may not have quite the ring of the Burns episode, but even so it leaves the matter of the level of recognition open to question.

Robert Louis Stevenson, another restless spirit, has always been close to Scottish hearts. He flouted convention, rejected the sanctimonious narrow-mindedness of nineteenth-century Calvinism and moved to France, where he met his future wife, before moving on to America and eventually ending up in Samoa. But it was not simply heroic adventurousness that made their sons so dear to the hearts of Scottish people. Walter Scott, a lawyer and conventional Scotsman, more in the Cronin mould, is also highly regarded in Scottish literary circles, and even has a railway station – Waverley in Edinburgh – named after one of his novels, together with a monument in Princes Street.

Yet in my own journeys around the localities where Cronin lived and studied, I can report a very vibrant and healthy interest in him. In Cardross I stopped a couple in the street to enquire the whereabouts of his birthplace, and within half an hour I was

ensconced in the living room of the ex-vicar and his wife. A couple
of phone calls later I was able to view the cottage in which he was
born, as well as the house that the Cronins later occupied. An hour
after that I was in another living room – this time in the company
of the current vicar and his wife – discussing other aspects of
Cronin's life and works. Then, on another visit, members of the
golf club showered me with email addresses and telephone numbers
of people who would, they were sure, know something special and
exclusive about Cronin the man, as opposed to Cronin the writer.
In Dumbarton itself, on a similar mission, a chance meeting in
the street with a second- or third-generation Irish Scot who, like
Cronin and Cronin's parents, was himself in a mixed marriage – as
well as the product of a mixed marriage – led to a guided tour of
Cronin's haunts, after which I was deposited with a retired local-
newspaper editor – yet another settee in yet another living room
– who sharpened my ideas of how to proceed with my research.
Later still, my presence in Dumbarton Library soon got around,
and complete strangers wished me luck and promised to buy the
book if it ever got published. In response to newspaper adverts
people corresponded, offering what little they knew. In western
Scotland, at least, I have witnessed, and can report, a healthy and
genuine interest in Cronin among ordinary Scottish folk.

Why public officials, whose occupation is to promote Scottishness
and Scottish achievements, have consistently ignored Cronin is
incomprehensible to me. It is not as if there was uncertainty
about his roots. In Cardross, the house in which he was born
still stands, as does the house his parents later occupied. The
building housing the Cronins' Helensburgh flat still exists, along
with Willowbrook in Round Riding Road, Dumbarton, his
grandfather's house and home to Cronin and his mother during
his formative school years. The original Dumbarton Academy
building, now no longer a school, still proudly commands a
place of importance on Church Street, and St Aloysius' College
in Garnethill is an even more impressive organization than in the
early years of the century, when Cronin was winning recognition
for his English essays.

It is not a case, therefore, of the area lacking wall space to erect
a plaque, or not being sure where to place it, any more than there
is a shortage of library or reading rooms that would comfortably

accommodate his name over the door. It is true that after gradu-
ation he left Scotland, but he did not turn his back on his country.
On the contrary, one of the main literary criticisms in this book is
that he spent too much time reminiscing about Scotland and the
problems of growing up in a sectarian environment at the expense
of wider issues. Western Scotland was in his blood, like the souls of
his most memorable characters – James Brodie in *Hatter's Castle*,
Lucy Moore in *Three Loves*, Andrew Manson in *The Citadel*,
Father Chisholm in *The Keys of the Kingdom*, Robert Shannon in
The Green Years, Gracie Lindsay and David Moray in *The Judas
Tree* and, last but not least, Dr Finlay.

His characters exported Scotland to every corner of the civilized
world. The least he deserves, in acknowledgement of his considerable achievements, is some public recognition, as a token of the
nation's favour. In the world of letters, even today, the human
impact of some of Cronin's work would undoubtedly complement
any study of modern social history, and that alone, quite apart
from his obvious narrative powers, should guarantee him a place
in twentieth-century British literature.

Many references have been made to Cronin's humanism and
social realism, obliquely suggestive of a latter-day working-class
champion. Born in Victorian Scotland, his life ran parallel with
the radical reforming movements of the twentieth century which
brought freedom and equality to previously dispossessed sections
of society, including his own. Almost genetically liberal, he was,
nevertheless, no espouser of causes. His ecumenical instincts, perversely co-existing with an uncompromising faith in the Catholic
Church, depicted humanity in its broadest sense, providing the
canvas on which he sought to make his mark, both as an impartial
observer and an explorer of the human conscience. He both loved
and despised the human condition – cruelty and love, poverty and
riches, ignorance and sophistication, failure and success – and he
grappled frustratedly to understand the implications of both sides
of the equation. To that end, he was always resolutely prepared to
question and judge life's experiences in a never-ending search for
truth. In the end, his place in the pantheon of British literature
rests delicately on the vagaries of chance: "Many are called, but
few are chosen."[8]

Chapter One

It is necessary to go back to the generation of Cronin's great-grandparents to understand the man himself, as well as to appreciate the meaning of certain key references in some of his books and unravel many of the claims made about his life and personality. In the early- to mid-nineteenth century, the main characters in the Cronin story were drawn to western Scotland from a wide area of the British Isles – County Armagh in Ireland, Edinburgh and Berwick-upon-Tweed in England – eventually converging on Glasgow, where the skilled and industrious could always find work. As a result, Cronin's genetic make-up was half Irish, three-eighths Scottish and one-eighth English.

On the paternal side, his grandfather Owen and his grandmother Bridget (née McShane), both staunch Catholics and founders of the Scottish dynasty – if that is not too grand a term – were born in Ireland in about 1826 and 1832 respectively. Owen Cronin's origins have not been verified, since his parents never left Ireland. However, his wife's parents – McShane and Smith – are known to have hailed from Annaghmore in County Armagh.[1] It is not known if Owen was from the same region, nor if he and Bridget McShane knew each other before emigrating to Scotland. Owen's surname, however, when he arrived in Scotland in about 1850, was Cronague, changed to Cronin in 1870. He married Bridget McShane in Eastwood, Renfrewshire, in January 1851.[2]

Their first child, James, was born in Glasgow in about 1854, and sometime after that date, but before 1861, the Cronagues set up business in Alexandria, north of Dumbarton. Initially hawkers – another name for rag-and-bone men – they were later described as "glass and china merchants" as they became more sophisticated and affluent. In that area they raised a further eight children, and in 1881 the entire family comprised:

James	25 years	Clerk, later Publican
Mary	23 years	Dressmaker
Ann	19 years	Yarn Picker
Joseph	18 years	Cabinet Maker
Thomas	16 years	Emigrated to USA
Patrick	13 years	Scholar, later Salesman [A.J.'s father]
Francis	11 years	Scholar, later RC Priest
Edward	9 years	Scholar, later Wine Merchant
Margaret	5 years	Scholar, later Housekeeper

By 1891, the date of the next census, only three children were at home: Patrick – later to marry Jessie Montgomerie – Edward and Margaret. Frustratingly, Owen Cronin disappeared from official Scottish records after 1891. However, though a precise date cannot be found for his death – suggesting he may have returned to Ireland – it is known that he predeceased his wife Bridget, who died of heart disease in 1894. It is significant that neither of Cronin's Irish grandparents lived to see their son Patrick marry, nor did they meet or directly influence A.J., Patrick's one and only child.

Much has been written about the Irish Catholic invasion of Scotland and the subsequent sectarianism, bigotry and racial conflict – sadly, not always objectively. When they decided to uproot in the mid-1800s, the Cronins would have been just two more unfortunate souls swelling the vast army of emigrants to the west coast of Scotland. Some made the move to better themselves – greater opportunities, higher wages, steady employment. Others, less welcome, moved for reasons of self-preservation. They had nothing and hoped to find something. Unfortunately, for the latter category, too often the "parish" beckoned – public assistance doled out by Poor Law Guardians or, in extreme cases, the workhouse. The Cronins, clearly able to look after themselves and intent on integration, as is evidenced by their change of name, belonged to the former group. As an attempt to gain acceptance by the host nation, a change of name was not an uncommon practice: other examples would have been changing from Seamus to James or dropping the "O" from the Irish surname.

It is, however, often forgotten that at certain stages in Scotland's industrialization Irish labour was vital, especially the "navvy" who dug their canals and roads and laid their railways. There was a saying in the Irish community that "Paddy sows what Sandy reaps". But that was only part of the picture. In the coal industry in particular the presence of migrant workers had the effect of depressing wages, weakening trade-union support and breaking strikes. It was hardly surprising, therefore, that real animosity ensued on economic as well as racial grounds. Perversely, the truth behind these issues is irrelevant, because it is perception that drives prejudice, not reality. It is difficult to appreciate accurately the conditions of those times and the attitudes of the opposing cultural factions.

There are brief references to racial prejudice in Cronin's first two books, in the characteristic venom of James Brodie against his daughter's Irish lover in *Hatter's Castle* and again, perhaps more reflectively, by Richard Murray, Lucy's somewhat sanctimonious and stuffed-shirt brother in *Three Loves*, on her impending marriage to Frank, an Irish immigrant:

> They came to Scotland, these Irish, to beget their prolific progeny, a mongrel breed; supplying chiefly the navvy and the labourer, or in its higher flights, the bookmaker and the publican; a race unwanted, and uncouth.[3]

But, if there was even a grain of truth in the myth of the feckless Irish, it did not apply to the Cronin family, whose children all went to school and were in employment at the time of the censuses, if they were of working age. They were, therefore, responsible citizens and industrious by nature. Indeed, in their day they would have been described as a go-ahead family. Owen, the patriarch, was a china-and-glass merchant, a dealer in rags and skins, and a hawker, to whom the old Yorkshire saying – where there's muck there's brass – certainly applied. The historian J.E. Handley makes a more general point that fits Owen perfectly: "By way of huckstering, hawking and dealing in rags, bones, metals and old clothes, many of them rose from the wage-earning class to comparative prosperity. For some, indeed, the old clothes trade... provided a competence beyond the reach of shopkeepers engaged in more conventional businesses."[4]

James, the first-born, started adult life as a clerk in the Turkey Red Dye Works, but around 1890 turned to the wine-and-spirit trade. "Cronin's Pub" subsequently became a thriving institution in the Vale of Leven, and it is possible that many years later James may have used his comparative wealth (discussed in more detail later) to help the young Cronin at a critical point in his career.

By contrast, Cronin met and lived with his two maternal grandparents and three of his great-grandparents in Dumbarton. His great-grandfather, Robert, head of the Montgomerie family in western Scotland, was born in Kilmaurs, Ayrshire, in about 1818, a rural area of the Scottish Lowlands, about twenty miles south-west of Glasgow. By trade a shoemaker, he and his wife Ann raised five children in Kilmaurs before moving to Oxford Street in the Gorbals district of Glasgow, where they appear in the 1871 census with five children. Their oldest child Archibald, Cronin's grandfather, twenty-four years old at the time, was described as a journeyman hatter (the same profession as that of the character often considered to be Archibald's fictional alter ego, James Brodie in *Hatter's Castle*). It is difficult to be precise about the meaning of the term "journeyman", but it suggests that he was employed by a hatter to sell his wares. Archibald Montgomerie married Margaret Perry, from Edinburgh, in 1872, and by the time of the 1881 census they had moved from London Road in Glasgow to Dumbarton with four of their eventual seven children. The second of these children was Jessie, A.J.'s mother. They took up residence in the recently built Levengrove Terrace across the river from the High Street, where in 1877, at number 145, Archibald established himself in business as a hatter and hosier, taking on a partner – a certain Donald MacLeod – in 1885. They remained in Dumbarton until his death in 1912, but changed houses twice – firstly moving to 1 Allan Place, the first property in a row of stone-built terraced houses (now demolished), some time before 1890, and then after 1906 to Willowbrook, the last house on the right-hand side before Boghead Farm, in what was then Cemetery Road, changed later to its present name of Round Riding Road. At the time the house, a substantial semi-detached red-sandstone property, would have been surrounded by fields, with views to the north of the Kilpatrick Hills, heights that enclose the south-eastern shore of Loch Lomond. As well as moving some time between 1885 and 1900, Archibald gave up his hatter's business and took up a position as a commercial clerk in Denny's shipyard.

Cronin's other great-grandparents were his grandmother's father, Francis Perry, a journeyman blacksmith from Berwick-upon-Tweed, and his wife Jessie, born in Edinburgh. They had lived for a time with her parents in Edinburgh before moving with their family to Dover Street in Glasgow, on the opposite bank of the Clyde from the Montgomeries. In the fullness of time, Cronin's grandfather, Archibald Montgomerie, offered all three great-grandparents a home, first at 1 Allan Place and then at Willowbrook, where Cronin became acquainted with them.

Over a period of forty to fifty years, therefore, the two families first made for Glasgow and then branched out to the outlying town of Dumbarton, home of the Montgomeries, and the Vale of Leven, home of the Cronins. Both places stand roughly adjacent with the River Leven, not far from its confluence with the Clyde, about fifteen miles downstream from Glasgow. From the early 1700s to the mid-1800s Dumbarton's chief occupation was glassmaking. Following its decline, the greatest impetus to the development of the town was shipbuilding and marine engineering, both becoming synonymous with the Clyde for a hundred years or more, during which time all kinds of ships came out of its yards, as well as aeroplanes and hovercraft. Even the first helicopter was constructed in one of the shipyards in 1909 – when Cronin was a pupil at the Academy. William Denny and Brothers, where Archibald Montgomerie worked as a shipyard clerk, was the last surviving shipyard, eventually closing in 1963. Before the final demise of the shipbuilding industry, Dumbarton fast became a centre for whisky production, but this too did not last, falling foul of takeovers by international conglomerates. With its decline, Dumbarton has increasingly become a commuter town for Glasgow.

Incredibly, after such a long and involved journey for the two families, the immigrant, industrious, Catholic Cronins and the sober, conventional, Presbyterian Montgomeries finally settled less than two miles apart in an area of land about three miles north of the River Clyde, and one cannot help wondering if they were aware of each other before the intended marriage between Patrick and Jessie, Cronin's father and mother – a marriage that was across the religious divide – rocked both households. Dumbarton and the

Vale of Leven were small communities in the 1890s, in which any whiff of scandal would have raged like a forest fire.

Crucial to an understanding of Cronin's childhood is the courtship and marriage of his parents – emotively referred to as a "mixed marriage", i.e. between a Catholic and a Protestant – and the subsequent family conflicts. There are many assumptions about the reactions to the marriage, but no facts. In general terms, at that time in history, marriages "across the divide" caused problems within families, the severity of the difficulty depending on the innate bigotry of the individuals concerned. All that is known of Patrick Cronin's marriage to Jessie Montgomerie comes from an unpublished account of their meeting and brief courtship written by Cronin, and the several references in Cronin's novel *A Song of Sixpence*.[5] From the unpublished account we learn that Jessie, his mother, was a Montgomerie, spelt, according to her father, not with the corrupt and plebeian "y", but with "ie" – a name that shone through the pages of *Debrett's* and the annals of history. It seems undeniable that Archibald Montgomerie was proud of his name and ancestry, although he lived humbly in a small villa on the outskirts of Levenford – in reality, Dumbarton (Cronin used fake place names in these real-life accounts just as he often did in his novels). Not only did he love his daughter, but he was immensely, perhaps inordinately proud of her, treasuring her as his very own. In the mornings he liked to walk with Jessie to Dumbarton Station, where their paths separated: he took the train to work, while she walked to Dumbarton Academy, where she worked as a pupil teacher. At the end of her day it was her habit to buy the *Scotsman* for her father, but on one occasion, sometime before her eighteenth birthday, that particular newspaper had not been delivered. Miss Duthie, the shop assistant, was most apologetic – at which point a young man, who had just got off the train from Glasgow, overheard the conversation and offered Jessie his copy. He was none other than Patrick Cronin, described by Jessie as "distressingly handsome, with a fair complexion, eyes of light hazel and well-brushed, reddish-brown hair that exactly matched his suit".

After the customary pleasantries came the introductions, which Patrick felt required some explanation:

"My name may shock you, Miss Montgomerie. I am Patrick Cronin."

"It's an odd name," she smiled. "Are you German?"

"No, Miss Montgomerie, much worse. I am of a race that is despised, even hated, in your country. I am an Irishman."

The story, touchingly told by Cronin, then unfolded, with Jessie ending up totally smitten. Next day she received a note from Patrick, begging her to meet him the following Monday for a drive around Loch Lomond in a friend's car, and telling her that he had been thinking of her day and night. Jessie lied to her mother and invented a walking trip with her friend Jean Douglas. And so the die was cast.

Patrick, a charming, handsome and well-set-up man of the world, was obviously touched with the blarney and well able to sweep a girl off her feet. Indeed, he had done it many times before. He was well in with Jules, the head waiter of the hotel he normally frequented, and was practised in the art of greasing palms swiftly and unseen. Jules, as a result, was attentive in the extreme, and at one point during the meal quietly asked Patrick if he required a room for the afternoon as he had obviously done on previous occasions. His reply was, "Of course not, Jules, you ass. This is altogether different."

After a fresh-salmon lunch with Chablis – her first taste of wine – they had coffee in the garden, where Jules presented Jessie with a long-stemmed red rose. Then, on the way home, Patrick proposed, and to the age-old four-word question she replied, "I will, Patrick, I will. This very minute" – whereupon she flung her arms around his neck. At the same time, she confided to him that her father wanted to pledge her to a fat, pimply old man, a minister of the Church, who had already had one wife.

Nothing was said to her parents, but the next week she left home with an explanatory note behind her, and they were married in a registry office in Blythswood, south of the river, with a solicitor friend, Robert Scott, as witness. From there they went to Patrick's brother – Father Francis Cronin – at the Catholic Presbytery in Gourock for their honeymoon. Miss O'Reilly, Francis's housekeeper, installed them in the best room, with views of the Firth on one side and the lovely gardens on the other. Francis insisted that their marriage be confirmed in Church, assuring Jessie that it would be a simple ceremony, little different from that of her own church. And so began married life.

The unpublished account is much fuller than that in *A Song of Sixpence*, though the connection with Dumbarton railway station still exists, as does the obvious, mutual attraction: "As they looked into each other's eyes, the damage was done."[6] In both versions, therefore, Cronin describes a case of love at first sight. In the published book, Laurence Carroll, who is in many ways Cronin's proxy, commenting on his mother's attachment to his father, says, "I am convinced she would have willingly accompanied him to a Hindu Temple had he professed that faith."[7]

It is likely that some of these events, from both accounts, really happened. Patrick would have needed to change trains at Dumbarton to proceed to Alexandria, and Jessie would almost certainly have passed the station every day on her way to work. Official documentation confirms their marriage in the Blythswood registry office. The trip around the loch and the salmon lunch with Chablis, however, though a lovely story, are more unlikely, while the honeymoon at his brother's Catholic presbytery would almost certainly never have been allowed.

Sectarianism and racism were potent forces in people's everyday lives at that time, and so Patrick and Jessie's love and intended marriage could only have caused heartache and dismay. Whether it is true that Jessie's father had planned for her to marry a Protestant minister will perhaps never be known, but accepting his serious allegiance to the Presbyterian faith, he was hardly going to welcome the prospect of an Irish Catholic marrying his favourite daughter – especially a Cronin. As mentioned earlier, the two families lived only a few miles apart, and while the Montgomeries lived a respectable, conventional, low-key existence, their perception of the Cronins may have been coloured by the existence of "Cronin's Pub", owned by James, the eldest son of the family, which fast became an institution in the Vale of Leven. That kind of notoriety, in addition to their Catholic faith, would hardly have endeared them to Archibald Montgomerie, who was probably a teetotaller. Unfortunately, nothing is known about Jessie's parents, neither psychologically nor physically. There is no reason to suppose that they were anything but typical of their generation – in which case Margaret Montgomerie would have been a dutiful,

A.J. Cronin
(1896–1981)

Agnes Mary ("May"),
A.J. Cronin's wife

Margaret Jennings ("Nan"),
A.J. Cronin's secretary and
companion in later life

A.J. Cronin with his wife May, his mother Jessie ("Mandy") and his three sons
Vincent, Patrick and Andrew in Blue Hill, Maine, 1941

Rosebank Cottage, the house where A.J. Cronin was born

Tighcruachan Villas, the house
to which the Cronins moved
after a year in Rosebank

7 Prince Albert Terrace. The Cronins
occupied an upstairs flat. Cronin's
father died here

Willowbrook Round Riding Road, the home of A.J. Cronin's grandparents

Dumbarton Academy, the school A.J. Cronin attended until 1912

St Aloysius' Catholic School, Glasgow, which A.J. Cronin attended from September 1912

Levengrove Terrace, the first property occupied by Cronin's grandparents in Dumbarton following a move from Glasgow

Cat's Castle, a house outside Cardross on the Dumbarton Road, which may have been the inspiration for Brodie's house in Cronin's first novel, *Hatter's Castle*

152 Westbourne Grove, the house
in which Cronin had his
London practice

3 Eldon Road, London,
the Cronins' Kensington flat

Sullington Old Rectory in Storrington, Sussex, the country
house Cronin purchased in 1935

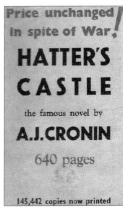

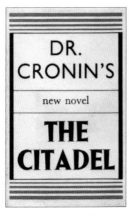

A wartime edition of
Hatter's Castle, Cronin's
first novel

First edition of Cronin's
second novel,
The Stars Look Down

First English edition
of Cronin's third novel,
The Citadel

The front cover of the June 1935
issue of *Cosmopolitan*, in which
The Stars Look Down was serialized

A poster for the film adaptation
of *The Stars Look Down* (above);
the US Armed Services edition
of *The Green Years* (below)

For dearest Nan in gratitude for her never failing cheerfulness, encouragement, and devoted affection to the 'maister'.

A.J. Cronin.

Kastanienbaum
Sept. 1961.

A.J. Cronin's dedication to Nan in a copy of
The Judas Tree

subservient wife whose main function in life would have been to produce and raise children in the time-honoured ways, keep house and support her husband. Archibald's role would have been that of head of the household, breadwinner and spiritual guide. It would be all too easy simply to accept the widely held belief that Archibald Montgomerie was a "stern", "strict" or "staunch" Presbyterian, implying an implacable unreasonableness bordering on domination – characteristics that provided the foundation for one of Cronin's best-known literary characters, the ogre James Brodie in *Hatter's Castle*. Equally, any suggestion that there were strong similarities between his real grandfather and the fictional James Brodie should also be resisted, except that they were both Victorian fathers. Whatever Archibald's temperament, it was not unusual in the mid-1890s for parents to have a considerable influence over their children's marriages, even to the choice of partner. Objecting to his daughter marrying a Catholic, therefore, was not only predictable, but perfectly reasonable.

There are contradictions between the two available versions of events – the unpublished account described above and the novel *A Song of Sixpence*. However, while some claims in the unpublished version can be proved to be wrong, the fictional account conforms to expectation and is probably not far from the truth. In the novel, it is explained to Laurence that his mother's parents

> …were dyed-in-the-wool Presbyterians, true blue, couldn't have been stricter, and she was the apple of her old man's eye, who, to make it worse, had a Scotch pedigree that went right back to William Wallace… so here was a lovely girl, well thought of in the town, helped her mother in the house, sang like an angel in the church choir, never put a foot wrong… when they found out she was going steady with an upstart Irish RC, blood brother to a publican and, God help us, a priest, hell's bells, man, did they raise the roof. Prayers and tears. For weeks there was the devil to pay while they tried every mortal thing to keep them apart. It couldn't be done, man. In the end, with never a word… they just up and off to the registry office. She knew her folks would never speak to her again…[8]

Undoubtedly, the affair would have hit the local headlines, engulfing not only the main protagonists, but the entire Montgomerie household, and it probably would have been impossible to contain the scandal within the walls of 1 Allan Place. Jessie had only two options: continue the relationship, defying convention and ignoring her parents, or give up Patrick. Courageous or foolhardy, genuinely in love or blindly infatuated, she took a great risk and chose the former. In the unpublished account of events, it is claimed that Jessie was not yet eighteen when she left home to marry Patrick, and that she was a pupil teacher at Levenford Academy. In fact, neither is true. She was twenty and worked as a telephone operator. But, more to the point, she was seven months pregnant. She married on 19th May 1896, and gave birth to her son two months later.

Jessie was, therefore, underage. From 1753 the age of consent to marry without parental permission was twenty-one, and the fact that the marriage required a sheriff's licence indicates that either permission was never sought or it was refused. The licence was issued on instructions from two witnesses – William Lees, a spirit salesman of 73 Sinclair Street, Helensburgh, and Jessie Buchannan or Lees of the same address. They must have been friends of Patrick, and one cannot help noting the fact that they were obviously living together in an unmarried state.

It is, of course, possible that Jessie never mentioned her love for Patrick at all, concealed her pregnancy and carried on as usual until she could hide it no longer, then simply left home with or without an explanation. Ignorant of the facts, her parents would have been both bewildered and upset, but at the same time suspicious. Eventually, they would have discovered the truth and would have become reconciled in their own way. If, on the other hand, they knew, they would have been shattered at the prospect that she was about to marry a Catholic, and even more distraught that she was pregnant. But why did Jessie leave it so late? At seven months pregnant, concealment would have been virtually impossible, given that the fashions of that period were wasp-waisted or hourglass. And how could she have hidden other tell-tale signs of pregnancy from her mother, who had borne seven children of her own? To add to the difficulty, Jessie was only 5' 2" tall and slightly built, and also – admittedly in unpublished references only – the baby she was carrying was big and possibly in a breech position.

The alternative that her parents were ignorant of the affair is unconvincing, mainly because of the inherent difficulty in keeping relationships secret in a large family and in small communities. It is more likely that her parents knew of the affair early on, and were in the process of persuading or cajoling her to give him up, hoping that the longer they worked on her the greater their chances of success. The conduct of that household over many months will remain a mystery for ever, as will Jessie's reason for waiting such a long time before acting. But the unanswered question remains – did Jessie admit to the pregnancy before she left? And, if so, when? If her parents knew, then it is possible they might have been grudgingly prepared to forgive her, and that together they might have devised a plan for concealment, involving Jessie giving up work and staying mostly indoors, until she could be moved away temporarily, perhaps to a distant relative, for the birth. Researchers of the period tell us that families went to great lengths to keep their guilty secret under wraps, such was the shame they felt.[9] If such a plan was ever devised, it was clearly scuppered by a change of mind, Jessie presumably realizing that she could not give Patrick up. On the other hand, Jessie may have delayed telling them until the very last minute, giving them little time to marshal their thoughts and no time to develop a plan. In conditions of such extreme urgency Jessie may have received a resigned and disappointed farewell, or she may have been shown the door in disgrace. In neither case is it clear whether her parents considered marrying a Catholic or bearing a child out of wedlock to be the greater sin.

It is impossible for one generation to relive the thoughts and passions of others. From a modern perspective, with sex outside marriage almost the norm and illegitimacy destigmatized, it is easy to underestimate the shame and frustration that would have been felt by her family, not to mention her father's righteous abhorrence of the violation of his daughter, which would have been relayed throughout the close-knit, moralistic community. "Our forebears placed great emphasis on the bonds of marriage, and those who deviated from this social norm faced condemnation from their community."[10] Implicit in that reference to the bonds of marriage is the expectation of purity and virginity before marriage. Those who only managed to get to the altar in the nick of time were not free from disapproval. Historical references demonstrate the uncompromising moral attitudes in nineteenth-century society: "Lots of foundlings were illegitimate. A look at the assize records for the nineteenth century and you'll find that half the murder victims were little babies... we don't think twice about illegitimacy now; it's really hard to get your mind around the idea that the shame was once so awful that women were prepared to kill their babies."[11]

Archibald Montgomerie, Cronin's grandfather, is generally considered to be the villain of the piece in this whole episode, in some quarters blamed entirely for the alleged hardship of Cronin's and his mother's life up to and after the death of Patrick. But the old man perhaps gets a worse press than he deserves. If only partially true, the claim – in both *A Song of Sixpence* and the unpublished account – that Jessie was the apple of her father's eye would explain his reaction. Rules were strict in Victorian Scotland, conventions were not flouted with impunity, virginity was valued and sex before marriage was castigated. No wonder there was consternation in Jessie's family, especially as the culprit – which is how they would have viewed Patrick – was an Irish Catholic. Some years later, even Emmeline Pankhurst was alleged to have been in "deep shock" when her own daughter gave birth to a son outside marriage.[12]

The only factor Jessie could not account for was ill health, and sadly it was such an occurrence that eventually dealt a blow to her future prospects. It would seem helpful, in this connection, to touch briefly on child welfare. Jessie obviously felt safe with Patrick, and it probably never occurred to her that there might be any risk in her chosen course of action. Child welfare, brought about by the appalling conditions in which the children of mainly working-class families were found, was the subject of increasing concern and regulation at this time. By 1884, parishes were permitted by law to separate illegitimate children from their mothers and place them in foster care, in the interests of both parties. And they did not shrink from enforcement. It was a big problem in Glasgow, and the exodus of children to other areas of the country and abroad was enormous. Such children were deemed to have been "rescued". Interestingly, it was the bourgeois ideal of "family" that was used as a benchmark for assessing what was best for the child.

Whatever the truth of Jessie's abrupt departure from home, she and her husband ended up in Cardross happy and contented, her son went to the village school and the future seemed set fair until the hopes of these three people, not unreasonably expectant of worldly success and personal happiness, were cruelly dashed by ill health and death.

Archibald Cronin – there is no mention of Joseph, his second name, on his birth certificate – was born at 3.45 a.m. on 19th July 1896 at "Rosebank", Cardross, on the northern shore of the Firth of Clyde, about fifteen miles north-west of Glasgow, and only a few miles from the southernmost point of Loch Lomond, an area of outstanding natural beauty. His birth was registered by David Smith, Registrar, on 8th August.

His parents' marriage certificate says that his father's occupation was that of a clerk. Elsewhere he was referred to as a mercantile agent, which probably means he was a clerk in a mercantile-insurance office. He was born in about 1868 in Alexandria, Dunbartonshire, and at the time of the 1901 census was still living in Cardross and had become a commercial traveller selling the newly developed Dutch product known as margarine. His wife was born in Glasgow in about 1876.

"Rosebank" is a low single-storey dwelling perched on the side of a grassy bank overlooking the River Clyde, an area referred to by some locals as the "wee wood". About half a mile from the centre of town, it can be reached by a narrow unadopted lane off the A814 Dumbarton–Helensburgh road, which also serves Geilston Farm, or by the direct route along the shore. Due to its relative isolation, it is not surprising that the family later decided to move into town.

At the end of the first year at "Rosebank" their new house in Cardross was ready. Patrick had it fitted with carpets throughout, and all of superior quality, helped in no small degree by his connections in the business world, from whom he was able to buy at wholesale prices. The house, standing opposite the railway station, perfectly situated for Patrick's travelling needs, was one of two pairs of semi-detached dwellings called Tighcruachan Villas in Station Road. Cardross, now a thriving, neat, well-manicured little town, was little more than a village in 1901, with no more than 750 inhabitants. *Tigh* is Gaelic for house, while *cruachan* derives from Ben Cruachan, a mountain in the western Highlands, five miles east of Oban, standing 3,689 feet above sea level. The builder, Colonel McIntyre, in naming these houses, must have been trying to instil, by association, a sense of grandeur. In a way he succeeded, because they are still standing and occupied today.

At the turn of the twentieth century in the west of Scotland it would have been difficult to find a more suitable place in which to settle and bring up a child than Cardross, yet there are claims that the Cronins were neither welcome nor happy there, by virtue of Cardross's strong Protestant affiliations. "To most neighbours and relatives in the small, strictly moral and sternly Protestant town of Cardross, Jessie's marriage and conversion were considered a disgrace, and upon her son they inflicted the inevitable ridicule and persecution."[13]

This fits perfectly with many other "poor boy makes good" and "rags to riches" articles that have been bandied about in magazines over the years. Cronin was, of course, a product of a mixed marriage, which some reviewers have likened to an affair almost as heinous as a marriage of black and white in the dark past of the southern states of America. But, as with all controversial aspects of life, much depends on the circumstances and personalities involved. Jessie did convert to Catholicism, but at what point during their time in Cardross is not known. However, the fact that they stayed in such an allegedly hostile environment for six years, and then left purely on the grounds of Patrick's deteriorating health, certainly leaves room for doubt.

As we have seen before, there were no relatives living in Cardross: they all lived either in Dumbarton or in the Vale of Leven, about four miles away, and for the first year of their stay in the village the Cronins lived in an isolated cottage on the shore of the Clyde, with no real neighbours. Up to the age of five, when Cronin got his first taste of education in the village school, he would have spent most of his time in his mother's care. Had any Protestant bigots wanted to vent their religious spleen on the little lad, they would have been hard put to find an opportunity. But the proposition itself that the village of Cardross was scarred by the kind of religious or racial conflict that afflicted other areas is difficult to sustain. It was both in character and make-up far removed from the Lanarkshire coalfields and the overcrowded streets of working-class Glasgow, where economic sectarianism was rife. Also, the Cronins were probably the only Catholics in Cardross – something of a novelty in a solid

Protestant community – who offered no threat to their respect-ability, temperance, peace or stability. They were law-abiding, hard-working and God-fearing members of society, even though they worshipped outside the town.

Over the course of my research I enlisted the help of a Scot-tish newspaper, the *Lennox Herald*, which printed my plea for information about Cronin in May 2008. A gentleman came forward whose mother, Mary Purdie, had been in the same class as "Archie". He was familiar with Cronin's work, and was able to recall the tone of conversations between his mother and her sisters, who all attended Cardross Primary School. He was adamant that there was no hint of anything dark, sensational or even unusual in their reminiscences. He remembered them talking of "Archie" possibly moving on to Keil School – an expensive private school in Dumbarton – but nothing more. If such a move was ever contemplated by Cronin's parents, nothing came of it. The same gentleman, without prompting, consid-ered it most unlikely that anyone, child or adult, would have received anything less than a warm welcome in the village and the village school. Though reminiscences are not evidence, a native of the village is surely better able to judge the collective mood of his own locality than critics revisiting the subject after a lapse of eighty years. Furthermore, Mrs Cronin's Scottish ancestry should not be forgotten, nor that Mr Cronin was a first-generation Scot and that both of them clearly exhibited all the generally acceptable middle-class virtues that the people of Cardross would have related to.

Crucially, no evidence of distaste, ridicule or persecution has ever been provided, simply the vague implication that because racial and religious bigotry and discrimination existed at that time, then it must have been prevalent in Cardross and directed at the fam-ily, with profound consequences for the young boy. It seems likely that the basis for the assertion is Cronin's own novel *A Song of Sixpence*, in which Laurence Carroll, aged six, on his first day at the village school is branded "the wee pope" by one of the older children. However, only two paragraphs later, Laurence himself, having reached the classroom, says: "Already I felt better, since I had recognized our teacher – a warm-looking girl with soft brown eyes and an encouraging smile – as one of the two daughters of

Mr Archibald Grant, who kept the store. Her younger sister Polly never failed to give me a butterscotch drop when I went to the store on errands for my mother."[14]

Laurence's immediate rehabilitation is also supported by more examples – though all from unpublished data – of sympathetic acceptance around the village. The rental of Rosebank cottage was conducted with Mrs Ross at the post office in the main street. When Patrick, Cronin's father, asked about signing the contract, she was mildly offended, pointing out that if she couldn't recognize folks of character who didn't need contracts it was a poor look-out, and that if he'd care to pop round once a month with a five-pound note, everybody would be more than happy. The good post mistress, no doubt a hardy Presbyterian Scot, then proceeded to lay on a good strong girl plus a handyman to clean up the place before the Cronins moved in.

Another example concerns Cronin's birth, which apparently was difficult by virtue of his size and breech position. The village doctor, Dr Cairns, was, from years of practice, a wise and skilled obstetrician, one of the old school who believed in letting nature take its course. He was against using forceps, except in the most extreme cases, allowing a few drops of chloroform only when the mother's pain became too much to bear. He and Mrs Cronin became firm friends, and in succeeding years he did all he could to assist with Patrick's chest condition. Cairns was another God-fearing Protestant.

The sympathetic behaviour of Polly Grant, Mrs Ross and Dr Cairns, together with the factual reminiscences of Mary Purdie and the length of the Cronin residency in Cardross, seem to con-tradict the assertion that they suffered "sectarian antagonism, not far short of that which has erupted in recent years in Northern Ireland as violence".[15]

So what was life like for the young Cronin in his early years in Cardross? Unfortunately, apart from his birth certificate and the census report of 1901, there are no records of any kind. The school he attended was demolished, and though records exist as far back as 1875, those for 1901 are missing. Though unpublished data tell us nothing of his schooldays, they paint an idyllic picture of life outside the classroom. Free to roam safely in a picturesque region of Scotland, able to go trout-fishing in the Gaelston burn with his father – a passion he took into later life – and loved by both parents, he seems to have enjoyed an enviable existence in the serene atmosphere of rural Cardross. But it was his father's gift of story-telling that truly captivated the young lad. With the boy on his knee, beside a roaring log fire, Patrick would weave magical tales to an entranced, imaginative listener. How could the child fail to have been spellbound with the adventures of his heroic central character, "Wee Goodshot" – clearly a representation of Archie himself – never daunted in his adventures, which ranged widely amongst Red Indians, cannibals and man-eating tigers, yet never in real danger because of his guardian angel Jumbo, the elephant, who followed him everywhere and rescued him from innumerable scrapes? So good were the stories that Cronin never wanted to go to bed. Despite the pleadings of his mother, he would invent any number of rituals to delay bedtime – including, last of all, satisfying himself that a boa constrictor was not coiled up beneath his bed.

There is, however, one aspect of his childhood that perhaps requires further comment. Increasingly, in modern times, research suggests the importance of meaningful communication with babies and small children for their future development. There was no such awareness back in 1896. Aside from ignorance of birth-control methods, the overriding rationale for creating large families was the addition of the earning power of children, males particularly, to the collective family pot. Cronin's father was one of nine, and his mother one of seven – neither case being unusual. It is, perhaps, not without significance that Cronin was an only child at a time when large families were the norm, leading to the not unreasonable conclusion that his prospects for a successful and happy future were enhanced by the daily attention of his mother and the combined interest of both his parents at all other times.

Sadly, Fate intervened to disrupt the happiness of the family. Patrick's health began to deteriorate, starting with a cough, which worsened with time and never left him. Medication – milk and cod-liver oil – and regular exercise were prescribed. Patrick took up golf at Cardross Golf Club, a nine-hole course in those days – another bastion of Presbyterianism which gladly embraced the Catholic Cronins. In those days the club was in a different place from its present location – on the estuary side of the A814 – nearer, in fact, to the Cronin house, but their records only reach back to 1905, by which time Cronin's father was dead. His membership cannot, therefore, be verified.

Only from unpublished sources have young Cronin's exploits come to light as he accompanied his dad on the course. On one hole, high above the green with a stream below, to have any chance of success the water had to be cleared. Even at the tender age of six, his father offered "a penny for you, laddie, if you clear the burn". It took time. At first the excitement of the challenge affected the boy's swing, and he failed badly, but he soon learnt to control his emotions, strike the ball firmly and win his penny. As mentioned before, years later, when he joined the Links Golf Club of New York, he was playing off a handicap of three.

Unfortunately, diet and exercise had no effect on Patrick, and the Cronins were forced to leave the low-lying estuary on which Tighcruachan Villas were built for an apartment in Prince Albert Terrace, Helensburgh. There, it was hoped, the elevation and drier air would help his bronchial condition. But the condition was by now too well established, and Patrick eventually succumbed to phthisis pulmonalis, a generic term for tuberculosis or a similar wasting disease, on 26th September 1904. The authorities were informed of the death by his brother James, the publican, who at the time was living in Alexandria at 59 Bridge Street. His name appears on the death certificate. Since nothing is known of the relationship between Patrick and Jessie and their respective families after their unpopular marriage, it raises the question of how James had come to know of Patrick's death.

Information from a distant maternal relative of the Cronins (Bridget McShane's sister) revealed that a John Connelly, Patrick Cronin's cousin on the maternal side, worked at Denny's shipyard in Dumbarton with a relation of Jessie. That relation was almost certainly James Montgomerie, the oldest of Jessie's siblings, who was apprenticed at Denny's as a ship's carpenter. One day James approached John Connelly enquiring if the Cronins in "The Vale" – a local term for Alexandria – knew that Patrick was ill. They did not. Connelly subsequently visited Patrick and reported back to the Cronin family that he was suffering from tuberculosis.[16]

What is most intriguing, however, is whether news of Patrick's illness had reached the ears of Jessie's mother and father via James, either at work or at home. Jessie's father also worked at Denny's shipyard, and through James a channel of communication might have opened up, regardless of their alleged estrangement. Whatever the truth, one thing is certain – that for Jessie, now aged twenty-eight, suddenly left with a son of eight and no obvious means of support, life took on innumerable twist and turns.

The move to Helensburgh, spa town and seaside resort, a town of broad avenues, piers, promenades and graceful architecture, had taken place in about 1902. The Cronins occupied 7 Prince Albert Terrace, an upstairs flat in a Victorian townhouse. Helensburgh's early success as a town owed much to the ferry service linking it to Greenock, allowing those who could afford it to earn a living on the southern side of the Clyde and live on the more attractive northern bank. Its proximity to Rhu, the main yachting centre of the Clyde estuary, also made it the residential choice of the wealthy cigarette and whisky barons of Glasgow.

Locals claim that Cronin attended the now-demolished Grant Street School (whose records have been lost), which they referred to as a "ragged school". This term requires some explanation. In 1847, the Rev. Thomas Guthrie, Minister of Free St John's, Edinburgh, having seen the vast number of waifs and strays roaming the city streets seeking any means of subsistence, published a pamphlet entitled *Plea for Ragged Schools, Or Prevention Is Better than Cure*, in which he proposed the establishment of schools where such destitute children might be clothed, fed and taught. And so, in the same year, at Ramsay Lane, Castlehill, the original Ragged School for boys, girls and infants was established. The children arrived early in the morning, left their rags in the fumigating chamber and, after a bath, put on the school dress before classes began. They were fed a breakfast of oatmeal porridge, a dinner of broth and potatoes and a supper of porridge. At the end of the day the children removed their school dress, picked up their rags and went home.

The promoters of this experiment had stressed that its success depended on a non-denominational form of teaching. Guthrie, however, was anti-Catholic, and his Protestant teaching offended the Catholic parents. After much discussion, a compromise was reached to have separate religious instruction. Since Catholics constituted the bulk of the entrants to these schools by virtue of their economic position in society, in time these schools may have been referred to simply as Catholic schools.[17]

This was not the case in Helensburgh. A Catholic church had been established there in 1880, with its own parochial school in Grant Street. The term "ragged" applied to that school was, therefore, not strictly correct. However, for the majority of Catholic parents, Grant Street was the only option. Unless they could afford any one of a number of expensive Catholic fee-paying schools in the area, they were forced to take what was on offer, which meant better-bred Catholic children had to attend Grant Street School, where the mix of pupils included children of poor Irish immigrants, some possibly from the despised "tatie howkers",[18] as well as others who were on the "parish" – their parents receiving handouts, in some cases clothes made from rough-spun cloth which were readily distinguishable and openly proclaimed their origins. As mentioned above, no school records exist about the composition of the pupils of Grant Street, nor how the school was run. But, whoever his schoolmates were, and whichever system of teaching was adopted, it would have been Cronin's first taste of life beyond the serene and sheltered existence he had enjoyed in Cardross – and for that very reason represents one of the many turning points in his life.

Researchers, reporters and writers alike have, almost without exception, attempted to explain this period of Cronin's life by stressing the adverse effects of sectarianism, poverty and loneliness. Salwak, Cronin's first biographer, writing in 1985, highlighted aspects of his life using much emotive vocabulary: "poverty-stricken", "ridicule", "persecution" and "alien", ending up with a claim that "Cronin was marked permanently by an environment that was noisy, quarrelsome, profoundly unhappy and emotionally dramatic…"[19] Another writer (unfortunately unidentified) states unequivocally that "as the only child of a mixed marriage, Archibald had a difficult childhood. He was sent to Grant Street School in Helensburgh… he hated this, and desperately longed to mix with the children of the rich Presbyterian community, but because of his background he was not accepted…"[20] In a 2008 article for the Helensburgh Heritage Trust we find a similar observation: "He hated these schooldays and desperately longed to mix with the children of the better-off Presbyterian community, but because of his background he was not accepted. He became a lonely and unhappy child..."[21] Similar references can be found in several Scottish newspapers which reviewed Cronin's life after his death in 1981. Yet virtually nothing is known of Cardross or Grant Street schools. Records do not exist and the buildings were demolished years ago. No locals were found who had first-hand knowledge of either. Therefore, the claims made about Cronin's early education almost certainly come from his book, *A Song of Sixpence*, in which Laurence Carroll, the hero, is thought to represent Cronin. Even so, it behoves readers to examine the text more carefully. The differences between Grant Street and Cardross school are immediately evident. According to the descriptions in *A Song of Sixpence*, the establishment was of "raw red-brick construction, practical, but starkly indicative of restricted means... so, too, amongst the schoolchildren, did this sad note of poverty prevail..."[22] But despite recognizing that "the general effect... was depressive",[23] Laurence Carroll still admits to finding goodness there, and there is no mention of hating it. On the contrary, far from experiencing any form of blind emotion, the text suggests the embryonic stirrings of social awareness brought on by the absorption of his parents' middle-class values. In Cardross dreams were realized, only to stall temporarily in Helensburgh. Initially a square peg in a round hole, there was a genuine promise of greater things, foreshadowed first in the words of Laurence Carroll's mother: "It's for your good, dear, and it won't be for long. You must just put up with it for the time being..." – and then those of his father: "Rising in the world... an unmistakeable promise of prosperity implied in his words... his manner, his elegant, well-groomed person... in excellent spirits announces: 'Don't worry, my boy. St Mary's is only a stopgap. Things are going to turn up trumps for you pretty soon...'"[24]

Such a growing sense of social ambition, strongly emphasized in *A Song of Sixpence*, would explain the attraction of the neighbouring Beechfield School, where the better-off Protestant children were found: "in their varying fascinating house colours, ranging from scarlet to vivid blue, [the children] thudded balls about, ran, passed, tackled and scrummed, in a manner to be expected of boys who would go to Fettes, Glenalmond, Loretto or even... to the best English public schools."[25] In secrecy, behind a hawthorn hedge, the boy watched their games "with a burning, envious longing".[26] But to deduce from that remark that Cronin became lonely, bitterly unhappy, persecuted and alien, as suggested earlier by other reviewers, is stretching the bounds of literary interpretation too far. The text of the novel is clear on this point: that it was not necessarily the rich Presbyterian children that he wanted to mix with and be accepted by, but anybody he could relate to. "Lack of companionship was my greatest cross," Cronin wrote in the book, implying that he would not have cared who they were or what section of society they came from.[27]

If *A Song of Sixpence* is to be believed – where Laurence says that his mother "could not bring herself to allow me to be friendly with boys who, as father put it, had no backside to their trousers" – it was his parents who would not allow him to spend time with his poorer classmates, and it was their attitude that led directly to his "lack of companionship" and boredom.

As an adult Cronin was an innately private man – a tendency that would have manifested itself as a boy. A contemporary of his at his next school after Grant Street says of him: "He was rather a withdrawn lad, who was a wee bit aloof and did not mix much with the other boys."[28] Loneliness is a sad, desperate condition, often unsought, not to be confused with solitariness. Loners derive comfort from solitude of their own choosing, yet can as easily handle society. Cronin was a loner all his life, and the telling appraisal of his school friend, more than any other, probably reflects the reality of his time at Grant Street School.

But the defining moment of Cronin's life as a child was not his frame of mind or the social milieu of his school, but the death of his father. Cronin was eight years old when his father's death forced his mother to give up the flat in Helensburgh, leaving behind her dreams and hopes for their future.

Though now in the Edwardian era, Britain was still essentially Victorian. The aristocracy and the middle classes, by this time in history enjoying a degree of peaceful co-existence, thought in terms of careers for their children, and were able to enjoy the benefits of the many fine private schools that had been built to cater for their needs. But working- and even lower-middle-class families generally had no such aspirations. Some sought trades for their children, but many were content for them simply to find employment, bringing home much-needed extra money, and parents were prepared to let their children leave school as soon as possible to achieve that end. However, gradually the pressure exerted by educationalists and liberal thinkers to extend education down the social scale began to bite. It took the form of lowering fees, instituting bursaries and offering incentives to schools to offer free places to indigent children on the basis of ability. Cronin's school life coincided with these moves, and by virtue of his abilities they worked to his advantage.

The key to social progress was Cronin's obvious intelligence; the motivation was the middle-class aspirations of both sides of his family. His grandfather Montgomerie had been in business in Glasgow and Dumbarton, and lived comfortably in one of the better-off areas of the town. Though the Cronins were Irish immigrants, his paternal grandfather had been resourceful and enterprising, sufficiently so to build up a business in Alexandria that eventually yielded relative wealth. His example undoubtedly fired Patrick's ambitions: not for him the humdrum existence of the factory floor or the sweat and noise of the Clyde shipyards. But for his untimely death, his genial and outgoing temperament would have raised him above the obvious limitations of his background.

Nor should Jessie Montgomerie, the most crucial piece in the puzzle, be forgotten. Was she just another love-struck girl, a victim of her own passion, who got "caught" by an older experienced man, or was she a woman before her time, prepared not only to challenge the conventions of the day, but also to pursue a path that few before her had dared to tread? She provided the other half of Cronin's genes, and after her husband's death supported him on the way to educational emancipation and social progress well beyond all reasonable expectations. It turned out to be a uniquely caring relationship.

What thoughts must have crowded in on Jessie Cronin's mind when her worst fears rose up to haunt her with the realization that, following the death of her husband, none of their plans for the future, most importantly their son's education, seemed likely to be fulfilled, and that she was on her own with no financial buffer for a rainy day? In her blackest moments, her vulnerability as a single parent without employment must have exercised her mind as sharply as her spiritual inclinations. As a newly converted Catholic, one wonders if her adopted faith was a sustaining or subverting

force. The circumstances of her marriage and parental estrangement must have weighed heavily on her already troubled mind,
fomenting hopes, perhaps, that divine Providence would somehow
condone her past guilt and mitigate retribution. Yet, however tenuous her future may have seemed, she clung tenaciously to all she
had left of her marriage – her only child – and there developed
between them a bond of mutual dependency that lasted the rest
of their lives. That bond is one of the keys to an understanding
of A.J. Cronin.

The first verifiable data of Cronin and his mother – assuming
she was with him – are to be found in school reports, which place
him at his grandparents' house in Round Riding Road in 1907.
That leaves a two-year gap, 1905 to 1907, which has given rise to
a number of theories. Some observers could not accept that Jessie
and her son simply packed up and returned to the parental home
immediately after Patrick's death, no doubt because of their belief
in the autobiographical nature of *A Song of Sixpence*, even though
the book is in many respects very unrealistic. In it, Grace Carroll
(who in many ways stands for Jessie Cronin) is approached by
her brother, who suggests that she might reconsider their father's
offer to return home:

> "I don't want to press you again, Grace. But won't you reconsider
> Father's offer?"
>
> "What's the use?" Mother said. "Am I to go back and pretend that
> I'm sorry, that I made a terrible mistake, but now I'll be good and make
> up for it?"
>
> "I think I could promise you'd be welcome. You'd have a comfortable
> home again, your own folks around you."
>
> "But on their terms? I couldn't bring myself to accept them."[29]

It was probably from that passage that the idea of Jessie's Her-
culean spirit and indomitable courage started. From there it was
a short step to misreading other sections of the narrative, specifically the claim that she took her husband's job as a "traveller"
in the grocery business. There are also those who go further and
assert that taking up such an appointment, at a time when married women were expected to stay at home, demonstrated great
courage and strength of character – qualities which first exhibited

themselves when she defied her family and married across the religious divide. Others go further still and portray her as some kind of super-woman, juggling the duties of breadwinner and mother, with Cronin as possibly one of the first latchkey children in Britain.

Unfortunately, there is not a shred of evidence to support any of this, and there is every reason to believe that its origins may be found firstly, as mentioned above, in *A Song of Sixpence*, in which Grace Carroll takes on the agency for selling yeast that her husband, Conor, had established with a Dutch firm called Hagemann, and secondly in *Three Loves*, in which Lucy Moore carries on her husband Frank's rounds selling produce, including margarine, to the baking industry. Cronin's penchant for producing cocktails of two parts fiction to one part fact is beguilingly evident. A Dutch firm, Jurgens, had in fact exported margarine to this country, having bought the formula from the Frenchman who discovered it in about 1871, but the need to import from Holland would have stopped in 1889, with the building of the first margarine factory in Britain. They would still have needed salesmen, of course, but it seems unlikely that they would have employed a woman.

In a later passage of *A Song of Sixpence*, Grace Carroll explains to her son that "the agency is finished... it was no work for a woman, at least not for me..." She goes on to explain to Laurence that he will be sent to his uncle Leo in Glasgow while she takes up a position as a music mistress in St Monica's Convent in Monmouthshire, and that in her leisure time she intends to take an intensive course of study to become a public-health visitor. "Four of these appointments, a new departure open to women, were to be made in Winton and... she had been promised one of them if she could take her training and get her certificate within a year." Why Cronin chose to send Grace Carroll to Monmouthshire is not clear: unless he still carried a picture in his mind of Abergavenny Abbey, where Vincent, his first-born, was christened. As to the appointment as a music teacher, readers may be assured that, although Grace in the novel was an accomplished pianist, his mother was not musical and did not play the piano.

In Cronin's unpublished papers there is an account of Mrs Cronin securing a position as a health visitor with the Glasgow Health Department, obtaining her certificate after a crash course with Dr Cairns, the doctor who brought Cronin into the world in Cardross. But it is the timing of the appointment, in line with other events in their lives, that is crucial to an understanding of that period. In this version, her daily duties and experiences among the poor of the Anderston district of Glasgow are enumerated, including a reference to the smart uniform she was required to wear – a navy-blue costume with a navy deerstalker hat. The Health Department were also responsible for her obtaining a flat in Yorkhill. Cronin recalls that he and his mother would leave the flat together in the morning, walk to Radnor Road tramway stop, where she would board a tram to the Anderston district, while he walked across Kelvingrove Park to the university. Except that Radnor Road is an imaginary name, this version seems to accord more closely with reality.

Mrs Cronin was, in fact, employed by the Burgh of Glasgow, in the sanitary inspector's department, but that was years later than 1904, the year of her husband's death. It was not until she and her son had moved out of the parental home in Dumbarton to take on the flat in Esmond Street, Glasgow, following her own father's death. Her name first appears on the employment lists in 1913–14, which ties in with Cronin's admission to St Aloysius' College and Glasgow University. She was employed as a Sanitary Inspector, working under William Roy, Superintendent of the Central Division, along with nine other inspectors, including another woman, a Miss Dewar. In the entire organization there were ten female inspectors, indicating that she was not the first female public-health inspector. Yet despite the existence of official records, most reviewers, including the *Glasgow Evening Times* of 5th December 1984, the University of Glasgow Roll of Honour, other newspaper reporters and biographical sketch-writers, casually accepted the fictional version of her appointment in *A Song of Sixpence*.[30]

Returning to the year of her husband's death, 1904, realistically there were only two options open to Jessie. Firstly, she could have made representation to the local parish board who, working with the Catholic Church, may have been able to find some form of temporary respite within the Helensburgh area, or even further afield in one of the Catholic homes in Lanark and Glasgow, which offered refuge for children at that time. Alternatively, she could have sought refuge with her parents. Most agree that this is what she did, but not all agree on when and how it happened.

Two very similar articles, both contained in the Cronin file in Dumbarton Library, have put forward a "rejection theory".

The first one says: "His father died young, and so he and his mother left Helensburgh and she went to live with her parents in Dumbarton. However, initially his grandparents refused to allow young Archibald to live under their roof, and he was sent to live with relations of his father... after a change of heart, his grandparents eventually allowed him to live in their home with his mother, but no love was shown to the boy, and he had to cope with being transferred from the strong influence of his father's relations into the staunch Presbyterianism of his mother's family... Archibald's grandparents made it possible for him to attend Dumbarton Academy despite continuing to show little affection."[31]

The second article says: "His father died young and his mother went back to her parents in Dumbarton. At first, they refused to accept the boy, who was sent to Greenock to live with relations of his father. The young widow pleaded constantly with her parents to allow her son to live with them. Eventually they relented, but showed him no affection and the lad found himself catapulted from the strong Catholic influence of his father's people into the staunch Presbyterianism of his mother's family."[32]

Neither article provides dates, names, timings, evidence or even reasoned arguments for the assertions. No explanation is given as to why the Cronin side of the family was the preferred choice to offer support when it is much more likely that Jessie would have turned to her own brothers and sisters. The second article, attempting to be more specific than the first, refers to relatives living in Greenock. Cronin is by no means a common name, but extensive searches of church records, old issues of the *Greenock Telegraph*, census books and Post Office directories have failed to reveal that there were Cronins living there. Not far from Greenock, however, was Father Francis, Cronin's uncle, the priest of the small parish of Gourock, but discussions with Church authorities confirm that allowing outsiders, even family, to live in the presbytery would have been "exceptionally unusual", and that any attempt would almost certainly have been vetoed by the Bishop.

Further searches for suitable foster parents among the Cronin family reveal few other candidates. James, the oldest uncle, was by that time fifty years old. He at least lived within reach of

Helensburgh, but the pub he kept was hardly the atmosphere Jessie would have wanted for her son. His aunt Mary married a Glasgow spirit merchant, Donald McDonald, in 1887, and they moved away from the area. Ann, working as a stay-maker in Glasgow, was un-married and lodging at 22 James Street. Thomas emigrated to the USA. Joseph, a cabinet maker in 1881, and Edward, an assistant wine merchant in 1891, both living at the family home in Alexander Street on those dates, are untraceable in official Scottish records after 1891: emigration is, therefore, a possibility. Margaret, the youngest, was a housekeeper who would probably have lived under her employer's roof. The articles' proposition, therefore, rests on the unlikely presumption that Jessie, still in shock and grieving for her husband, was prepared to leave her eight-year-old son, the only tangible thing left of a loving marriage, in the hands of James the publican, the only available Cronin relation, whom she would not have known well.

There are other reasons for questioning the reliability of both articles. They state, for example, that Cronin's *grandfather* owned a pub in Bridge Street, when it was in fact his uncle; that his mother became the first female public-health visitor employed by Glasgow Corporation, which official records contradict; that Cronin's nickname at Dumbarton Academy was "wee pope", when it is known that the nickname itself, though fiction, was coined in Cardross; that he practised in Harley Street, when it was in fact Westbourne Grove, Bayswater; that *The Stars Look Down* was set in South Wales, when it was Northumberland; finally, that the suc-cess of *Hatter's Castle* so enraged his grandfather that it brought to an end the relationship between them – which is implausible, as Grandfather Montgomerie died in 1912, a full nineteen years before the book was published.

The lack of suitability of a foster home, as well as Jessie's almost certain refusal to be parted from her son, naturally shifts the focus to 1 Allan Place, Dumbarton, the Montgomerie home. Proponents of the "rejection theory" maintain that his grandparents – in real-ity Archibald Montgomerie, the head of the household – were prepared to accept their daughter back into the fold, but not their grandson, a claim that never appears to have been challenged. There is no doubt that Victorians held virtue in high esteem and, despite suggestions to the contrary, there was no hypocrisy in their distaste of promiscuity. They had made great strides in reducing the incidence of illegitimacy from 7% in 1845 to around 4% at the turn of the century.[33] But for either or both grandparents to direct their moral outrage against an innocent child, when it was their daughter who had brought shame on the family, has never been explained. Only by resisting the temptation to identify Archibald Montgomerie with the fictional, villainous figure of James Brodie – justifiable in the light of Cronin's own admission that "Brodie is a cumulative… a combination of the more odious attributes of his age"[34] – may the relationship between him and his grandson be viewed in a different light. This also allows a different perspective on Jessie's return. Whatever emotions were stirred up by her leaving in 1896 – shame, anger, disappointment – time would have soothed them. The prying eyes of neighbours would have dimmed with faded interest. All reports of this episode affirm unequivocally that, for the sake of her child, it was Jessie who begged to be taken back, but it is possible that her father might have made the first move, especially if he had not wanted the split in the first place. How desperately might he have wished to restore his relationship with his once-favourite daughter? It is likely, although not provable, that as a reconciliatory gesture he also offered to pay his grandson's fees at Dumbarton Academy. After all, it should not be forgotten that forgiveness was as much a part of Victorian Christian teaching as of puritanism. At school Cronin's intelligence and work ethic could hardly have failed to impress his serious-minded grandfather, and even if religious matters separated them, other things brought them together.

They shared, for example, a common interest in football, and were both Dumbarton supporters. On one particular occasion Cronin remembers his excitement as Dumbarton scored an equalizer in a cup match against Celtic: "My grandfather, sitting in the stand opposite, saw me practically dancing the Highland Fling on the touchline with joy!"[35] On another occasion one of his aunts recalled seeing him with his grandad walking up Round Riding Road. Victorian men in general tended to be distant and undemonstrative, but there is no evidence to support the claim that Cronin was shown no affection by his grandfather.

As we have seen before, Cronin's father died towards the end of September 1904, in the middle of a school term. Whether Cronin and his mother left immediately or waited until the end of the year is not known, though it is likely that he will have joined a class at the start of the first term in 1905. His name first appears on the 1907 prize list of the senior department of Dumbarton Academy's Elementary School. He was then eleven years old, and that same year he entered the senior school. But the Academy took in younger children in their middle and junior departments, so it is quite possible for him to have started his education in the junior classes of the elementary school. School policy dictates that records are destroyed every ten years, so that may never be confirmed. But the next eight years proved to be immensely fruitful for the young Cronin. His time in Dumbarton laid a solid foundation for his future success.

Unfortunately, he left no reminiscences of his life with his mother and grandparents, or his school years in Dumbarton. Professor Salwak, however, seems determined to find deep psychological undercurrents in his time at Dumbarton Academy:

> Cronin's talent also meant he would suffer the emotions of premature loneliness that so often afflict an unusually bright boy. He was highly regarded by his teachers, but other students – and their parents – sometimes resented his abilities. One father, whose young hopeful son was beaten by Cronin in an examination, became so enraged that years later [he said]: "*Hatter's Castle* took shape around his dominating personality."[36]

In the same paragraph Cronin's early novels are also mentioned, in which "for the most part humour is dimmed by gloomy memories of his own neglected childhood".

This cause-and-effect approach – he was bright, therefore he must be rejected and, therefore, he must become lonely – is open to question. There is also a danger of overstating his undoubted academic abilities. In the Dumbarton Academy Prize List for 1910–11, a golden year for Cronin, he was one of no fewer than forty-five special-prize winners. He secured prizes in English and mathematics, which demonstrated an impressive range, plus a Gold Medal for an essay in the County Schools Competition. But he was not the only multiple winner. A certain Agnes Gordon, senior to Cronin, received the Denny Gold Medal for English as well as the

Kennedy Prize for duces in French and German. Another young lady, Euphemia Grandison, secured the Overtoun Gold Medal for Classics, the Kennedy Prize for French and the Walter Brock's Prize for Art. Finally, William Forrest got the Rector's Medal for the best athlete, the John Ward's Prize for Science and the M'Ausland Gold Medal for Mathematics.[37] This was clearly a school where excellence was not in short supply, and so Cronin's achievements, while laudable, were being matched by others. There is also a danger of exaggerating Cronin's natural aloofness. A classmate remembers that "he was a good-looking young fellow with red hair, and I recall that he was one of the best wingers the school football team ever had... he was a good athlete and very clever at school... the last time I remember seeing him he was sitting on the wall of a house in Round Riding Road and as I passed he nodded and winked at me. He would have been about sixteen at the time."[38] The young Cronin was certainly not a reclusive, absent-minded swot, but a lively, talented all-rounder, as demonstrated by his ability on the football field.

In the lists of disadvantages that allegedly blighted Cronin's life, poverty was never out of the spotlight. In 1984 the *Glasgow Evening Times* ran the headline: "Poor boy who was to become the wealthiest writer in the world". Another reputable source, Dale Salwak, in one paragraph alone, juxtaposes "penniless mother" with "poverty-stricken home of her parents", followed by "the next ten years were to be a period of unbelievable hardship".[39] Ironically, Cronin himself added support to their cause. In his will he reminded his children of the many benefits that were bestowed on them, contrasting sharply with "the poverty and hardships that were my lot following the untimely death of my father..." Cronin's view carries no more weight than any other, of course, and it still requires the scrutiny of social and historical perspective.

Jessie's financial situation, penniless or not, is not entirely relevant. She sought help from her parents and earned her keep either by assisting her mother in the home or by getting herself a job. 1 Allan Place, the house occupied by the family until about 1905, has been demolished, but Willowbrook, in Round Riding Road still stands, in a sought-after area of Dumbarton, with no shortage of luxury cars in the driveways. The house itself is a solidly built, well-proportioned sandstone property, occupied in 1964 by the Burgh Chamberlain. In 1900 it would have been grander than it is today, and the area would have been surrounded by green fields. Grandfather Montgomerie – proud, independent and hard-working – was anything but poor, and he would probably turn in his grave at the "poverty-stricken" tag.

Poverty-stricken homes, of the kind referred to, were not in short supply in Scotland, particularly in the teeming tenements of Glasgow, in such areas as the Gorbals, Govan, parts of Yorkhill and Anderston. The haves and have-nots in those days were clearly identifiable:

> One of the most distinctive features of Scotland's transition to an industrialized economy was the level of overcrowding experienced by the urban working-class population. In 1901 around half of Scots were housed in dwellings of one or two rooms, and 11% lived in just one room. The notorious "single end" – one small room in a four-storey tenement containing kitchen and sleeping accommodation – was roundly condemned as a breeding ground for immoral conduct and ill-health, but it continued to house a large proportion of Glasgow families. 20% of these "single ends" were occupied by five or more people in 1911, and the vast majority of their inhabitants shared sanitary facilities, such as they were. The infant-mortality rate – higher in Glasgow than in any other British city – was even more pronounced in overcrowded housing conditions. 32% of all infant deaths in Glasgow in 1905 were babies from "single ends", and there was little improvement until after the Second World War.[40]

Conditions at the time were such that Catholic families living in a desperately poor and crowded area of Glasgow did not even possess their own cooking utensils, but did their cooking on a shared and timed basis. At certain times of the day, children, fleet of foot and well-practised, could be seen "running up and down the closes" transferring the one and only frying pan from one kitchen to the next, so that each mother could get the meal on the table in time for the head of the household's return from the daily toil. There was also another level of hardship at that time in our history, when it was not just the immediate risks that caused problems, but the slow, inexorable deterioration of health brought on by inadequate and unwholesome food, together with unsanitary housing – both leading to debilitation and premature death. There are many examples of such cases in Victorian and Edwardian Scotland.

Cronin lived in a dream world by comparison. Throughout his entire life, he never experienced "unbelievable hardship" – though, later in life, he might have implied it for effect. Blessed with a dry sense of humour, he would not have been averse to twisting journalists' tails just for the fun of it. For years they were always eager to print anything sensational about him – a Cronin story was always good copy. In real life, his father had provided well for them until his premature death, and his grandfather, in regular employment, did the same after his father's death. Tenement dwelling represented "unbelievable hardship", not Round Riding Road. In his youth, his most pressing concern was not where his next meal was coming from, but how best to triumph over his social superiors. His homes, even by today's standards, are middle-class dwellings. Even outside the desperately impoverished city areas, industrialized Britons inhabited terraced houses, often back-to-back, some with no running water. Bathrooms were unheard of, lavatories were outside, of the non-flushing variety – sometimes humorously referred to as "the thunderbox". There were literally thousands of such properties in the mining valleys of South Wales, where Cronin himself first practised medicine, and in the cotton-spinning and wool-weaving towns of Lancashire and Yorkshire, and on into Scotland itself. Anyone living in the kind of property Cronin occupied would have been considered a "toff".

The type of dwelling often also determined the expectations of its occupants. Further education and a university career were inconceivable to generations of uneducated youngsters from tenements and back-to-backs. Their inheritance was a self-perpetuating cycle of under-achievement. Cronin understood that better than most. How else could he have created the indomitable Martha Fenwick in *The Stars Look Down*, who refused to be impressed by her son's election to Parliament because it cut across the grain of working-class convention?

Class mobility was a slow process, its watershed the 1944 Education Act, but forty years earlier the barriers for entry to fee-paying schools like Dumbarton Academy were being breached by the granting of bursaries to pupils of exceptional ability. It has never been established if Cronin, whose school results suggest he was an exceptional student, secured a bursary. The popular view in the Dumbarton area is that he did not, and that his grandfather paid his fees. Many years before, his grandfather had given up his business as a hatter and secured a position as a shipyard clerk. There is also a reference to him as an overseer, suggesting that his position entailed a measure of responsibility beyond simple administration. A list of average salaries in 1911 helps to throw some light on the subject.

Solicitor	£1,343
Police Constable	£70
Doctor	£265
Teacher	£176
Train Driver	£78
Coal Miner	£83
Fitter	£125
Brickies Labourer	£47
Compositor	£96
Clerical Worker	£229

The one thing that stands out very clearly from these statistics is the high regard in which clerical workers were held and the correspondingly high level of reward.[41]

Unfortunately, no records exist for Dumbarton Academy to help analyse these salaries in relation to school fees, but the fees to St Aloysius' College – Cronin's next school – in 1911 were £7 a year, which to a clerk earning £229 a year represents three per cent of his gross annual income. Though his grandfather had wider familial responsibilities, his ability to pay cannot be doubted, casting further doubts on any reference to poverty and hardship.

During my researches in Dumbarton, conversations with interested locals, while welcome, became tediously pat. All were anxious to deliver the message not only of a poor boy, but also a highly intelligent, fatherless, persecuted Catholic lad – persecuted at home by a stern grandfather, who at first refused him entry, and then, having relented, showed him no love, and later at school, where he was the only Catholic in the strongly Protestant Dumbarton Academy. But apart from his academic and sporting achievements and a few comments in local newspapers, which mention his natural aloofness, nothing is known of his time at Dumbarton Academy. Consequently, there is no evidence of sectarian strife beyond the passage in *The Green Years* in which Robert Shannon (assumed to be Cronin) is given a miserable time in his first few weeks at his new school "for being a dirty little papist".[42] Readers may remember that the "wee pope" epithet served as evidence for persecution in Cardross village school where Laurence Carroll (Cronin) attended as a much younger boy.

There is, of course, a considerable Catholic population in Dumbarton – probably higher than the national average of 16% – and towards the end of the nineteenth century the town suffered sectarian riots that involved loss of life. Even today there is evidence that Catholics in Scotland are marginally disadvantaged in some areas – home and car ownership and white-collar employment[43] – and so it is, perhaps, not surprising that locals gave weight to this aspect of Cronin's upbringing. If it happened in wider society why not in schools?

But sectarianism, like all indefensible philosophies, suffers from contradictions. Just as there were inconsistencies at a denominational level, which allowed Protestant Irish and Catholic Scots freedom from intimidation, so could individuals gain a measure of insulation by resemblance to their hosts. Cronin and his family had set their hearts on an education that would raise his social status and open new horizons: the very ethos that the school embodied. A youngster of his bearing and ability would surely have fitted in easily and felt at home there.

Besides, it is, perhaps, not generally known that he was not the first Cronin to be educated at the school. Two older cousins, John and Edmund, the sons of James Cronin, the publican in Alexandria, attended the Academy before transferring to St Aloysius' in August 1903 for the final two years of their secondary education. Also, another cousin, Thomas, followed the same path in 1916. The school was, therefore, used to Cronins and it is even possible, considering that Dumbarton lacked a Catholic school of similar quality, that other Catholic parents, seeking a good education for their children, followed suit, resulting in a minority of Catholics in the staunchly Protestant Dumbarton Academy. Cronin's isolation, with its implied trauma, may, therefore, have been imaginary.

Certainly the school offered him everything he needed to display his all-round talents, leaving nature and his mother to add the finishing touches to his developing personality.

Finally, he professed to having warm memories of the town, as a letter dated 3rd March 1972 to Mr Storey, the chairman of the Dumbarton Football Club, clearly shows:

> I am happy to join in the 750th anniversary of the award of the Royal Charter to the Burgh of Dumbarton. Although I have travelled the world over I may say in all sincerity that my heart belongs to Dumbarton, which indeed has figured largely in most of my novels and these, as you may know, have also travelled the world over, being published in as many as 23 different languages. In my study there is a beautiful 17th-century coloured print of the Rock of Dumbarton. I even follow with great fervour the fortunes of the Dumbarton football team, which now seems to be rising towards the top of the league. I send you, and all Dumbartonians, my warm and friendly greetings.

Chapter Two

Who knows where myths start? Over the years Cronin seems to have collected more than his fair share of old chestnuts. Some refer to people whom he is supposed to have used as models for his characters, the most notable being his grandfather as the model for James Brodie in *Hatter's Castle*, his great-grandfather for Alexander Gow in *The Green Years* and his uncle Francis Cronin for Father Chisholm in *The Keys of the Kingdom*. Others relate to events in his early life that are presumed to have had a significant impact on his adult personality. Examples of these can be found as early as 14th August 1964 in an article in the *Helensburgh Advertiser*, in which the twin evils of Catholicism and poverty are juxtaposed in an effort to justify comments such as: "Free of his father's dominating Catholic influence Archie became an acceptable Academy boy" – or: "The Grant Street urchin had made it".[1] Later, the *Glasgow Evening Times* – in articles by Alasdair Marshall in December 1984 – and Salwak in his 1985 biography went even further in promoting the notion of sectarian antagonism, following the mixed marriage of his parents. From that inauspicious union, romantic yet frowned upon, emerged a host of subsidiary issues – ridicule, persecution, family rejection, poverty and deprivation – that were used indiscriminately to explain the kind of adult Cronin eventually became and the reasons for his incredible life and success. The snowball effect can be seen in subsequent reviews, yet the single most pivotal event in changing the course of his life was death.

As we have seen in the previous chapter, the loss of his father was followed by a period of uncertainty and confusion until, under his mother's wing, he was adopted into his grandparents' home in Allan Place, and later distinguished himself at Dumbarton Academy. The Montgomeries obviously set great store by education, with a daughter a qualified teacher and a son training as an

61

accountant. It was that environment, ambitious and supportive, that first shaped Cronin's life, with the prospect of university and a chosen career beyond – until fate tragically intervened again, on 20th August 1912, with the death of his grandfather, Archibald Montgomerie.

There is no evidence to establish who paid Cronin's fees to Dumbarton Academy, but the most likely candidate is his grandfather. Educating a young boy, of course, involves a great deal more than paying fees, and so Jessie Cronin's arrival with her son at the parental home added to the already considerable burden. At that time, Archibald Montgomerie was also responsible for his wife, both his wife's parents, his mother and his youngest child, Harvey. His wages, supplemented by board and lodging from those children still at home and at work, constituted the only known source of income to the household. It is not known if Jessie found employment or helped her mother at home.

The loss of his income would have dealt the family a body blow. In those days there was "no help but the Poor Law... when the breadwinner of the family died". It took another fourteen years before widows' pensions became state-funded, set at ten shillings a week in 1926, and even then they were woefully inadequate.[2] Archibald Montgomerie had, of course, been in business as a hatter in Dumbarton. If the business was sound, its sale might have provided a nest egg for his future, with possibly an insurance policy to cover his death. On the other hand, adverse trading conditions may have forced the sale on him. The state of the Montgomerie finances is, therefore, unclear, but Cronin's grandmother managed to remain in Willowbrook until at least 1919, suggesting that some provision had been made for her, or else her children assumed financial responsibility for domestic affairs. It was from that house that Annie, a schoolteacher, married in 1917, and Robert, an accountant, married in 1919, the year when his grandmother finally left to live with Annie and her husband, an officer in the Gordon Highlanders, in Monifieth, Angus, where she died in 1937. It is interesting to note that Cronin was a witness at his uncle's wedding, which suggests that the family remained united despite Jessie's past indiscretion.

Accepting responsibility for running Willowbrook, however, did not extend to paying school fees for the sixteen-year-old Cronin, now at a critical juncture in his academic career, and what happened next demonstrates the priority his mother accorded his education. Within thirteen days of his grandfather's death, on 2nd September 1912, he took his place in the fifth form of St Aloysius' Catholic School, and at the same time he and his mother moved into a flat at 29 Esmond Street, Yorkhill. Calmly planned or a last-minute action, the move in so short a space of time, with a family funeral intervening, was quite an achievement. Confident that his future lay in his eventual attendance at university, the flat, within walking distance of the school and university, avoided the tiresome journey from Dumbarton to Glasgow.

St Aloysius' was a grant-aided school at that time, in receipt of funding from the Scottish Education Department and Glasgow City Council, which would have kept the fees low by comparison with a public school. But fees still had to be paid. Bursaries were available, often awarded on the recommendation of the local parish priest, but school records do not confirm how Cronin's costs were met. The most widely held theory is that his uncle, Father Francis, paid them. In 1912 he was officiating at Mossend, no more than eight miles from Yorkhill. It is known that over and above his sacerdotal duties he found time to become involved in educational matters as a member of the school board there.[3] Such an appointment might have placed him in a privileged position for helping his nephew gain a place at St Aloysius', even perhaps a bursary, but whether his stipend would have stretched to paying school fees is another matter. There is no reason to doubt that he took an active interest in Cronin's life at that time, but one wonders why his presence was not more obvious in 1904, at the time of his brother's death and Jessie's greatest need.

Another possibility, never before considered, is that James Cronin, the publican, might have offered help. After his father's death, as the oldest surviving child, he might well have assumed the unofficial role of head of the family. He was, for instance, the brother who had been on hand in Helensburgh to witness and report Patrick's death. He was also familiar with the routine at St Aloysius', having sent his own sons there. And an added bonus would have been the removal of Cronin and his mother from the Presbyterian influences of Dumbarton and returning them to the Catholic fold. Moreover, with his business prospering, he more than any other family member, particularly Francis the priest, was in a position to meet the fees without hardship. It is interesting to note that, despite his relative wealth, he lived a frugal life, and on his death he caused a considerable upset in the family by leaving all his money to charity. For a man so inclined, what better way to employ charitable instincts than by helping out a brother's widow?[4]

The most likely possibility, however, is that Jessie did not seek any help after her father's death. It would have been quite in character for her to have arranged everything herself, including employment as a public-health inspector. Just as she had relieved her mother of the burden of their presence in Willowbrook, when her father died, so she struggled on, free of outside influences, for the next nine years in their new home in Yorkhill. She was not estranged from her family, as their attendance at her brother's wedding shows, but this was the first time in their lives that mother and son experienced a form of isolation. Thrown together by unfortunate circumstances in strange surroundings – a new job for Mrs Cronin and a new school for her son – there developed a close mutual dependency.

From unpublished data we know that their flat was on the top floor, which they both considered to be an advantage, because it gave them a feeling of seclusion, freedom from the noise of other inhabitants and "a superb view of the Lomond Hills, etched against the setting sun in the western skies".[5] It was a small flat: one bedroom and one other room which served as a kitchen, with an alcove containing a built-in bed, which could be curtained off, a boiler behind the range supplying hot water and, finally, a bathroom with a porcelain bath. How they must have missed the comforts of Round Riding Road. In these same reminiscences Cronin claims that there was a telephone in the flat, but the years must have played tricks with his memory, because there is no record of it in the telephone directories of the time.

As we have seen, much emphasis – mostly misleading – has been placed on poverty in the formative years of Cronin's life and its motivating effect on his character. It was, in fact, at this stage in his life, during the two years at St Aloysius' and later at university, as he approached adulthood, that he would have experienced a certain degree of hardship. However, although not well paid, his mother's job was permanent and secure, as was his university bursary and so, at whatever financial level they were forced to operate, budgeting at least would have been a relatively straightforward task. But they managed together – a fact that had an enormous influence on their future relationship. The links that bind parents to children are primarily instinctive, but it is possible for circumstances to forge bonds that transcend nature itself. It was in Yorkhill that Cronin, a serious-minded and responsible young man, and his mother developed a very special Darby and Joan-type relationship. He accepted his share of the domestic burden, starting dinner if he was the first home in the evening, and helping out in other ways. Despite the difference in their ages, he became a confidant and remained close to his mother for the rest of her life. Once established as a doctor and later as a writer he looked after her, including her as part of the family as they moved to America and Switzerland and on all long vacations.

After excelling at Dumbarton Academy, Cronin's academic prowess continued at St Aloysius', where in five terms he was fourth in class in his first term, second twice, and first twice. His education at this stage covered a wide spectrum of disciplines: algebra, geometry, trigonometry, religious education, English, repetition, literary French, and dynamics and science. His English essays during the period 13th September 1911 to 14th March 1914 never received less than A-. One in particular, written in May 1912 and entitled 'The Loss of the Titanic', received a special commendation. The teacher, who took a keen interest in Cronin's writing ability, singled out one section for praise: "Lower and lower she sank, till at last, with a crack like a breaking nut, and a hiss of steam on water, that slowly elaborated production of a thousand brains and hands, the latest and completest expression of technical skill, broke completely in two…"

Cronin's literary potential went beyond the sinking of the *Titanic*. In the course of her work Mrs Cronin witnessed extremes of poverty and degradation in the slum areas of Glasgow, experiences which, at the end of their day, they shared. One in particular touched them both deeply. It concerned a young boy who suffered from rickets, but despite his condition was cheerful and optimistic, and "with his little legs bent under him" used to sing "in a sweet little voice: 'Bluebells I gather, take them and be true'". Mrs Cronin recounted, with tears in her eyes: "God knows, he'll never see a bluebell wood, let alone put a foot in one".[6] That report must have had a profound effect on Cronin, because he used the incident as the basis for an essay at St Aloysius', dated 12th November 1912, entitled 'A Child of the Slums'. In his schooldays Cronin wrote many fine essays with appropriate commendations, but the master's comments about that particular effort are particularly poignant: "I am glad you wrote that. Good to read."[7]

After St Aloysius', in 1914, aged eighteen, Cronin secured a Carnegie Foundation Scholarship to study medicine at Glasgow University. Why medicine? In later life he admitted it was not a "calling", but he explained that in school his ability to win prizes for his English essays was taken by friends and family "as a manifestation of something wrong with my head". He went on: "The Scottish view is very practical... there is always a choice: you can have medicine or you can have divinity! I chose the lesser evil."[8] True or not, he was an accomplished student, appearing frequently on the prize lists for merit certificates. In his first two years he gained merits in zoology and physiology, then took a year out to enlist as a sub-lieutenant in the Royal Navy Volunteer Reserve in the Great War. On his return, he gained a commendation in clinical surgery, and second-class certificates in systematic surgery, the practice of medicine, midwifery and psychological medicine, finally graduating in 1919.

Over many years observers never failed to refer to Cronin's social conscience and his seemingly natural rapport with ordinary folk. He, of course, insisted that he never knowingly represented any social group and, in fact, consciously strove to avoid partiality in his writings, but there is little doubt that the years spent at Yorkhill with his mother, struggling for survival in difficult circumstances, were morally uplifting and accelerated his developing maturity. His mother's daily grind in the slums and his own straitened circumstances, compared to his mostly affluent and carefree university colleagues, were constant reminders of the fundamental injustice of early-twentieth-century society. They spent many hours discussing not only the medical basis of real-life cases, but also the insidious effects of slum conditions on the poor and undernourished. Perhaps that lay behind Cronin's eagerness to obtain a Diploma in Public Health to add to his medical degree.

At university, Cronin's personal circumstances emphasized the immensity of the goal his mother and he had set themselves:

the medical faculty was dominated by the well-off. The ideal of educational egalitarianism was gaining ground, bursaries were increasingly available – the only route open to Cronin – but the amounts they offered were small and survival was hard.

In unpublished documents, Cronin mentions that he did not join the union, because he could not afford to, going instead to the library to work. He recalled that the students in his year were a boisterous lot, types whom he naturally avoided. He said to his mother: "Of course, there were a lot of cards... I gave them a wide berth." His mother's reply was illuminating: "Don't mix with any but the best."[9] Was there a hint of snobbery in that remark, or was it a demonstration of her steely pursuit of substance as opposed to affectation? Jessie's visionary nature and constancy were beyond the ordinary. Hers was the light that guided Cronin's aspirations, the orchestrating hand that overcame all obstacles, and the imprint of her quiet determination was evident everywhere in her adult son.

Their lives in Yorkhill settled to a manageable routine. When Cronin was at school and university, he and his mother attended church every Sunday – a church near St Aloysius' College. There is no reference to the strength of his faith at this time, but more importantly no mention of its diminution, as is suggested in *Adventures in Two Worlds* – a book that, as was noted earlier, has often been considered autobiographical. On one particular Sunday – according to unpublished material – he became reacquainted with Father Challis, one of his former teachers from St Aloysius', who also happened to be a dear friend of Father Francis Cronin. The priest took an immediate interest in Jessie and promptly invited himself to tea the following Saturday. Like all women of Jessie's breeding, she went to extreme lengths to make everything perfect – choosing a dress of yellow shantung silk that her husband had greatly praised, black soft-leather shoes and pale-grey silk stockings. Cronin himself was suitably scrubbed and polished, and on display were the best, monogrammed linen tablecloth, the finest Minton china and a silver cake stand. The meal was all home-baked and served with Twinings tea – her husband had never drunk any other blend. The priest was concerned at her solitary life, and since she was a Montgomerie, he offered his help in introducing her to ladies of her own class from his congregation, with a view to forming some kind of relationship. The upshot of the visit was that she received a call from a Miss Eleanor Fenton, which developed into a friendship. Together they attended the opera at the King's Theatre, with dinner beforehand at the Carlton – and so, joined by other friends of Miss Fenton, Jessie's social life took a decided turn for the better. She began to lead a life of her own, and with Cronin heavily committed to his medical studies – cutting and staining specimens for mounting on slides in her absence – their respective interests dovetailed nicely into a comfortable existence.

But perhaps Cronin's imagination is running a little out of control here. Theatre trips and hotel meals were luxuries that do not fit squarely with the financial constraints he and his mother were supposedly living under.

As mentioned earlier, two years after the beginning of the Great War, Cronin decided to interrupt his studies, firstly to take a midwifery course at the famous Rotunda Hospital in Dublin (founded in 1745 and reputedly the first ever maternity training hospital) and then to join up.[10] There was no conscription at that time, so it was not compulsory. Many medical students were enlisting, some out of patriotic sympathies, others to gain the invaluable medical experience peculiar to war, and still others attracted by the lure of a gratuity at the end of their stint. Two years into his medical course, in 1916, Cronin joined the Royal Navy Volunteer Reserve, aged twenty, as a surgeon probationer. He was sent to the Royal Hospital Haslar in Gosport for a month's extra training and then posted to a brand-new destroyer, the *Melampus*, based at Harwich. He spent a year in the navy before resuming his studies, finally graduating with a commendation in October 1919.

Cronin was still living in Esmond Street when he was appointed physician in charge of out-patients at the Bellahouston Hospital. Subsequently, in 1921, he accepted a live-in appointment – albeit for a brief period – as medical superintendent at Lightburn Hospital, Shettleston. He was at Lightburn when he married Agnes Mary Gibson, also a doctor, on 31st August 1921.

Until now all that was known of their courtship and marriage is what is recounted in *Adventures in Two Worlds*, published in 1952. This version of events, which has become accepted, is as follows.

Agnes Mary Gibson, known as May, was eighteen when she met Cronin at Glasgow University. She was a high-souled young woman bent on becoming a doctor attached to one of the foreign missions in Africa. Cronin, recently returned to medical school after a brief spell in the navy, cut a considerable dash in his uniform, and he admits that on his part it was love at first sight. He was so astounded on being noticed by her that his mind went blank and all he could say by way of an approach was to utter a tongue-tied comment about the weather. However, they got on famously, spending hours talking in the Glasgow tearooms in the winter, and on most Saturdays in spring and summer they escaped to the woods and lochs of the western Highlands. Sometimes he would borrow a friend's motorcycle and they would go tearing down to Helensburgh for an expensive lunch at the Royal Caledonian Hotel.

They were happy in each other's company, but in their more serious moments they realized how impossible their relationship was. Not only were they temperamentally opposed, but they were the last two people in the world, for every practical purpose, to contemplate a union. Cronin was extremely ambitious, so an early marriage would only be a drag on him. He was also a Catholic, while she was a strict Nonconformist, holding pious hopes of converting the natives of the Congo with kind words and castor oil. So, many a time, they agonized and wept and parted for ever, but no sooner had they got home than she reached for the telephone to beg him to come round, only to find that he was already on his way. The one irrevocable thing Cronin did was to sign on for a cruise to India as a ship's surgeon in an attempt to clear his infatuation. But it was no use. Her long letters followed him, and when he returned they married.

This account of the Cronins' courtship and marriage contains certain inconsistencies. The stated difficulties for a continuing relationship and possible marriage at that stage in his career – Cronin's ambition, lack of funds and their contrary religious beliefs – are not difficult to understand, but they were not unique and are certainly unconvincing as reasons for not marrying. Marriages across the divide were not that uncommon any more. Furthermore, the notion that they were "temperamentally opposed for every practical purpose" is immediately contradicted by vivid descriptions elsewhere in the account of carefree times together.

Another version of his courtship and marriage, to be found in Cronin's unpublished notebooks, differs from that given in

Adventures in Two Worlds. It tells us that on his return from the war, still with his mother in the Yorkhill flat, Cronin became something of a celebrity at the university. His naval service had rounded the edges of his personality, rendering him more extroverted and worldly. He even overheard a remark from a fellow student who had known him previously: "I say, hasn't the navy done Cronin a hell of a lot of good… you wouldn't know he was the same man." He now joined the student union, which he had previously shunned, and began to socialize. As an illustration of the kind of relationship he enjoyed with his mother, on the occasion of his return home from the navy he jokingly asked how she had been behaving while he was away. Her response that she had been introduced to a number of nice people by Miss Fenton prompted him to reply, sternly: "No men, I trust?" She replied: "Haven't I told you there's no room in my heart for anyone else?" A short time later he received a £200 gratuity from the navy, which he promptly shared with his mother.

During one particular lecture he became aware of a pair of bright eyes to his left, and then suddenly a small, nicely manicured hand slid a piece of paper across the top of the desk, which read: "Were the seas rough, Captain?" Amused, he accepted an invitation to tea at the Cadena (a famous chain of tea and coffee shops) with the young lady and her small group of friends. He discovered that the pretty, brown-eyed, slim girl was May Gibson, obviously the leader, and the other two were introduced as sisters, Jane and Madge Duncan. At this stage in his career he was applying himself very seriously to his studies and was making rapid and substantial progress but, at the same time, the relationship with May began to develop. Her father was a successful baker serving a wide area in and around Glasgow, and Cronin found it pleasant to leave the torrid city and visit their lovely villa on the outskirts of Hamilton – her address was "Glenesk", 49 Miller Street – where he basked in the euphoria of well-cooked meals and the caresses and kisses which May was only too willing to give, and indeed seemed to anticipate.

But he was foolish, he later admitted, not to reflect on the dangers of such intimacies. To him it was no more than a student friendship, yet May soon made no secret of her desire, openly expressing her love for him, and making more of the relationship than she had any right to assume from his somewhat casual attitude. Then, as his finals approached, visits to May stopped. He took four subjects: medicine, surgery, midwifery and public health, an unusually ambitious endeavour, but he passed with distinction in all four, and on the strength of his results gained the enviable position of superintendent of Lightburn Hospital, a small fever hospital, mostly for children, in lovely countryside on the eastern outskirts of Glasgow. His salary was £200 per annum with free meals, board and lodging. He had now moved out of the Yorkhill flat, but he and his mother remained close, meeting regularly for Sunday lunch, and he looked forward to the day when he would be in a position to free her from the necessity of earning her living.

Despite his casualness, May began to figure prominently in his life again. He found her devotion flattering, though he realized that, almost against his wishes or intentions, "I had become fixed, unnaturally, in the emotions of this beautiful but hyperactive young woman." Had he been more experienced with the opposite sex he might have backed off, but he allowed the relationship to drift along, as he thought, aimlessly. Then one day she invited him to lunch, mentioning how lonely she felt. Out of sympathy for her, not out of love, he accepted her invitation. The meal was exquisitely prepared by May herself – lobster salad, strawberries and cream and champagne – and eaten in the beautiful surroundings of her father's garden, her father and older sisters being conveniently elsewhere. They ate their fill, and at her suggestion went to relax inside the house, soon finding themselves upstairs in one of the bedrooms. There, she removed all of her clothes and suggested he did the same, urging him: "Come on, stupid," as she threw herself on the bed. Somewhere at the back of his mind a little voice murmured: "Be careful, you bloody ass! But I was too far gone to listen. In ten seconds I was stripped and beside her." On his return to the hospital he became racked with guilt. A deep depression settled on him, and that night he could not sleep. He tried to tell himself that the events of the day would soon be forgotten, but he could not shake off the foreboding that there was trouble ahead. "I did not for an instant realize that my folly of the afternoon would change and distort my entire life and culminate eventually in a fateful and tragic disaster."

The account goes on to tell us that the next day he received a telephone call from May's father expressing his delight that his daughter and he were in love and wished to be married. The news naturally astounded Cronin, who had no wish to be tied down with marriage so young. The older man assured him that he would be delighted to help in any way with his future in medicine, tossing promises about, including the grandest wedding and honeymoon money could buy. He said he was prepared "to go all the way in setting Agnes and you off on your united life". Speechless, Cronin hung grimly to the end of the receiver, eventually agreeing to meet Mr Gibson the very next day to discuss details. Cronin does not say whether he had a plan to follow, but even if he had it would not have taken into account the news May gave him when she met him at the station – she had missed a period.

An old man when he wrote this account of the early days of his relationship with May, Cronin's pen was working faster than his brain. Only two days after having had sex May could not possibly have known if she was pregnant. She was, after all, a doctor herself. Cronin, recalling the event many decades later, had obviously mixed up the timescale of the fateful lunch, May's plan and her father's decisive phone call.

In an instant, after receiving the news, he realized his fate was sealed. Not only was he being pressurized into marriage, but his job at Lightburn would also be lost, since that position was for a single man. May's reaction, however, was gung-ho: "Don't sound so gloomy, darling. Who wants Lightburn when we'll have all the world before us?" Cronin's world for the next two weeks, virtually penniless and without a job, took on an air of feverish unreality. Saddened at losing him, it was the matron at Lightburn who pointed Cronin in the direction of South Wales, to a position that needed no capital, and so his frantic search for employment ended with an offer of an assistantship in a practice in Treherbert, a mining village in the Rhondda valley, to start at the earliest day possible. That suited him, because he had only thirty-five pounds and a few shillings in the bank. He would have packed and left immediately, but May and her family were determined on a big wedding.

The problem of their different religions was now brought sharply into focus. Professor Salwak, taking his cue from *Adventures in Two Worlds*, claims that "May's father would never have allowed her to marry in a Catholic church. As it happened, Cronin's faith then burned low, and he felt no compunction about agreeing to wed in the church where the Gibsons regularly worshipped..."[11] In the light of events, this is not sustainable. Cronin was probably equally emphatic on the subject, and in the end a neutral venue was agreed. They married in St Enoch's, one of the best Glasgow hotels, with the occasion reported in the local newspapers, making much of Cronin's bravery in the war and his great medical success.

The few references to this period in Cronin's life all ignore the one crucial element in his eventual success: his long-suffering mother. Cronin was now twenty-five, at the end of a hard nine-year journey from that day when he and his mother had left the security and comfort of Willowbrook, with nothing but an uncertain future, Jessie's indomitable vision and their undoubted mutual strength of character and determination to succeed. No doubt plagued by thoughts of the trauma her own questionable marriage had wrought upon her life, Jessie could hardly fail to have been heart-broken; history was repeating itself with her only child. There is no evidence to tell us whether the pregnancy was discussed at any stage, but later revelations from the unpublished documents show that Cronin's mother disapproved of his choice and was distraught at his decision to marry so early in his medical career. There is no mention of her attending the wedding – which itself indicates the depth of the rift between them.

The wedding went as planned, but the next morning Cronin was awakened by a tapping at the door. It was the minister who had performed the wedding ceremony. The little man had at first been suspicious of Cronin, thinking he had latched on to May for her father's money, but having learnt of his war service and his undoubted abilities he warmed to him and was sorry for his unworthy thoughts. He then drew him to one side to offer his Dutch-uncle advice: "It's only right for ye to ken that Agnes is a very sensitive, nervy and highly strung lass. If she's treated nicely, quietly and calmly she's right as rain. But if she's not so treated and is used roughly or angrily or given too much sex... then you'll be in trouble." The "trouble" referred to a "couple of turns" May had had, "not exactly breakdowns, but..." The minister went on to tell Cronin that the Gibsons' family doctor had assured everybody that when she was married to the right man she would be fine, and that both he and May's father were confident that Cronin was the right man. The conversation ended with an even bigger revelation:

that May had been mistaken in thinking she was pregnant, but the minister assured him that she had not purposely deceived him. Cronin's reaction was perhaps a little surprising. He said that the news dulled slightly his present elation and sense of well-being, but he was also mightily relieved that there was no baby.

But the matter did not end there. On honeymoon in the High-lands the difficulties began, with May ignoring Cronin for long periods while she played cards with a group of older ladies, losing more and more money as the days rolled by. Cronin spent much of his time out walking in the hills, and on his return he enjoyed the company of a Dr Crawford, Regius Professor of Psychiatry at Aberdeen University. Crawford had read about Cronin in one of the newspapers and had been quietly observing the newly-weds since their arrival. Then one day, having drawn him out on the subject of his marriage, and feeling that he had his confidence, he volunteered that he felt Cronin was in for a rough ride with his wife's condi-tion. "God damn it," the doctor said, not wishing to give offence. "There never was a baby, except in the neurotic imagination of an undeveloped, unstable young woman." They talked at length, the professor expressing his view that May's tantrums were a mani-festation of paranoia, but that with careful handling they should pass. His advice was: "Be quietly firm with your wife, but never, never argue with her, for once she has an idea in her head all the logic in the world will not convince her…" When the honeymoon was over, the professor accompanied them to the village station, and as he shook hands with them he whispered, as he pressed his card into Cronin's hand: "You've a hard road ahead, laddie. But you have a good heart, and if you are wise, you'll come through. If ye should be in trouble, get in touch with me."

The Cronins moved to Treherbert in South Wales immediately after their wedding, his first appointment in general practice, an experience that would later influence both *The Stars Look Down* and *The Citadel*. Cronin was assistant to a Dr Hinde, with whom he and his wife lodged at Tynewydd House, which still stands today (not, incidentally, at 63 Bute Street, the address stated in the Medical Directory for 1921).

The 1976 autobiography tells us that Mrs Cronin's problems worsened on their arrival. She did very little around the house, leaving everything to her willing landlady, took little interest in

Cronin's work and hardly ventured out of the house. It was not long before Cronin's eyes turned to the attractive Company Medical Secretary, a girl called Mary. Like Cronin she was a Catholic, and before long their friendship turned to something deeper. She attempted to put him off: "Don't let us ruin our friendship. I am now a completely sexless person. And if I were not I am wise enough to realize the folly of falling in love with you... you will never stay in Treherbert. If my heart were broken once again I would never survive it." His response was: "I was humbled... any idea I might have cherished of sharing her chaste little bedroom dropped from me as something obscene..." But working in close proximity they could not avoid each other, and so they agreed to attend Mass together the next Sunday morning at a nearby Catholic church, reached in her two-seater Singer car. There was no Catholic church in Treherbert or Treorchy in 1921, and so their choices were either Tonypandy, lower down the valley, or the Church of Our Lady of Penrhys, which was nearer, in Ferndale. Cronin's confession to the priest is illuminating:

> I told him I had behaved foolishly and sinfully, that I had abandoned my own Church to marry a woman I did not love, that I had brutally hurt my dear mother whom I deeply loved and to whom I owed so much, that I had betrayed my teachers and the good education they had given me. That I had felt myself so lost my thoughts and inclinations had become sinful. However, I wanted with all my heart to amend, to free myself from the mess I had created...

He continued to attend Mass with Mary, now uninhibited in his confession:

> I did my best to pray sincerely. It was difficult. I had made such a mess of my life, encumbered by a wife I had never wanted, and now falling more and more in love with this splendid girl I could not marry. Still it was a joy to go forward with her to the altar to receive Holy Communion...

After one service he and Mary lunched with the priest, and it was during that meal that he learnt of Mary's decision to enter the order of the Carmelites. Having been completely unaware of her intention, he was obviously dumbfounded, his desolate reaction prompting a desperate explanation from her: "What else is there for me... I soon see that you are falling in love with me while I am equally in love with you. But we cannot marry... there is a refuge for sad, disappointed and frustrated women who still believe. That is the one I shall seek..."

That same day, on their return from church, he was called to the stationmaster's wife's confinement and took Mary with him. The woman's baby was brought back to life after having been taken for dead, with Mary praying throughout the delivery for the life of the child. Then, in the early dusk, after the birth, Cronin accompanied Mary to her home, and there, standing close together, neither knowing what to say, she put her arms around his neck, kissed him lovingly and then was gone. He walked home slowly, not knowing how he would survive without her, telling himself: "I loved her, yes I loved her." At home he knew he must face his wife cheerfully, thinking that perhaps she might share his joy at having just delivered that lovely baby, but all she was interested in was the new card game their landlady had just taught her and the total of the scores she had made...

At this point, a pause may be appropriate to highlight the preceding events' relationship to *The Citadel*. Any readers who are keen to discover more about Cronin, the man behind the books, as opposed to Cronin the story-teller, will have found in their searches – whether from internet references, thumbnail sketches in several articles or, more importantly, from Dale Salwak's biography – the view that *The Citadel* is autobiographical or at least semi-autobiographical. Many American reviewers also refer to the biographical and autobiographical content in the novel.[12] Those readers may have been surprised – shocked even – at the revelations in the 1976 autobiography, since *The Citadel* is often seen as a love story as well as an indictment of questionable medical practices presumably witnessed by Cronin himself in his early career. They could, therefore, be forgiven for thinking that the courtship and marriage of Christine Barlow and Andrew Manson mirrored that of Cronin and May Gibson. Such a view will have been further endorsed by the 1938 MGM film and the British television series, both portraying their relationship as a love match. The fact that the directors of the MGM film strayed so widely from the plot, allowing Christine Manson to survive, perhaps emphasizes the point.

Ironically, the strongest autobiographical reference to Cronin's marriage is, in fact, to be found in *The Judas Tree*, published in 1961, twenty-five years after *The Citadel* was written. One of the main characters, Doris Holbrook, is, like May Gibson, "a highly strung girl, not exactly difficult but, well, kind of moody and, though mind you she could be very lively and outspoken at times, inclined occasionally to get depressed."[13] She too is determined to move her relationship with David Moray along, using all her feminine wiles to ensnare him. Her parents also, like the Gibsons, are happy to generalize about her problem: "Doris is a fine girl. And I'm sure she'll grow out of her little difficulties..."[14] Bert Holbrook, her brother, also weighs in, articulating the problem from a different angle, similar to the vicar's message to Cronin at the Glasgow hotel the morning after the wedding: "I've talked it over with Ma and the old man. We all think you're just the fellow for Dorrie. You'll steady her down... she needs a bit of ballast, for off and on she's had a spot of trouble with her nerves..."[15] And so, against David Moray's better judgement, they marry, and as time goes on the psychotic tendencies he should have noticed on that fateful voyage worsen until finally she is diagnosed with paranoid schizophrenia and committed to hospital, eventually dying there.

The similarity to Cronin's own situation is clear. David Moray is first ensnared by the pleasures of the flesh, followed by persistent though gentle family pressure, just as Cronin had been duped by May's sexual favours, a phantom pregnancy and a father-in-law's promises. Why he felt compelled to relive the event in *The Judas Tree* is a mystery – an overflow of remorse, perhaps, or the purifying therapy of disclosure. In literary terms, neither David's marriage to Doris nor her paranoid schizophrenia are germane to the plot: an accident or one of any number of physical ailments could have brought on Doris's demise. But Cronin seemed compelled to live through the detail, as if to elicit sympathy for David and, perhaps, himself: "Gradually, through increasingly erratic and intractable moods, fits of violence and periods of amnesia, she passed into depressive delusions..." Then "she will have to be certified" and "for fifteen years, he had been the man with a wife in a mental clinic... enduring the whole hopeless muddle..."[16]

May's condition, of course, was nothing like as severe as Doris Holbrook's, but we now know from the 1976 autobiography that the marriage had been the cause of a rift between Cronin and his mother. His feeling of contrition, after one particular Sunday morning confession, was so overwhelming that he was moved to seek a reconciliation with his mother by writing her a long letter. He said: "It was from the heart, so I will reserve its contents, but I did mention where I had been this morning. I also expressed the hope that I would not be much longer in Treherbert – the dead end of all my ambitions..." He would have needed all his literary powers to heal the breach. After years of selfless devotion, a sudden marriage to an unsuitable girl, an unwanted pregnancy, his departure to an unknown and possibly inferior position in a remote Welsh valley did not match the dreams she had once harboured for her beloved son...

Returning to the 1976 autobiography, the Cronins' stay in Treherbert quickly came to an end. Apart from his address and the name of the doctor whose assistant he became, little is known of his time there, nor what lay behind the short duration of his tenure or his reason for leaving. It may, of course, have had something to do with the conditions under which he was expected to work, if a description provided in *The Citadel* has any bearing on reality:

> There are one or two things about this place you ought to know. You won't find it conforms to the best traditions of romantic practice. There's no hospital, no ambulance, no X-rays, no anything. If you want to operate you use the kitchen table. You wash up afterwards at the scullery bosh...[17]

In 1922 the couple left for Tredegar, in the Rhymney Valley, taking up residence in "The Glen". Cronin's appointment with the Tredegar Medical Aid Society meant that he was not an independent practitioner charging fees for his services, as was customary in those days, but was employed on a salary by the Society. Nye Bevan, a contemporary of Cronin, who was born in Tredegar and went down the pit at thirteen years of age, later became Chairman of the Hospital Management Committee and used his experiences of the Medical Aid Society as a model for the NHS thirty years later. It was not the only fund in the valleys, but it was probably the most ambitious and successful of its kind in the country:

> All persons employed by the Tredegar Iron and Coal Company, who contributed 3d in the pound sterling deducted from their wages, were entitled with their families to free medical attention and free medicines and appliances. The employees would also be granted sick pay on a scale, which varied for men, women and boys under the age of sixteen… no relief would be available if the illness or accident was caused by drunkenness, fighting or any other misconduct whatsoever…[18]

Cronin's appointment was made possible by the resignation of a Dr Dunlop, who was leaving to take up a position in Cambridge. The committee interviewed a shortlist of four doctors, from which Cronin was selected by twenty-three of the twenty-nine votes. His age is recorded in the minutes as twenty-nine, whereas he was actually twenty-five. Prior to taking up his appointment the committee had agreed to build a roadway to the house, The Glen, and add new iron gates, and on 28th January 1922 agreed a sum of £8 for decoration. At a meeting on 25th February only three rooms had been finished, and Cronin was asked to get the work completed as soon as possible or else the cheque would not be paid. Not long after arriving, even Mrs Cronin became involved, engaged for one week only to assist the dispensers.

The committee met regularly, at least once a week, and sometimes more frequently. There is no doubt that from the patients' point of view the scheme was years ahead of its time and was of untold benefit to people who would otherwise have found it impossible to afford an equivalent level of medical care. It employed a chief medical officer, who was also a surgeon, up to five doctors and even a dentist, and it was prepared to send patients anywhere in the country to obtain specialist treatment or itself engage outside help on a temporary basis. It also had X-ray equipment, a full administrative staff and drug dispensers. Costs and expenses were strictly controlled. For instance, when the Cronins' kitchen range failed in April 1922, it was discussed in committee and decided that it should be repaired and not replaced.[19]

The Society never stood still. As far back as 1901 it recognized the need for a hospital in the town, and the workers agreed to provide an extra half-penny per week to help swell the funds. The Tredegar Park Hospital was officially opened in 1904, but by the time Cronin arrived it had expanded several times to a capacity of forty beds, and during his first year the Tredegar Iron and Coal Company donated a new operating theatre to the hospital with modern anaesthetic and sterilizing rooms. With an eye to the future, the Society, which already owned a cottage in Church Street, bought two adjoining cottages, "and then demolished all three... to build an impressive new central surgery". The building contained "consulting rooms, treatment rooms, plenty of storage, a pharmacy, as well as a large waiting room on the ground floor. The middle and top floors provided spacious living quarters for three doctors and their families and a dental suite".[20] That was in 1911, ten years before Cronin's arrival.

There was a certain degree of freedom in doctors' contracts. They were allowed to practise privately, provided the Society's needs were paramount and that they did not use the Society's facilities. They were also entitled to seventeen days' holiday each year. However, the Society doctors did not enjoy the freedom of their counterparts in private practice, who were masters of their own domains in every respect. Many doctors simply could not countenance interference in their affairs from the state. In Tredegar there is no doubt that doctors employed by the Society were subjected to far greater scrutiny and discipline, not only with regard to expenses but also in matters of conduct. During Cronin's time there were several incidents.

For instance, on 27th May 1922 a general complaint was lodged at a meeting about the late attendance of doctors at surgery. This particular complaint seemed to surface at regular intervals, and even included the chief medical officer himself. At the same meeting one of Cronin's colleagues was reported by the husband of a patient for unsatisfactory conduct at his wife's confinement. That particular doctor seemed unable to avoid trouble, and about a year later, on 31st July, the committee saw fit to dismiss him.

At the same meeting Cronin was granted three days off to sit an examination for his Diploma in Public Health. In March 1923 he was given permission to erect a garage at The Glen and was told that he would be expected to remove it if he left their employ. It was clearly, therefore, not a permanent structure, and one wonders why it was needed. There is no evidence that Cronin owned a car in Tredegar, though it is possible that he would have had the use of the chief medical officer's car, for which the committee had agreed to defray the running expenses – just over £8 per month – provided he bought it, paid for the chauffeur and the chauffeur's uniform and made it available for assistant doctors to use on long-distance visits. When Cronin finally left Tredegar, the committee declined to buy the garage from him.

In July 1923 the committee wrote to him concerning the upkeep of the grounds and garden of The Glen. Cronin was presumably no garden lover, but the importance of the incident goes far beyond mere horticulture in demonstrating the intrusiveness of the committee beyond purely medical matters. Apart from the excitement generated by the sacking of one of the doctors and finding a replacement, the committee meetings for the rest of that year were uneventful.

During his time at Tredegar, as well as obtaining a Diploma in Public Health Cronin became a medical referee for the Ministry of Pensions and a member of the British Medical Association. In 1924 he became a Member of the Royal College of Physicians. With Mary finally out of his life, everything about the move to Tredegar – the house, the area and the practice – inspired optimism, but his wife's condition showed little improvement. Vincent, their first child, was born there on 24th May 1924 and baptized in Abergavenny Abbey. But, as the 1976 account tells us, May's problems persisted. Several times Cronin mentions that he had to bite his tongue to avoid arguments: "Rule 27... if your wife is in trouble through her own fault, don't even smile, just help her out." On one occasion, when he informed her that the chief medical officer in Tredegar, Dr Edwin Davies, was prepared to help him obtain his MRCP (Member of the Royal College of Physicians), she said: "Did he, dear? Oh, I wish you had brought him up to see baby in his new pram..." Cronin's reaction was: "I kept silence. I knew it was useless..." Dr Davies offered to lend him books, and also suggested that he attend some of his operations at the hospital to increase his knowledge of pathology. Cronin commented: "Why should I mention this to my wife? She would have forgotten three minutes after. Hitherto, I had accepted this careless inconsequence as part of her nature, but now I began to feel that it might have a deeper and more organic origin. But I dismissed the thought..."

Dr Davies turned out to be a great help, and on the day Cronin returned from London having gained the cherished MRCP, the senior doctor sent his chauffeur to meet him at the station, requesting an urgent meeting. He proceeded to tell Cronin that his wife had consulted him during his absence and that his diagnosis was that "she is not altogether normal". Cronin tells us that Dr Davies had given her the "Forbes-Ellison Test" – a name unknown in the psychiatric world. Whether Cronin invented the name to add credibility to his account or simply misremembered the details of his consultation all those years ago is not clear. The results of the test, however, were positive, meaning that "in effect she is living a life that is, in part, devoid of realism, and it is this absence of balance that induces actions of a distressing nature... you must be both watchful and wise in your relations with her. Above all, be kind and loving, never angry or aggressive..." He assured Cronin that the outlook was far from hopeless, and that she could continue for years with long periods of remission to normality. He also reasoned that rather than thwart her maternal instincts it would make sense for her to have more children. Cronin was slightly shocked, though Dr Davies's diagnosis confirmed what he had long suspected.

When he got home that evening, the house was locked and in darkness, forcing him to ring the bell and get May out of bed. But instead of remonstrating with her for locking him out, he greeted her with: "Darling, I'm so sorry to disturb you..." – and he proceeded to carry her upstairs to bed and cuddled her back to sleep. This new-found attitude was part of his resolution to understand her condition. He emphasized his tolerance towards her, never losing his temper and always trying to see her good side. He even began to call her Agnes, which he had apparently done in the early days of their relationship. On the first occasion she was reduced to tears, and he thought he had perhaps gone too far.

On 28th February 1924, out of the blue, Cronin sent in his letter of resignation to the Medical Aid Society. Unfortunately, there is no record of the letter and no details are given in the Society's minutes, except that a delegation was sent to discuss the matter with him. They reported back on 17th March that Dr Cronin expressed his satisfaction with the committee and Society generally, but that he intended to leave. In May a complaint was lodged against Cronin, concerning remarks made to a patient about her condition. What he is alleged to have said was not reported, but it could not have been too serious, because at the same meeting the committee agreed to extend his period of notice until September 1924.

There is no doubt that the Tredegar Medical Aid Society was a well-conceived and well-run organization with a solid agenda for progress and modernization, but it is easy to see how its regulatory atmosphere, common in committee-based ventures, would not have suited somebody of Cronin's independent nature. Doctors who sought employment in places like Tredegar were either young, lacking the capital to buy into a practice, or older, seeking security of employment. Apart from Cronin, the chief medical officer, Edwin Davies, was one of the most highly qualified physicians and surgeons practising in Wales. The working conditions, intrusive or not, obviously suited Davies's temperament, as he spent his entire working life with the Society, retiring after thirty-eight years in 1949. In his first year he performed 113 in-patient operations and 144 on out-patients, which included operations for strangulated hernia, the removal of tumours and other morbid growths, Caesarean sections, appendectomies, some amputations and the removal of enlarged tonsils and adenoids.[21]

Cronin left Tredegar in September 1924 to take up the highly prestigious position of HM Inspector of Mines for Great Britain. At the same time he was studying to gain an MD, the final qualification he needed to be, in his terms, "fit for anything". It was finally awarded to him in July 1925 by the University of Glasgow for a dissertation entitled 'The History of Aneurysm'. Apart from the written thesis, he was required to attend the university for an interview with the adjudicating panel, so the Cronins took the opportunity to visit their homeland. This was an important trip in other respects, as Cronin decided the time was right for making peaceful overtures to his mother. May and Vincent stayed with May's younger sister, Netta, who lived with her only son in Uddingston, having lost her husband in a cross-channel air disaster. Meanwhile Cronin, like the prodigal son, turned up at the Yorkhill flat he had previously shared with his mother.

Their reunion, described in the 1976 autobiography, was a poignant affair. He accepted he had been to blame, and was duly forgiven. He learnt that his mother had given up her position as a public-health inspector and got a job at a school in

Garnethill, keeping the registers and the housekeeping accounts as well as taking first-year pupils in religious instruction for an hour each afternoon. She playfully chided him that she was teaching the little ones what she had singularly failed to instil into her own son. This was the first time Cronin realized the depth of his mother's religious feelings. That first evening he wined and dined her in the best Glasgow restaurant, glorying in her brightness and animation. She overflowed with feeling: "How pleasant it is to dine out with one's big, handsome son... Thank you, thank you darling for a heavenly evening. And how heavenly, too, to think that tomorrow we go together to Holy Communion." Cronin was thus reacquainted with Father Challis, who took his confession. He then saw fit to add: "Those of my readers who deride our Catholic fetishes must admit that to acknowledge and regret one's iniquities and most horrible misdeeds to a saintly man is a purifying exercise... it was, therefore, a great joy for me to approach the altar with my mother and receive the sacrament with her. I had the joy of knowing that I had made her happy..."

After church, his mother diplomatically refused his invitation to a grand lunch in the city, preferring to return to the flat, where together they cooked lunch as they had done in the old days, one major difference being the improvement in the quality of the ingredients. For Cronin it was an uplifting experience: "This reunion with my mother, the return to the Church I had so long neglected... all these conspired to renew my faith in myself and to strengthen my purpose, my will to succeed." Refreshed by the restored relationship with his mother and delighted with the peace she had at last found, he took his sad farewell, leaving her with an envelope containing £250.

Cronin's memory takes a tumble at this point. He claims that it was when he left his mother to rejoin May that he applied for the position of Inspector of Mines, and that it was Netta who typed his application – but that cannot be, as we have seen that he took up his position with the Mines Department in September 1924, one year before gaining his MD degree.

May and Vincent remained with Netta in Glasgow, though sometimes they moved about the country with him, staying in digs, and Cronin visited them on weekends. But before he took his leave his sister-in-law opened up to him: "So long as you turn up regularly, Archie, it will relieve my mind... it's my duty to tell you that your wife sometimes worries me... sometimes she seems right out of her mind... she seems not to know who she is or where she is..." She explained that May's attacks could last three or four hours, after which she would emerge saying she had experienced an awful dream. There was little Cronin could do, except follow his plan to treat her sympathetically: "I was myself particularly gentle... in bed at night she would snuggle into my arms like a child, but there was nothing wifely in this embrace and fully aware that sex was repugnant, and would be harmful to her, I treated her soothingly as one might soothe an errant child."

Cronin soon realized that the job of Inspector of Mines was boring and unfulfilling, and that he was temperamentally unsuited to any kind of work within a government department. It was not long, therefore, before he began to seek other employment – a return to general practice in the London area. He finally settled on a practice in Bayswater, belonging to a Dr Tanner, who wished to retire to High Wycombe. It had four hundred patients, mostly panel but some private, spread over a wide area: Upper Bayswater, Hyde Park, South Kensington and Knightsbridge. The house itself, in Westbourne Grove, was on a corner, allowing two entrances, the side door for panel patients and the front for private patients. It had distinct possibilities, and Cronin was quite taken with Bayswater's air of old-world, faded dignity.

An uncanny coincidence helped seal the business in Cronin's favour. Cronin bore a striking resemblance to Dr Tanner's son, who had been killed in the war, so much so that when Mrs Tanner first set eyes on him she dissolved into tears. From that moment she and Dr Tanner were resolved that he should have the business. The asking price was £3,000, with the cost of the house to be negotiated. Realistically, Cronin could only afford £700, but he offered £1,000, with the remainder to be paid out of receipts. Dr Tanner admitted that had it been anybody else he would have refused, but then "with a faint smile on his face" he said that he would include the house in the £3,000 and accept a deposit of £700 plus annual payments of £700. Even more helpfully, he did not insist on a legally binding agreement, but was happy with a letter of intent signed by both parties.

Cronin rushed up to Glasgow to break the news. At first May seemed indifferent about his return, and he learnt from Netta that her moods had alternated between apathy and bouts of unusual liveliness. But on hearing the news of a practice in London she exclaimed: "London... shops and theatres, what a difference from this dull little hole. I detest it here, darling..." They spent about a week together before Cronin had to return to work, commenting: "how agreeable my wife can be when everything is going her way..."

The committee at the Mines Department, reluctant to see him leave, offered him the job on a permanent basis. When he refused, they assigned him to a different task: an investigation of the toxic effects and pathological changes in workers in haematite mines. Had he been given such interesting work at the start, he might never have gone back to general practice.

His first patient at Westbourne Grove was an elderly lady who asked if he would put her old cat to sleep. Apparently, the local chemist had told her that he would do it for 3/6d – 17½ p in today's money. He gave the poor creature a saucer of cream and then put it out of its misery, promptly refusing the fee. The practice turned out to be not as sound as Dr Tanner had led him to believe – not from any dishonest intent, but more from absent-mindedness. The Cronins' financial position as a result of the move, however, was nothing like as parlous as that depicted in *The Citadel*, a novel that describes the career of an idealistic young doctor called Andrew Manson.

When May eventually joined Cronin from Scotland – apparently after a terrible row with her sister – she took an immediate dislike to the maid, Elsie, who had served the Tanners well and had so impressed Cronin that he had made the decision to retain her without consulting his wife. Her initial reaction – "What may I enquire is that?" – prompted him to lose control. He caught her by the shoulders and shook her, exclaiming: "You supercilious bitch, drop your supercilious rot or I will throw you out of the house... that girl can be a great help if she's treated decently..." During tea, served by Elsie, who had baked a cake especially for May's arrival, May began to soften and she even congratulated Elsie on her performance. Then, after tea, she suddenly got up, flung her arms around her husband and, with tears streaming from her eyes, declared: "Darling, dearest darling, forgive me… you know how awful I sometimes am…"

It was now 1926. Cronin was back in general practice at 152 Westbourne Grove, where he stayed for the next four years. London suited May: her attitude changed dramatically and her condition improved. Cronin admitted that when his wife was in an ecstatic mood there was no resisting her. She became pregnant for the second time, giving birth to another son, Patrick, on 1st September. The practice flourished, and their lives began to take a better shape. The children attended a kindergarten in Kensington Square, and May felt permanently settled: "I am so happy, darling, with you and the little ones. I have never been so happy…"

By 1930, when Cronin was thirty-four years old, with a successful London practice, two sons, financial security and the prospect of a rosy future, he would have been justified in thinking he had made it. Those reviewers mentioned earlier who were persuaded by the notion that his urge to lift himself out of poverty energized his drive for financial success might also feel quietly righteous. Although the claims that he became a Harley Street doctor are false, his wife was in no doubt that, as he "was specializing more and more in eye work, attending several ophthalmic clinics and hospitals… I had an idea that one day, when he was more mature, he would move to Harley Street as an ophthalmic surgeon. But this seemed too far off to ruffle the even tenor of life…"[22] After Harley Street, the prospect beckoned of greater riches – fame, possibly a knighthood, an extremely comfortable, stress-free lifestyle in fashionable society, ending with early retirement and the opportunity to indulge in world travel or any pursuit that might take his fancy. After all, was that not what he had slaved for?

In fact, it was not. Challenge, not the benefits of wealth, drove Cronin. It was his lifeblood. Without it he became restless. In London from 1926 to 1930, once the practice was established, the inevitability of his future – bigger fees, better car, the social whirl – began to lose its attraction. Even his practice was changing, almost beyond his control. His wife put it very succinctly in a speech she made to a fashionable ladies' society in America:

I will not be hypocritical and pretend that this financial success was not gratifying to me – it brought many pleasant things in its train… there was a neat maid to open the door and a nice nurse to take the children out for an afternoon in the park. My husband made his visits in a new Austin Coupe and was able to escape occasionally for a game of golf, while I, without too many misgivings, could patronize the shops in Bond Street... Nevertheless, at the back of my mind, I was conscious now and then of a vague sense of dissatisfaction, almost of disquiet, as I perceived that the character of the practice was changing... more and more my husband was preoccupied by his "better class" patients, less and less with the poor... now that he was popular he could pick and choose... all sorts of complex and understandable ambitions entered into this selectivity: the desire to get on, to improve his position, to achieve a better social standing... yet even while I enjoyed the sweets of his prosperity... I could not help thinking of him as he marched along the rows of miners' houses in his oilskins and pit boots. And I said, almost in spite of myself: "You thought more of your cases and less about your guineas in Tredegar..." For a moment I thought he was going to blast me right out of the drawing room, but to my surprise he was silent, then, in a low voice he remarked: "I believe you're right. I mustn't ever forget those Tredegar days. They were well worthwhile..."

...And the remarkable thing is that he didn't forget... round about us were many practitioners who exploited their patients and commercialized their profession, yet A.J. never betrayed his real function as a doctor. And in the days that followed he seldom passed over a poor cause – it became a point of honour for him not to do so...[23]

The fact that she was unaware of his dissatisfaction with medicine and his secret urge to write may be seen either as an indictment of their relationship or as an indication of how close Cronin could be. They met as students and spent hours together in the Glasgow tearooms, as well as roaming the hills around Loch Lomond at weekends. It is not unreasonable to have expected them to have opened their hearts to one another, to admit their innermost feelings and ideas. Therefore it is difficult to understand how such a fundamental aspiration had been missed, especially in view of Cronin's earlier writing accomplishments at Dumbarton Academy. Yet, as the rest of her speech makes clear, it had been missed. "It's time we cleared out of here..." Cronin told his wife one spring day, after lunch in their Bayswater home, occasioning great anger and dismay. She could scarcely believe her ears:

What on earth do you mean? We're happy here, absolutely settled, with the children and everything. You've always had that bee in your bonnet, never content, wanting to dash off at a minute's notice. But I've had enough of it, I won't have it any more... in any case you could never sell the practice here – it's much too large and personal...

Cronin then made an even more startling revelation: "Please don't get mad... I'm afraid I have sold it..." He went on, in a low voice, apologetic yet firm:

I've always wanted to be a writer, ever since I was a youngster. But naturally if I'd told them back home in Scotland they'd have thought I was wrong in the head. I had to do something sensible instead. That's why I went in for medicine... Oh, I admit I liked it all right... I might even go so far as to say that I'm good at it. But all the time I've felt it wasn't my job... even as far back as the Rhondda days, I kept thinking what stories I could make out of it... Of course, I hadn't the time... we were always tearing so hard to get on. Well, now we have got on. I can take six months off, even a year, to give myself a chance... it's a million to one I'm no good. And if I'm not I can always come back to the treadmill...

It was Cronin's health, a stomach condition requiring prolonged rest, that provided the spur – "By Heaven! Gastric stomach or no gastric stomach, now I have the opportunity to write a novel"[24] – but how he set about it betrayed his nature. An obvious option was to play it safe, retain his practice and employ a locum. But that was not the Cronin style, nor did it reflect his mood at the time. He realized that the "enforced rest would eat into my savings, and the prospect of returning to a profession I disliked would not hasten my recovery",[25] but it was all or nothing. Overwhelmed by the need to "escape from the neat little pathways of the practice of medicine into the unconfined and infinitely more attractive pastures of literary art",[26] only the clean break of a sale could properly symbolize the end of one career and the beginning of another. Just after seeing the proofs of *Hatter's Castle*, the novel that was the result of this resolution, in February 1931 he confided to his publisher that if they did not "pull it off" he would "depart into the wilderness, uttering loud cries and rubbing handfuls of ashes into my hair..."[27] The success of the novel was his only hope.

In the unpublished 1976 autobiography Cronin contradicts all that has gone before regarding his reasons for giving up medical practice and turning his hand to writing. He recalls how he had been called to an emergency, to a young boy suffering from diphtheria who had difficulty breathing and would certainly die without surgical intervention. And so for the third time – at least in his literary career: such a procedure also occurs in *The Citadel* and *Adventures in Two Worlds* – he performed a tracheotomy and saved the boy's life. The boy's grateful father, a man called Pollock, instead of paying the normal fee for Cronin's services, offered him the chance to make a great deal of money in South African gold-mine stock by joining him and a few others in what today would be called "insider trading". Cronin accepted, speculating what he could afford, and the resulting operation made him £85,000 richer. They chose to celebrate with a champagne party, where late in the evening in an upstairs bedroom he was propositioned by Mrs Pollock. He was sorely tempted, but refused her overtures. The money – a fortune in those days – persuaded him to give up the practice, because, he claimed, the hard work was slowly killing him. However, there is no mention of a stomach ulcer.

With the addition of the sale of the business – £7,000 – the family moved temporarily to Dalchenna Farm, near Inverary on the shore of Loch Fyne. Elsie, the maid, moved with them. On their first night there, Cronin slept apart from his wife, in the spare room adjoining the main bedroom, as he was "in no mood for connubial bliss". He states quite clearly that he started writing on that first night, which conflicts with a version in *Adventures in Two Worlds* and a brief mention in one of his speeches, where he says that he experienced great difficulty in getting started, spending hours staring at a blank page. During their stay Elsie met and married a local lad. Cronin gave them a cheque for £300 as a wedding present, and soon after headed south to a rented cottage in Arundel where – he makes a point of mentioning – he regularly attended church.

Chapter Three

The fairy-tale start to Cronin's writing career is documented in *Adventures in Two Worlds*, but this account is too fanciful to be taken seriously: "As we sped along, that fine June day... lambs were frisking in the meadows... our children, released from the back seat, were gathering wild daffodils..."[1] Cronin appears to have got his seasons mixed up. From the unpublished documents, we learn that the Cronins packed their car to the gunnels with their belongings, with Elsie and their two sons, six-year-old Vincent and three-year-old Patrick both wild with excitement, and set off on a twelve-hour trip from London to Inverary in the Scottish Highlands to find their remote rented property, Dalchenna Farm. There, during August, September and October of 1930, Cronin wrote *Hatter's Castle*. This illustrates his amazing powers of dedication and capacity for work: in only three months he wrote a novel of over two hundred thousand words, a daily average of nearly two and a half thousand – prodigious by any standards, and even more remarkable for a man who, on becoming an established author, confessed to hating the actual business of writing. Before taking up his pen he was almost neurotically obsessed with the surrounding atmosphere: "If I am to string more than three sentences together I must do so in stony silence and a solitude best described as sepulchral..."[2] Even then he might falter: "This business of beginning a novel troubles me enormously... I enjoy immensely sitting in an easy chair before the fire, closing my eyes and rapturously envisaging the sweep, the drive, the sound and the fury of the masterpiece... but writing... that is a different pair of shoes..."[3] But once under way, he became totally absorbed, writing at a staggering speed, to the exclusion of everything else, until it was completed. He confessed that "one day the novel will finish me!"[4]

In *Adventures in Two Worlds*, Cronin provides a romanticized version of his introduction to authorship, containing references to his "private treadmill", his stubbornness and his relentless drive, day and night, to fulfil his promise to himself. While some of this is reasonably accurate, the rest is somewhat apocryphal. On the choice of publisher, for instance, one version – to be found in a biography of Victor Gollancz, Cronin's British publisher – suggests that his wife stuck a pin in a list of thirty publishers and Gollancz was discovered.[5] *Adventures in Two Worlds* claims instead that Cronin found Victor Gollancz's address in a two-year-old directory – hardly likely, as Victor Gollancz Ltd was not founded until the end of 1927. Cronin's persistence in adding drama to ordinary events – a tendency that remained unchanged all his life – is partly responsible for these inconsistencies, and is no better exemplified than in his treatment of the manuscript itself. In *Adventures in Two Worlds* we are told that, while on holiday in the Highlands, and "with a sigh of incredible relief", he "packed the manuscript in an old cardboard box, tied it with farmyard twine… then dispatched the untidy parcel and promptly forgot about it…"[6] The truth is that Cronin had already moved from Scotland and had taken up residence in "Eastcote", a small country cottage on the River Arun near Arundel in Sussex, before searching for a publisher. In a speech to an unidentified assembly he explained the events that led to his writing career:

> I wrote to four publishers, asking if they were prepared to read my manuscript… the first publisher stated that he would read my novel; the second that he would be pleased to read my novel; the third firm informed me that they would be very pleased to read my novel; but the fourth, ah, the fourth gentleman – he said that he would be delighted to read my novel. He then, in his courtesy, became my victim.[7]

This victim was Victor Gollancz, and the letter, dated 9th November 1930, starts:

> Dear Sirs,
>   I have just completed a novel which, although a first novel, I feel might interest you. I have named it *Hatter's Castle*, it is 150,000 words long, and deals with the history of a curiously isolated family who lived in an industrial town towards the end of the last century… By profession I am a physician…[8]

The contents of the letter to Gollancz are, thankfully, indisputable, except that the novel was over 200,000 words, not 150,000; but the writing has the scent of a typical Cronin red herring.

Although Victor Gollancz was a noted socialist and one of the founders of the Left Book Club – a subscription service set up in 1936 that distributed radical left-wing material to its members – his background was a relatively privileged one. Born in 1893, he was the son of a wholesale jeweller in a five-storey house in a middle-class area of north London. His outstanding academic ability won him a scholarship to St Paul's, even though his father could easily have afforded the fees, and from there he went on to New College, Oxford to read for a degree in classics. He moved in fashionable circles, courted friends wisely, joined the right societies, debated enthusiastically, punted along the Cherwell and became fervently political. After Oxford, Gollancz went on to work for the publishing firm Benn Brothers, where he was noted for his sometimes bullying temperament – accumulating enemies among staff, colleagues and even authors – as well as for the charm with which he dealt with those who were loyal and obedient.[9] In 1927 he formed his own publishing house, Victor Gollancz Ltd, and quickly established relationships with many authors whose left-wing political outlook matched his own, most notably George Orwell, whose *Down and Out in Paris and London* he published in 1933.

Although relations between the two men would be, on the surface, friendly and civilized over the years, their conflicting backgrounds and temperaments would militate against harmony. Until his death in 1967 Gollancz was locked in a constant struggle with Cronin over contracts, advances and royalties. From the outset they both must have realized there could never be a winner, yet over a thirty-year period, with individual vanity as much as commercial considerations dictating their shifting fortunes, there were countless misunderstandings, arguments and reconciliations. When imagination and inspiration coincide, authors are born, but at some point the conflict of interests between the creative and commercial sides of writing needs to be resolved. Obviously, in the early stages of a career, writers are at their most vulnerable. New to the business, not only do they lack the experience of the publisher, but also a measure of their own worth. Once published, however, life changes, as other issues – sales, marketing, contracts, royalties and above all business risk – enter the equation. Then, the conflict between publisher and author requires compromise to establish a long-term relationship. It is only natural that writers should think their contribution to be the more significant, but to Gollancz that kind of thinking smacked of ingratitude and a failure to recognize the scale of his contribution. His attitude was, of course, the reverse: "He published the books; they merely wrote them."[10] It was a difficult balance to strike. Interestingly, Gollancz never had a cross word with another of his star authors, Daphne du Maurier, "who was loyal and rather uninterested in money, but demands from less amenable people upset his *amour propre*".[11] But she was perhaps the exception that proved the rule.

Luck usually figures strongly in famous people's lives. Victor Gollancz Ltd had been trading for only a relatively short time when, quite by chance, Cronin chose to entrust them with his manuscript for *Hatter's Castle* in 1930. He was totally naive as to the credentials of the company to which he was committing such a defining document – his one and only hope for a monumental change of career and a vastly different future for his wife and family. He could not have chosen more wisely. At that time Gollancz was breaking new ground with innovative advertising methods as well as his trademark distinctive yellow dust covers. His ideas, considered brash and ungentlemanly by more conservative publishers of the day, were nevertheless achieving results. "The readers had spotted [*Hatter's Castle*] as a godsend and Victor had done the rest, throwing everything he knew into a March launch that made Cronin rich and famous overnight."[12] The overriding factor in his decision to take on *Hatter's Castle* was Cronin's narrative power, which Gollancz claimed the author never lost.

In the same speech in which he described his choice of Gollancz, Cronin freely admitted his "phenomenal luck", acknowledging his "blundering along in this first incoherent attempt at self-expression". He also accepted that "although the theme of the novel I wished to write was already outlined in my mind – the vague record of a man's egotism and bitter pride – I was, beyond these, naive, fundamentally, lamentably unprepared." But beneath Cronin's self-deprecation was a serious and earnest nature, as he was the first to admit: "I could never have gone through with that first novel without some powerful compulsion, some irresistible force driving me from behind."

The book, of course, turned out to be nothing short of sensational, as Sheila Bush (aka Sheila Hodges), an employee of Gollancz, recalls: "Once or twice in a lifetime of publishing a manuscript may perhaps appear out of the blue and become a world best-seller. That is what happened in the case of a very long novel which arrived in the post one winter's morning in 1930; it was *Hatter's Castle*, and the author was A.J. Cronin."[13] Tributes poured in: "The finest novel since the war" (Hugh Walpole); "Epoch-making" (*Daily Express*); "Almost overwhelmingly impressive" (*Everyman*); "Has a sweep and fervour that is positively awe-inspiring" (*News Chronicle*). The book was translated into countless languages, and sold in its millions. It was even chosen by the Book Society, an organization founded in Britain in 1929 by Alan Bott (who went on to found Pan Books in 1944) that, much like the Book of the Month Club in America, aimed to raise British reading standards by guiding readers towards books endorsed by a committee made up of well-known literary figures, including Sir Hugh Walpole and J.B. Priestley. To have a book recommended by the Book Society was a commercial coup for the publisher (Gollancz printed millions of individual bands saying "Chosen by the Book Society")[14] and a feather in the cap of the author. Overnight the Scottish doctor had become a literary phenomenon. An inscription in a personal copy of *Hatter's Castle* reads: "This, my first novel, a great success, removed the stethoscope from my hand and put a pen there instead."

Unfortunately, full details of the first contract between Gollancz and Cronin in respect of *Hatter's Castle* could not be found, nor the number of books sold – information necessary to calculate the precise impact of the book on Cronin's life. However, certain facts are known. Cronin himself, in one of his speeches, referred to a £50 advance from Gollancz on receipt of the manuscript, which would probably have been repeated on publication, making a total of £100. It is also known that Gollancz arranged the American rights with Little, Brown, who paid Cronin a £250 advance and a 10% royalty rate; split 75% to Cronin and 25% to Gollancz. He also arranged foreign and translation rights with publishers in Germany (Zsolnay: £20 advance), Sweden (Pideus: £30 advance), Denmark (Gyldendalske: £30 advance), Holland (Querido: advance unknown) and France (advance unknown). The book itself sold for eight shillings and sixpence in 1931, i.e. 42.5p in today's money.

Both Gollancz's biographers, Ruth Dudley Edwards and Sheila Hodges, refer to sales of *Hatter's Castle* amounting to millions.

If it is assumed that Holland and France paid a £30 advance, then Cronin will have received £490 in advance payments. Also assuming the same royalty rate of 10% in Britain as in America on sales of 100,000 – not an unreasonable estimate – Cronin will have earned a total of £4,740, excluding royalty earnings from America and Europe. Calculating the relative worth of money over time is a complex procedure, and is at best arbitrary, but using the services of Measuring Worth and the index of average earnings, £4,740 in 1931 equates to £927,000 in 2009. *Hatter's Castle* had, therefore, made Cronin a millionaire.

Set in 1879 in the fictional town of Levenford on the Firth of Clyde, *Hatter's Castle* concerns the life of James Brodie, a cruel and domineering patriarch and the titular hatter. When his eldest daughter Mary falls pregnant to her lover, the Irish Catholic Denis Foyle, the couple plan to elope. However, the secret is discovered by her father, who, on the night Mary falls into premature labour, beats her and throws her out of the house into a violent storm. Mary comes to within an inch of losing her life in giving birth to her child, who subsequently dies. Denis is then killed when – in an echo of the real-life Tay Bridge disaster of 1879 – the train on which he is travelling falls into the River Tay. The novel goes on to describe the collapse of James Brodie's business, the subsequent death of his wife and the elopement of his mistress, Nancy, with his son Matthew. As all these events unfold Brodie constantly urges his younger daughter, Nessie, to apply herself to win a scholarship known as "the Latta", in the misguided belief that her success will demonstrate the superiority of the Brodie name in the town as well as securing a victory over a rival of his, whose son is also in contention for the award. Becoming ill under the pressure applied by her father, Nessie secretly writes to her sister Mary asking her to return to the family home, something that Brodie refuses to allow. However, after discovering that his mistress has abandoned him for his own son, he relents. When she discovers that Brodie's rival's son has won the scholarship, Nessie hangs herself. The novel ends with Mary's marriage to Dr Renwick, the doctor who saved her life on that fateful night when she gave birth unaided.

As we have seen, Cronin's use of real-life situations as background and real people as models for characters has at times been an obstacle to an understanding of the life of the man himself. *Hatter's Castle* is a case in point. "Levenford", a name that is used many times in other novels, is identifiable with Dumbarton. In the Dunbartonshire Directories of 1877 there is a reference to Cronin's grandfather, Archibald Montgomerie, as a hatter and hosier at MacNeil Place, 145 High Street, and then, possibly with a partner Donald MacLeod, at 158 High Street in 1885 (only a short distance away from Church Street, where Cronin attended Dumbarton Academy in its original location). The business was, however, sold long before Cronin was born. Brodie's unusual house is the subject of disagreement between Dumbarton locals – who claim it is a representation of a house in Round Riding Road that displays a kind of turret in its design – and inhabitants of Cardross, who are convinced that its model is a house called "Cat's Castle", a stone-built, castellated dwelling on the outskirts of the village, which as a young boy Cronin might well have encountered as he wandered the fields and shoreline around the village.

As for the characters, the conviction that the hero, James Brodie – a ruthless, selfish ogre, devoid of any redeeming features, remorseless even in the face of death – is modelled on Cronin's grandfather has become part of Cronin lore. The likelihood of its being true, and the notion that Cronin was, therefore, treated badly in his grandparents' household, has been challenged in an earlier chapter of this volume. This eliminates the possibility of revenge in explaining the passion that rages fiercely throughout the book – the idea that the squalid treatment, firstly of his mother for marrying a Catholic, and then his own loveless reception, so burnt in the author's soul that a well of repressed hate burst forth in a scarcely veiled attempt to settle the score.

But if his grandfather was not the inspiration for Brodie, who was? After the publication of *Hatter's Castle*, something of a furore broke out in Dumbarton among some inhabitants, who were "affronted" at their supposed depiction in the novel. One young lady wrote to Cronin out of sheer disbelief, asking if he had really intended James Brodie to be taken seriously, implying that he was some kind of "gigantic hoax". Puzzled by such responses, Cronin replied in an article on the cruelty of Victorian fathers that appeared in the *British Weekly* of July 1931. In it he stated: "In the light of present-day relationships it is difficult to realize that less than half a century ago a man might not only dominate, but actually terrorize, his family into a state of abject submission." That observation is the foundation on which Brodie was built. Cronin admits he was a mixture of people, not photographic ("a combination of the more odious attributes of his age": see second note to p. 53) – a statement that dismisses any association with his grandfather. Then, moving from the general to the particular: "In the small Scottish township where I spent my early childhood the general tone of discipline was harsh even to severity, and instances were not few of dark and sullen punishment inflicted by elders upon their children." The small Scottish township referred to is Cardross, not Dumbarton. He went on:

> The weapon of castigation was the taws – a thick leather thong, well tanned and tongued at its end; and it was, I assure you, used unsparingly upon the slightest provocation... chastisement then was a matter, not of accident, but of habitude: a frequent prophylactic rather than an occasional remedy... vividly to this day I remember the actual case of one unfortunate boy. He was a failure at school, and at home he was "leathered" for his failure. At length matters became so humanly unbearable that in desperation he ran away. Two days afterwards... he was captured... haled back in open daylight by his father like a captive; and the stricken look upon his face still haunts me. He was to be thrashed within an inch of his life, the father averred... next day his body was washed up by the tide; he had run out in the night and drowned himself. This was the incident which formed the nucleus of Nessie Brodie's tragedy...

Witnessing that tragedy cut him deeply, but Cronin avoided the temptation to generalize from that particular incident. Instead, he argues that while cruelty was not "rampant in a sort of universal orgy... there can be a prevailing tendency, a cult, a fashion in conduct". He insists that his view was not reached by deduction but by example, that the Victorian age "produced a parent who maintained sternly an unqualified authority and exacted stiffly an unqualified obedience by the gloomiest and most uncompromising measures". The end of his thesis refers particularly to his novel:

It was the sublimated essence of such men that I threw into the character of James Brodie... I have offended many who demand that life should be represented as they know it or – filled with pleasant illusions – as they wish to know it. But I have written of life as I know it. And as I know that it has been...

The fervour and vision of *Hatter's Castle*, later to be recognized as Cronin trademarks, sprang from years of suppressed outrage against a type of man who exercised "in his milder manifestations an unnecessary severity and in his harsher a cold and studious cruelty".[15] There were complaints in some quarters of an excess of melodrama, but perhaps those critics lacked the imagination to accept Cronin's contention that a man like Brodie could exist. In a letter to Gollancz, dated 1st January 1931, he explained: "For my own part I consider that the physical unpleasantness gives an added force to the coarse brutality of the character of Brodie and, for that reason, was deliberately introduced."

But Cronin's compass was wider than Brodie himself. The hatter is a metaphor for the unshakeable monolith of Victorian morality, and his eventual demise mirrors its gradual decline. The book contains more issues than the mere destructive power of a man's egotism: liberal enlightenment, religious bigotry and racial hatred, all fermenting in a cauldron of simmering defiance. The choice of an Irish Catholic partner made by Brodie's innocent daughter Mary reaches out across the divide of religious and racial intolerance. Face to face with the young Irishman, Brodie spits out his invective: "You are low-down Irish scum, a nothing out of nothing, Your father sells cheap drink, and I've no doubt your forbears ate potato peelings out o' the pot"[16] – the humble potato in western Scotland in the nineteenth and twentieth centuries being a symbol of racial and economic inequality, as the poor Irish immigrants were forced to do the dirty work of potato picking that had become intolerable to the host population. That alone is sufficient reason to deny Foyle access to his daughter, but Brodie, exhibiting his unquestionable authority, continues his boasting: "I forbade her, and now that I've seen what ye are I still forbid her... I do not explain to her, I command."[17] And to his subservient, downtrodden wife he decrees: "Mary's not allowed out of the house. Not a step beyond the front gate. It's an order."[18]

Brodie's own daughter and the happy-go-lucky Denis Foyle are the main opposing forces to Brodie's wickedness. Foyle's confrontation with him – in which he tells the enraged hatter: "You belong to an age that is passing; you do not understand progress"[19] – symbolizes the radicalism of the period. Quieter, but just as effective, is the innate courage of his own daughter, whose will to resist her father, even as she is bodily thrown out of her home, represents the suffering that liberals were prepared to face for their cause at the turn of the twentieth century:

> "Now," he shouted, "you're going out and you'll never come back – not until you crawl back and grovel down to lick these boots that have kicked you."
> At that, something within Mary spoke. "I will never do that," she whispered from her pale lips.[20]

Mary gained no immediate and dramatic victory, any more than the suffragettes were immediately given the vote, but her personal struggle, like the struggle of campaigners everywhere, eventually secured a happier future.

The characterizations of Mary and Denis reach well beyond the novel. Strangely, while the link between Brodie and Cronin's grandfather became embedded in people's minds, less was made of the association of Mary Brodie and Denis Foyle with Cronin's parents Jessie Montgomerie and Patrick Cronin. It seems highly likely that Cronin modelled Mary on his mother. They trod almost identical paths: both fell in love with an Irish Catholic, both became pregnant and both fell out with their parents as a result of the relationship and left home roughly seven months pregnant. The only difference is that Jessie married and gave birth to a child, while Mary loses a husband and her child, and nearly her own life. Mary's and Jessie's pregnancies arose out of the ignorance and moral ambiguities of the time, and just as Cronin chose to expose other iniquities in Victorian society, he could not ignore sex and premarital relationships. Unlike today, when sex is discussed openly and largely practised without ethical restraints, Mary had nothing to guide her: "Mamma! Dear Mamma! I understood nothing! I didn't know I was wicked... I didn't know what I was doing."[21] The subject was a minefield of contradictions: male lust and female probity morally in opposition but instinctively compatible. Denis Foyle and Patrick Cronin may have been wicked by the standards of the period, but they were also open, loving and honourable, and they represented the changing nature of Victorian manhood. What happens between Denis and Mary in *Hatter's Castle* is not casual sex as we understand it today, nor the action of a flighty girl. It was "the first time she had kissed any man... she was perfectly innocent and entirely ignorant... her spirit rushed to meet his, swifter than a swallow's flight and together uniting, leaving their bodies upon the earth, they soared into the rarer air..."[22] Cronin argues for a relaxation in the over-pious Victorian attitudes to sexual transgressions through Brodie's excessive hate and cruelty to his daughter, implying that even the strictest application of morality has to allow for forgiveness. The hatter's inhumanity is challenged by no less a figure than Sir John Latta, the summit of Brodie's social aspirations: "You may have observed that I have not patronized your establishment since the beginning of last year... you behaved like a blackguard and a bully to your unfortunate daughter." Brodie's sullen response is: "I can do nothing... it's all past and done with now." Latta replies sternly: "You can forgive her... you can promise me that she shall have refuge in your house if ever she might require it."[23] Latta's insistence on forgiveness embodies the nascent spirit of change in Victorian society. It is also possible that in seeking forgiveness for Mary, Cronin is attempting to assuage the guilt of his mother.

Cronin clearly believed that love between men and women was not defined solely by sexual feelings. In *Hatter's Castle* Mary's love for Denis, in which physical desire is secondary to their spiritual union, is contrasted with the hatter's earthy passion for the pretty barmaid Nancy at the Winton Arms: "And as he surveyed her... a sudden, terrific desire for all the lustful pleasures that he had been denied rushed over him; he wished to rise immediately from the table and crush Nancy in his huge embrace, to feel a young, hard resistant body in his arms."[24]

Cronin was never prudish about sex, or blind to social trends. Joe Gowlan in *The Stars Look Down* blatantly uses his sex appeal as a means of social advancement, while Jenny, one of his conquests, in common with Lotte in *A Pocketful of Rye*, Claire in *The Minstrel Boy* and Doris Holbrook in *The Judas Tree*, never seems to be physically satisfied. In his later books Cronin adapts smoothly to contemporary life. In the 1960s, when romantic sentimentalism was anathema to the prevailing mood of Flower Power and free love in youth culture, he was able to inject greater realism into his books:

> His head was whirling, his heart pounding like mad. He began to search for the necklace, first in the yoke of her dress, then moving between her firmly nippled breasts, further down over the smooth flatness beyond... not here, you fool... in your room... in five minutes... stark naked... her body had an almost sultry warmth as she wound her arms tightly round his neck... quick... can't you see I'm dying for you...[25]

Towards the end of that same decade, Cronin reflected on the fact that the Swedes were known as prolific copulators. Lotte in *A Pocketful of Rye* tells Laurence: "I like you very much. We give each other much satisfaction... we must have a cigarette... then again we have much more fun-fun..." As the years passed, Cronin was not uncomfortable in dealing with the physical side of sex, but he makes it clear that nothing will fundamentally change his views:

> That, exactly, was the trouble with Lotte. Bliss when we made love, and afterwards nothing. No tenderness, no persistent sense of belonging, nothing of that yearning which springs not from the body but from the spirit... there should be something, a communication of the heart rather than the adrenals...[26]

How far Cronin's sentiments relate to his own life and relationships is a matter of conjecture.

Cronin's dependency on emotional impulses or literary coat hangers more than once left him and his publisher open to the danger of misrepresentation. When *Hatter's Castle* was first published, there were suggestions of plagiarism from more than one source, but one in particular – by T.J. Pringle, General Manager of the National Sunday School Union – was directed to Victor Gollancz himself: "I am particularly interested in this author's books because as a Scotsman I was extraordinarily shocked when I read *Hatter's Castle*, not because of the story but because of what looked like plagiarism." The book Pringle was referring to was *The House with the Green Shutters* by the Scottish writer George Douglas Brown, published in 1901. Pringle went on: "I read this book and it made a tremendous impression on me. It was truth written in a brutal way. *Hatter's Castle* is the same truth written in a cultured style."[27] Victor Gollancz had not read *The House with the Green Shutters*, but acknowledged that there had been a great deal of talk about it at the time of the publication of *Hatter's Castle*. He replied that he had discussed the matter with Cronin and as a result was able "to say quite definitely that there was no question of plagiarizing. If I remember rightly Cronin had read the book at least twenty years before he thought of *Hatter's Castle*; and any resemblances were at most a matter of subconscious memory. Such subconscious memory is, as a matter of fact, surprisingly common. We constantly get manuscripts in which there are startling resemblances to other books, and we find that perhaps an author of fifty had read the book in question as a schoolboy..."[28] The explanation, together with a presentation copy of *The Stars Look Down*, was graciously accepted.

But *Hatter's Castle* also incurred the wrath of Sir John Latta, a noted member of a famous mercantile family, for the use of his name in relation to the scholarship which Brodie's daughter was seeking. Cronin, in a letter to Gollancz, wrote:

I hear that our friend Sir John Latta will be suitably appeased if an insertion is made that the names are fictitious. As they clearly are fictitious I agree and leave the matter in your hands. But I assure you that had I been definitely established in the world of letters I should have resented the suggestion with considerably greater authority. I never heard of the gentleman nor do I consider that he has any legal monopoly in the matter of his name...[29]

Cronin obviously cannot now be questioned, but that statement is almost impossible to believe. Sir John Latta, born in 1867, was a well-known figure in western Scotland, chairman of Lawther, Latta & Co., shipowners and merchants. In 1896 he married Mary Short, thus forming an alliance with Short Brothers, the Belfast family of shipbuilders. There is a Latta Street in Dumbarton, which Cronin would have passed every morning on his way to school and every afternoon on the way home. The connection with shipbuilding is evident in *Hatter's Castle* itself, when Brodie expresses a feeling of pride at "receiving attention from the distinguished principal of the famous Latta shipyard". Even allowing for some strange aberration of memory, Cronin's petulant attitude after being "caught out", and his grudging response to a perfectly reasonable request, is difficult to explain.

Cronin took to business affairs early, like a duck to water. In January 1931, in a long and friendly letter to Victor Gollancz, in which amongst other things he sought to arrange a meeting to discuss his second book, he also returned signed agreements for *Hatter's Castle*:

> Finally, with regard to the agreement, I feel that whilst admitting your fairness to a completely unknown individual, I would gladly have waived all question of an immediate cash payment upon the publication of the book for a slightly increased percentage upon all succeeding works which might meet with your approval. However, I appreciate so much your spontaneous acceptance of *Hatter's Castle*... I make this respectful comment merely in passing and I enclose the signed agreements herewith.

Cronin's statement is perplexing. He had no idea at the time how successful his first book was likely to be, not to mention subsequent attempts, if there were to be any. Indeed, he later confessed that he wondered if it would be good enough even to warrant a second try and "justify postponing my return to medical work in order to write a second novel".[30] At that stage, not even Gollancz, one of the shrewdest publishers of the day, could be certain of the book's reception. Yet Cronin's remarks imply that he was already au fait with the complex workings of the publishing world – or else he was flying a kite. Nevertheless, the wily Gollancz must have been alerted to the fact that his newest author would be no pushover.

Cronin's first venture into the world of letters excited him beyond his wildest dreams. So powerful was his determination to quit medicine that he scarcely found time to lay down his pen. Between 9th November 1930, when he first introduced himself to Victor Gollancz, and 1st January 1931, he wrote a three-act comedy, which successfully passed two initial readers, and had outlined and started a second novel, *Three Loves*, on a theme he thought had never before been attempted. Unmoved by the tributes that had been heaped on *Hatter's Castle*, Cronin, naively perhaps, confided to Gollancz even before its completion: "I know it's a better book than 'H.C.' and makes a definite advance… yet I think – at least I hope – the vital spark is still there…"[31]

But *Hatter's Castle* was a hard act to follow, and his expression of confidence in *Three Loves* belied a deep anxiety, which Cronin later admitted: "Because the book represents a struggle between a natural impulse and a series of inhibitions set up by reviewers it cost me simply torture to write."[32] Cronin's clarity of expression appears to have deserted him on this occasion. Put simply, he found it hard to write (his natural impulse) with the burden of *Hatter's Castle* on his shoulders. Sheila Bush, who well remembered *Hatter's Castle* arriving at the firm's offices in Henrietta Street, recognized Cronin's dilemma:

> …but to sit down and write his second book must have been a daunting task. The reviews for *Hatter's Castle*, which filled column upon column of newspaper and magazine space all over the world with a lavishness and a degree of praise almost impossible to imagine nowadays, had greeted Cronin as a brilliant new star in the literary firmament, and there could have been no way for him to write his next novel without feeling the critics breathing down his neck.[33]

The rest of 1931 was largely taken up with finishing *Three Loves*. For most of the year, as far as their correspondence suggests, relations between publisher and author were as cordial as they had been at the beginning. In July, for instance, Cronin sounded particularly upbeat: "Many thanks for your letter… it's good of you to keep me in touch with what's going on… you'll be glad to hear that at present I'm considerably on the crest of an optimistic wave regarding *Three Loves*."[34] Then in August he took a holiday in France, and on the 26th wrote from Le Grand Hôtel in Paris: "On the day previous to the arrival of your letter the novel was finished… has gone to the typist… ready for me when I return from Brittany in a fortnight's time… a crude unpunctuated copy requiring pruning…" On his return from France Cronin was obviously heavily involved in that pruning process, and it was not until 26th

November that he was able to inform Gollancz that *Three Loves* would be with him on 1st December.

The reason for highlighting what might at first sight appear to be uninteresting detail is to establish the fact that up to 1st December Cronin and Gollancz were on good terms. However, relations between the two men changed markedly after a meeting in Gollancz's office on 8th December, in which the most pressing item for discussion was Cronin's second book. The mindsets of both men are crucial to an understanding of that meeting. Even before *Hatter's Castle* was published, Cronin had made up his mind that he could improve on his first effort: "It is with all the diffidence in the world that I say that I can, and will, do better work – much better work than *Hatter's Castle*."[35] Such enthusiasm was laudable, but his judgement was perhaps questionable: it was not for him to anticipate the response of the reading public, the critics or his own publisher. By the time of the December meeting, *Hatter's Castle* was the sensation of 1931. Cronin was obviously delighted, yet he still seemed to be harbouring unjustifiable expectations for *Three Loves*:

> I have taken infinite pains over it and at last I'm satisfied... don't think I'm anticipating your opinion. I hope you'll be able to read it yourself right away – and nothing will be sweeter than a note saying that you're really pleased...[36]

Gollancz, who had backed *Hatter's Castle* with a massive publicity campaign and, as he had done on previous occasions, helped to make it into a best-seller, was not impressed with *Three Loves*, an unfortunate fact that coloured his relationship with Cronin for the next few weeks. The tone and substance of that meeting will never be known, only the personal, biased recollections of two supreme egos. However, Cronin was goaded into action. On the afternoon of the same day he wrote to Gollancz:

> It was nice to see you again this morning and since then I have been thinking upon the topic of our conversation. I have quite made up my mind that I have sufficient to do in looking after the artistic end of my show and that in so far as the business side is concerned I am neither sufficiently experienced nor informed to cope with this. I feel it is high time I had an agent...[37]

Cronin explained his reasons for wanting an agent: "I want to be free to get on with my work, as distractions of any kind simply upset me and keep me out of the right vein... so I expect Peters will be getting in touch with you in due course..."[38]

"Peters" was Augustus Dudley Peters, a respected literary and talent agent, whom Cronin engaged to represent him in December 1931, though they first met at Cronin's rented cottage in Arundel soon after the Cronins moved south from Scotland in 1930. Peters, who had founded his company in 1924, approached Cronin and arranged a short lecture tour for him. The two men got on well, and Cronin signed a formal agreement. He judged Cronin's contract with Gollancz to be sound, but claimed he could have done better for him. It was on Peters's suggestion that Cronin bought 3 Eldon Road, the Cronins' Kensington flat, in November 1931, at a cost of £2,700. Peters died in 1973, but his company survived until 1988, when it merged to become Peters, Fraser and Dunlop (PFD), one of the biggest and most prestigious literary agencies in Britain.

Cronin's letter, though couched in civilized terms, has clear undertones of retaliation. It was a warning to Gollancz that from that date onwards the author would have support in his corner. Three days later Cronin returned the offending manuscript with a terse reply: "Certain parts polished and adjusted... I have been able to understand your notes... and I have put everything right."[39]

Engaging Peters appears to have made no difference to Cronin's involvement in business affairs. It was simply not in his nature to hand over details affecting his life and career to another person. In fact, his agreement with Peters appears to have been a very informal affair, as a letter from Cronin to Gollancz on 4th August 1933 suggests:

Many thanks for your two letters. I duly appreciate your agreement to my suggestions and hope that we may lunch together soon to discuss them more fully. In the meantime I do *not* want to make any move with regards to Peters. My relations with him are not yet in the melting pot and I prefer that our present negotiations remain confidential. Peters is not likely to approach you regarding my contract as he has not my authority to do so...

In fact, Cronin himself always dealt directly with his British and American publishers over contractual matters.

It was a bad time altogether for Gollancz. For a month or so not only had he been preoccupied with a libel case, but he had also lost a much-valued American author, Susan Glaspell, and was faced at the same time with rumblings of discontent from Ford Madox Ford. The last thing he wanted now was a row with a potentially great writer. But communication between the two men suddenly stopped until February 1932, when, free of some of his earlier pressures, Gollancz sought to bring matters to a head:

> I am seriously worried about our relations... before the publication of *Hatter's Castle*, and during the initial sales of that book, all was well as one could imagine: we met with reasonable frequency: you were cordial in your appreciation of what I was trying to do for the book, and you were kind enough to discuss with me your future projects. I am not conscious that, on my side, there was anything lacking: I think that any publisher would agree that I did the very utmost that could be done for *Hatter's Castle*... Then, at some point or other, something seems to have gone wrong. I made great efforts to see you at reasonable intervals, but was not allowed to do so...[40]

Gollancz's self-righteousness was, perhaps, too obvious. Cronin refuted the implication:

> I am awfully glad to have your letter. I was actually on the point of writing to you to say that, although I have obviously disappointed you, you might perhaps let us rally back to our old footing. For I will say that I've been very unhappy at your silence and have contrasted this mentally with the corresponding phase last year when your frequent letters were to me such a source of encouragement and delight...[41]

Nothing was gained by either man in that exchange, as each blamed the other. Gollancz then gave his version of the rest of the meeting:

> At our interview here at the office, after I had read *Three Loves*, you will recollect that I first ventured to make some purely artistic criticisms of the book; secondly, I expressed some doubts as to the magnitude of the sale, and coupled with this expression a tentative suggestion that you

might care to consider some reduction in the very big advance – making it clear that, in any event, I accepted the book on the terms laid down in the agreement. I then said that I was sure you would not connect in any way this suggestion with my artistic criticisms of the books; and was surprised and, to put it frankly, hurt, when you sat back in your chair and roared with laughter and said: "Do you expect the man who has written these two novels to believe that?" That you should be able to say this to me after what I felt to have been real evidence of goodwill on my part, seemed to indicate yet more clearly that something had gone wrong between us...[42]

Cronin attempted to maintain his dignity, despite his injured feelings:

Please do believe me when I emphasize that I am acutely conscious of all that you have done for me... but if you imply that this success has gone to my head, that my gratitude has evaporated into thin air, then really – you are mistaken... your reception of *Three Loves* was the biggest disappointment I've had in my life... and when you told me frankly that if it hadn't been for *Hatter's Castle* you wouldn't have been disposed to go ahead and publish... I did feel like dying...[43]

The version of events in their letters perhaps bears little relation to what was actually said or the manner in which it was delivered, but it is no secret that Gollancz was not the most tactful or sensitive of men and, though he was scrupulously honest in his business dealings, he was not averse to persuading authors to "take small advances or a lower scale of royalties than they were used to in order to leave more money available for advertising".[44] On the other hand, Cronin had obviously built up his expectations of *Three Loves* to an unreasonable level, and was probably over-sensitive to any form of criticism. In a nutshell, Gollancz thought Cronin was getting above himself, while Cronin, shattered by Gollancz's poor opinion of the book, felt that he was surreptitiously trying to worm his way out of his contractual obligations.

In the end Gollancz, who was clearly worried about Cronin's willingness to take advice from Peters, tackled the vexed question of agents:

> I have known no case in which relations between an author and myself, having begun as cordially as ours did, have gradually practically ceased altogether... is it perhaps that you feel relations between an author and his publisher ought to be on a purely formal footing – all business matters being transacted through an agent... this is, of course, a tenable point of view, but I can't think it a wise one...

Gollancz had no time for agents. To him they were "parasitical nuisances put on earth to foment ingratitude among Gollancz authors".[45] He preferred to deal directly with authors, behind their agents' backs if he could get away with it. Happily for him, it was not in Cronin's nature to relinquish control of his own affairs completely, and so for years Gollancz had little contact with Peters – just as well, because they were not on the friendliest of terms. He and Peters had not seen eye to eye over *Three Loves*, and they also became embroiled in a row over Cronin's next novel *Grand Canary*, which is dealt with in detail later. Neither Cronin nor Gollancz, however, was prepared to push their disagreement to the point of breakdown – each was too valuable to the other – and so both sought a way of ending the row amicably. Gollancz provided the cue with an olive branch of sorts: "I am really unhappy about the situation, and I feel I must be at fault in some particular or particulars of which I am unconscious..."[46] That allowed Cronin to respond in kind: "I know I'll never get anywhere if I'm at variance with my publisher... I have the most cordial feeling towards you and I hope that you may one day entertain a vestige of this for me."[47] New to the business, Cronin realized he could not afford a serious disagreement with his publisher and, sensibly, attempted to retrieve the situation:

> Please understand I hate flattery but I am on the other hand terribly sensitive of the opinion of anyone whose opinion I really value. It was for this identical reason that I hesitated to approach you when the work was still unfinished. I was seething with ideas (and trouble) but I was too diffident to bother you...[48]

He ended the letter with a plea: "Let's wipe out the whole sad misunderstanding and start afresh. I've been struggling for the last six months but now I feel that I've found myself."[49] Cronin was learning the hard way that there was more to being an author than inspiration and creativity, but he was a quick learner and, even at this early stage, it is not unreasonable to wonder if the obvious slice of humble pie was genuine or whether he was keeping his powder dry for future encounters.

Nevertheless, Cronin was not the best judge of his own work. At times his expectations were unreasonable. He persistently rated his latest effort as his best, despite critical reaction and public response. Not that Gollancz was without his foibles, wanting every book he handled to be a best-seller. That was equally unrealistic, as Sheila Bush, Gollancz's trusty lieutenant, observed:

> None of Cronin's subsequent books caused such a stir as *The Citadel*, but every one of them had an enormous sale not only in England and the United States but also in translation and in paperback, especially on the continent, where there was always an eager market for them...[50]

Happily, the vital spark in *Three Loves* was present, and the American readers loved it – though the book, perhaps not surprisingly, lacked the passion and vitality unique to *Hatter's Castle*. The novel is not as bleak as *Hatter's Castle*, despite one reviewer's observation that "it is almost as if Mr Cronin were more at home with abnormal psychology than with sanity".[51] There are moments of humour in the laid-back character of Frank Moore, the blustering Joe, his publican brother, and Polly, his fat sister-in-law, and the narrative is compelling. There were suggestions of melodrama in *Hatter's Castle*, something Cronin was careful to avoid a second time: "Melodrama was not open to me," he explained to Gollancz.[52]

The source of his inspiration for *Three Loves* is close to home. The setting is Ardfillan (Helensburgh). Lucy Moore is a Scottish Catholic, with proud Murray blood in her veins and a Jacobite strain in her pedigree. She is married to an Irish Catholic, Frank, a salesman in margarine. They have one child, Peter. Lucy drives Frank from his home after becoming obsessed with his suspected infidelity with her cousin Anna, and he drowns. Lucy is left to bring up Peter alone, reminding us of Cronin's early years in Helensburgh and the subsequent struggles of his widowed mother. Indeed, Lucy works extremely hard in order that he may become a doctor. As the book unfolds, events stray from reality and become too extreme to have any autobiographical significance. After her son's marriage, Lucy devotes herself to God, becoming a novice in a Belgian monastery. However, when she can no longer tolerate the bodily mortifications she subjects herself to in her religious fanaticism, she is sent home. While waiting for Peter to meet her from her train, she collapses, is hospitalized and dies.

Some felt that Lucy shared the psychological profile of Brodie in *Hatter's Castle*: both are driven to extremes of human behaviour in order to achieve their own ends, and both fail in the process. *Hatter's Castle* is arguably less complex than *Three Loves*, because, in the context of those times, Brodie's self-centredness is easier to understand than Lucy's possessiveness.

Cronin told Gollancz that in *Three Loves* he would find "the theme bigger, the characterization richer, the satire more subtle".[53] But Cronin's satire is, at times, perhaps too subtle to follow. Lucy's character destroys everything she cherishes – her husband, her son, her religion and eventually herself – yet despite her dogmatism and intransigence her essential goodness shines above the foibles of the other characters and even of the Holy Church. Is her love selfish or selfless? Is it possible that Lucy is right and the rest of the world wrong? Is Cronin telling us that true goodness is unrecognizable in the modern world, just as it was when Jesus himself was spurned? And, finally, is Lucy's stay in the convent Cronin's first challenge to ecclesiastical authority, and is she the intrepid forerunner of Father Chisholm in *The Keys of the Kingdom*?

The *Times Literary Supplement* observed that: "Cronin seems drawn to the exploration of the tragedies which come from human presumption; and for the spirit that cannot yield there is no rest so long as life is in the body."[54] Thus, the irredeemable Brodie perishes in the same fires as Lucy. The *Manchester Guardian* on 16th March 1932 was equally negative:

> None of the story makes pleasant reading, for the characters are never allowed any of the virtues, even if they manage in an aimless way to avoid the vices. The abnormal may be of absorbing interest to the student, but the amateur may be pardoned for wishing for more frequent opportunities for studying the normal...

Arguably Cronin's most remembered heroine, and one of his strongest characters, Lucy Moore was unquestionably modelled on his mother. Thankfully, unlike Lucy, Jessie did not pay the ultimate price, but lived to enjoy her son's success, receive her due gratitude and die in the knowledge that her sacrifice had been appreciated. She once told her son that *Three Loves* made her cry. Ironically, eighteen years after the book was published, Cronin's mother had spiritual experiences as a boarder, firstly in a convent in Boston and later in Switzerland, where she died in 1962. In that one respect, her life was so uncannily like the story of Lucy Moore, except the tragedy, as to make one believe in Cronin's prophetic powers.

Cronin's first two literary efforts might reasonably be referred to as "psychological" novels, each dominated by a single character through whom the vicissitudes of life – action and reaction, pain and pleasure, reason and emotion, right and wrong – are minutely examined. His third book, *Grand Canary*, published in 1933 – conceived on a voyage that Cronin and his wife took to the Canary Islands – is possibly less of a single-character psychological study, but nevertheless of the same genre, dealing not with decline but with rejuvenation.

Despite his claim that *Grand Canary* was a light novel, Cronin still seemed unable to avoid extremes of human behaviour: in this case the slow recovery of Dr Harvey Leith from alcohol-related neurosis to normality during a voyage to the Canary Islands. Leith's asceticism, nurtured by years of tireless research in serum therapeutics, leads him to suppress all human aspirations – money, happiness, love, beauty, even nature – in favour of his work. But when he is faced with the deaths of three patients – all resulting from the unsuccessful use of his discovery – criticized by a hostile press, rejected by jealous colleagues and abandoned by authority, his resolve fails him and he takes to drink. Ironically, on the cruise intended for his recuperation, his rehabilitation is initiated by love, an emotion he once dismissed as no more than a biological necessity. Lady Mary Fielding, the object of his desire and his saviour, is a beautiful Englishwoman also searching for meaning in her life beyond a genteel, loveless, aristocratic existence. The transformation in their lives is both unexpected and sudden, his physical recovery coinciding with her belief in the predestination of their meeting, which endows their mutual attraction with an almost mystical inevitability. On the island, Mary contracts yellow fever and, faced with death, is saved by a blood transfusion from Harvey: "A strange sense of possession had now taken him... when he felt the current of his blood stream languorously into hers."[55] On a symbolic level, he has given her back the life that her love had returned to him. Rescued from the despair of his monkish past, Harvey is at last awakened to the beauty of the world and a humanitarian vision of the future.

For a love story, *Grand Canary* does not have a conventionally happy ending. The two changed characters return to England, but circumstances thwart their future together. They resume their past lives: she, maturer and wiser, determined to make more of her existence, while he, free of his smugness, is possessed by an intense desire to work humbly for the future: "A new faith was in him – a new inspiration."[56]

Cronin blew hot and cold over *Grand Canary*, displaying a side to his nature not previously seen, full of doubt and indecision. His initial reaction to the book suggests his confidence was not fully restored following the unenthusiastic reception of *Three Loves*. Before leaving for a holiday in Scotland, he felt compelled to get a letter off to Gollancz:

> I must write you before I go... you may remember that I had a very distinct enthusiasm towards *Grand Canary*. I felt that it might have a certain popular flavour, but we decided that after two very solid novels this might not come amiss... Peters, I presume, has told you... about a certain qualm which I had entertained towards the novel. Now I want myself to give you certain definite and confidential information on this subject...[57]

He went on to explain that his agent had managed to sell the first half of the manuscript for serialization in America, which led him to think: "Ah! Then it is popular – in fact it's much more so than I thought."[58] But when Cronin got back to London in the middle of a heatwave to finish the book, he changed his mind again: "I slogged at it in all that gruelling weather until at last – completely enervated – I finished it. Then of course I felt that it was less than popular – in fact I felt it was completely unworthy."[59] At that stage, only an American editor had read it, and then only part of the novel. Cronin continued:

> Now I have had the thing read and have received (please treat this as confidence) a very favourable opinion thereon. This of course completely alters the complexion of the case and incidentally my own opinion of the book. I now think it is popular and damned good. This sounds sheer lunacy – I mean this reversal of my own view – but you know the psychology of the author's mind!!![60]

He expressed the hope that Gollancz would like the book, and finished with: "I apologize for this long scrawl but I did very much want to let you know the whole business and I did also want to pass on to you what I regard as very happy news."[61]

Cronin's diffidence, and at the same time his treatment of Gollancz almost as a father figure, is uncharacteristic. His gratitude for making *Hatter's Castle* such a success obviously still weighed heavily with him:

> Please do believe me when I emphasize that I am acutely conscious of all that you have done for me. I'm fully aware that where six other publishers might have sent me back the manuscript with a polite refusal you accepted it and by most lavish (and for a first novel unheard of) publicity secured for it... a remarkable success...[62]

In the event Cronin's equilibrium was soon shattered by Gerald Gould's condescending and spiteful review in the *Observer*. Gould, a poet, essayist and novelist in his own right, was also a book reviewer and one of Gollancz's most respected readers. The review opened with an acknowledgement that "literary comparisons suggest themselves frequently as one reads, and yet the skill with which the whole is fashioned is highly individual, and provides us with an admirably compelling story".[63] Having established that it was an old-fashioned and unoriginal plot, he then labours the point, naming the relevant works – Harold Frederic (*The Damnation of Theron Ware*), Somerset Maugham (*Rain*) and Robert Louis Stevenson (*The Ebb-Tide*) – though stopping short of accusing Cronin of plagiarism. That was followed by a sugar pill of sorts:

I should not be surprised if Dr Cronin were able to declare that he was wholly uninfluenced by any particular precedent. My point would indeed be made stronger by such a declaration; for it is that these characters and situations have a general diffused existence in the world of literary convention...[64]

Gould then finishes somewhat dismissively:

I do not think that any character, except perhaps a minor one, the stilted and peppery captain, is quite human and real. But then I do not know that it was the author's purpose to give us humanity and reality. The sea, the sun, the tropics, the fever – they compose into a unity of their own...[65]

Cronin had not yet learnt to ignore the specious opinions of the superior breed of reviewers such as Gould who went out of their way to needle authors if they sensed a weakness to be exploited. When Cronin read the review he became "so hurt, indignant (and infuriated by its injustice) that I took the logical step of consulting my agent".[66] Peters's advice was to insist on some kind of retraction. Gollancz, who after all was not responsible for Gould's opinions, was not prepared to be bullied by Peters and resisted his suggestion, whereupon a wrangle developed between agent and publisher. The unfortunate business dragged on for weeks, until it was finally rescued by Cronin himself, who took the matter out of Peters's hands and appealed to Gollancz directly:

We are all wandering down futile alleys of recrimination and imputation. Let us chuck it for Heaven's sake! To my mind the acid test of a publisher lies in his ability to sell a book, not in his ability to control reviews. For the rest you know that our relations are friendly. Long may they continue so.[67]

It turned out to be a salutary lesson, one that was quickly learnt. A mere fortnight later he chose not to react to Graham Greene's review in the *Spectator*, which was even more scathing than Gould's. But he became hardened as a result of the experience, deciding there and then to adopt a defensive mechanism in future by cutting the natal cord immediately he finished a book. He was forced to admit that:

At the outset of my career no young novelist subscribed with greater reverence to the press-cutting agencies than did I. But I found myself reduced to a state of such dithering confusion by the fact that one reviewer's meat was so apparently another's poison, I decided that writing a novel was sufficiently exhausting without the subsequent shower of brickbats that in trying to please everyone I must end by pleasing nobody. And so I resolved forthwith to let the little clippings alone, do my best, and leave it at that...[68]

Looking back on Cronin's remarkable career, it is too easy to be so confounded by the magnitude of his success as to overlook critical episodes such as this. It is universally acknowledged that Gollancz worked wonders with *Hatter's Castle*, and the part his unique approach to marketing played in launching Cronin's career should not be underestimated. Ruth Dudley Edwards, Gollancz's biographer, tells us:

Victor planned the publicity campaigns that were to turn unknowns like A.J. Cronin and Eleanor Smith and modest sellers like Daphne du Maurier and Phyllis Bentley into household names. It was his showmanship – visible even in the green ink "V.G." signature to his letters – that took English publishing... from the "pony-and-trap" period into the automobile epoch... Instead of the dignified advertisement list of twenty titles set out primly in a modest space, there was the double or triple column, with the title of one book screaming across it in letters three inches high... the competitors might copy him... but they had the persistent problem that Victor's innovativeness and publicity instinct kept him always several jumps ahead...[69]

Gollancz was not interested in modest sales. He wanted all his authors to become household names and, based on his own instinct for the potential best-seller, was happy to lavish advertising money unreservedly: "When he spent money he spent it on a grand scale... in his first year or two, rivals could console themselves that he would burn himself out... then as best-seller followed best-seller, authors deserted them or grumbled that they would sell better with Gollancz... By the early 1930s even the most optimistic competitor could no longer dismiss Gollancz as a flash in the pan..."[70]

Yet even he could not turn water into wine. Cronin's second and third books – *Three Loves* and *Grand Canary* – were not runaway successes. Cronin was still regarded as the author of *Hatter's Castle* – society ladies in Sussex greeted him with that felicitation. Both men could not have failed to realize that they were at a crossroads. Cronin had to produce something spectacular if he was to remain a force in his chosen career.

Despite the negative reaction from some critics, *Grand Canary* became the first of Cronin's novels to be adapted for the big screen. The film was produced by the Fox Film Corporation and directed by Irving Cummings, starring Warner Baxter as Harvey Leith, and was released in the US in July 1934. Adapted by the screenwriter Ernest Pascal, the ending of the film departs widely from the book. In the American version, Lady Mary Fielding, on her return to Britain from the Canary Islands, tells her husband that she is in love with Dr Harvey Leith. Like a true English gentleman he obligingly gives her a divorce so that they can be married. In the British version, truer to the book, Harvey and Mary return home and unhappily part to lead their separate lives. The finale is guilty of mild invention, in that Dr Leith triumphs at last in his medical research and receives a telegram of congratulation from Mary.

Although *Grand Canary* was the first of Cronin's full-length novels to be filmed, in March 1934 Columbia Pictures released a film called *Once to Every Woman* in the US, based on a short story of Cronin's, 'Kaleidoscope in K', that had appeared in *Cosmopolitan* in 1933. Cronin's story is set over a twelve-hour period in a London hospital and concerns the sometimes tense relationship between a young surgeon, Dr Barclay, and his superior, Dr Selby. In the film the two characters were played by Ralph Bellamy and Walter Connolly respectively, with Hollywood "scream queen" Fay Wray making an appearance as nurse Mary Fanshawe.

The two 1934 films represented the beginning of what was to be a long relationship with Hollywood and the broadcast media. Throughout his long career, motion pictures, television and radio added greatly to Cronin's fame and fortune. In all, eleven films were made of his books, mostly starring leading actors of the day. When he emigrated to America later in his life, he became a regular visitor to Hollywood, taking advantage of California's climate to

offset the harsh New England winters. He rubbed shoulders with
the stars, but never became too closely involved in film-making or
the larger-than-life world of the movie icons. He is credited with
having cooperated in the screenplays of three films, yet contrary to
his somewhat proprietorial nature, he allowed the directors considerable latitude in their interpretation of his books – or perhaps,
contractually, he was in no position to object.

The Cronins left Dalchenna Farm in Scotland at the end of 1930
and moved south to a rented cottage, "Eastcote", in Arundel,
Sussex. Their stay in Arundel, however, was less than a year, and
their next move was to the Kensington apartment at 3 Eldon Road
in November 1931. Their children – Vincent, now seven, and
Patrick, five – attended one of the local schools. Cronin's fame
was spreading, and his new lifestyle is possibly best described by
Mrs Cronin:

> By this time, my husband had come to submit, rather unwillingly, to the
> penalties of his success. He had been elected to several of the London
> clubs, was on the Board of Governors of two hospitals, and sat on the
> Council of the Authors' Society. Much against the grain he presided at
> official dinners, opened bazaars and book fairs, appealed for funds for
> aged ladies and shipwrecked mariners, all of which, I may now reveal,
> were written out beforehand and carefully learned by heart! It was, in a
> popular phrase, *a full and interesting life* which often made A.J. groan,
> "Oh Lord, why can't they leave us alone."[71]

Chapter Four

The first three books of Cronin's British period, which can be described as "psychological" novels, represent the first phase of his writing career; three frantic years in which he explored the extremes of human nature and behaviour. The next phase, from 1933 to 1942, lifted him to another level, and was the most rewarding both financially and in terms of prestige, setting the seal on a reputation that endured for the rest of his life. The three novels Cronin wrote during this period – *The Stars Look Down*, *The Citadel* and *The Keys of the Kingdom* – were regarded by most critics and readers as works of literary significance. Those books move from a psychological to a sociological sphere, from the relatively narrow, personal compass of his early novels to a wider canvas, where communities replace people as the axis on which the plot turns and in which characters are developed over a longer time frame in a specific historical context.

The inspiration for the first of the three novels, *The Stars Look Down*, came from the author's three years as a practising doctor in South Wales and a year as Inspector of Mines in the early 1920s. At that time mines were privately owned, run purely for profit. Following one of his many inspections, Cronin recalled:

> At that precise moment, emerging from the mine, it was not so much the danger or the dirt or the wretched recompense offered to the miners which struck me. What appeared so extraordinary to me was the calm and casual acceptance by the great, the generous-hearted British public of the services rendered by this long-suffering body of men... I reflected that the production of coal was of vital necessity to the community. It was not merely the process of getting coal, but a unique, a basic industry which provided the material for half the prosperous industries of the country. And yet the men who produced this vital commodity, under appalling conditions, at the risk of their lives, and

at a wage which barely kept them from penury, were taken for granted, regarded by their fellow citizens as no more than ordinary labourers...

That moment left an imprint on his mind: "Subconsciously at least I had an intention, an idea, posted unawares in my brain-box... here is a major thesis for a novel." From the outset he always harboured a strong desire to write the book but – "for many complicated reasons" – it remained in his head until 1934.[1]

Cronin set out to write "a human account of the miners and their everyday affairs, against the background of a small north-country mining town",[2] but with industrial strife and the nationalization of the mines constantly in the headlines, he found himself, almost against his will, writing a novel with a political dimension. A work of such scope, he explained, could not be "complete, or even authentic, without entering the political arena. For every mining village has been... a political cockpit... and the conditions of life of the miners are no more than the prolonged and reverberating echo of political strife and political betrayal."[3] It was not simply compassion for the dispossessed or propaganda from either side that prompted his concern, but rather the evidence of his own eyes:

> The more I looked into the matter the more convinced did I become. Royal Commission after Royal Commission had solemnly brought in findings which successive governments had solemnly ignored. Promises had been made only to be broken. One government following another – Tory, Liberal and Labour alike – had failed deplorably to implement assurances given to the miners upon the hustings. On the question of royalties alone, a principle which had been for twenty years condemned as iniquitous, millions of pounds were still being diverted annually from the industry into the pockets of hereditary owners whose only claim to such fabulous incomes was the titular possession of tracts of land, superficially worthless, often gifted to their ancestors upon a royal whim at some remote period in history, through which access to the mineral was now obtained...[4]

Even today the unjustified ownership of land is a live, though largely forgotten issue. But as a result of such pronouncements, together with the humanitarian drift in many of his novels, Cronin is often regarded as the champion of the weak and underprivileged, which was expressly not his intention. In explaining the basis of his character James Brodie, from *Hatter's Castle*, for instance, he was at pains to declare his impartiality in any moral debate about Victorian fathers, pointing out that he wrote about life as it is, not how he wanted it to be. Later, he expanded the thesis to include *The Stars Look Down*:

> I have always had a profound distaste for those sermons in tomes which undertake to redress a social evil... in plain truth, there is nothing more infernally dull than conscious rectitude. And the author who rams virtue down his readers' throat is apt to produce, not the spiritual purge intended, but a genuine physical emesis... when the idea of a novel of British mines first entered my head it was not derived from any noble desire to champion the underdog, but rather from a simple and direct compulsion to put before people... an honest presentation of this aspect of the contemporary scene...[5]

The message could scarcely be clearer that Cronin is not consciously giving away anything of himself in his books. Therefore, those who presume from reading *The Stars Look Down* that he must have had socialist sympathies, or from *The Citadel* that he must have been in favour of nationalized health provision and possibly a wider welfare state, should reconsider. Cronin's political affiliations are not known. During conversations I had with Cronin's eldest son Vincent at his home in Normandy, he spoke of him as having liberal tendencies, while Andrew, his youngest, in a letter to me dated April 2009, felt he would have voted Democrat had he been allowed the vote in America. In fact, for most of his adult life Cronin appears to have been disenfranchised.

Towards the end of 1933 Cronin could barely contain his excitement over his new novel: "I do indeed feel that I have got on to something very big," he told Gollancz. "I have the plan of the thing almost completed. It will take me a long time to do, and it will be hell doing it... but you wait and see... just one thing – I am not quite sure of the title. Isn't it, well, quasi-poetic? You know what I mean. I'm inclined to alter it to *Men upon Foot*."[6] Presumably, Gollancz talked him out of that idea. Within a few months Cronin, now in great demand, found himself submerged in offers, so much so that it was beginning to affect his writing. He informed Gollancz:

I have been taking stock during the last few days and have reached an important decision. Since the beginning of the year I have been crowded out with work which has seriously interfered with the new novel. Only this week I have been asked (a) to contribute a weekly article to the *Sunday Chronicle* and (b) to take up a fortnightly broadcast on new books at the BBC... This is all very well, but if it goes on I shall not write the book I want to write. As a result I have definitely decided to cut everything, isolate myself in the country for the next three months, and really let myself go over *The Stars Look Down*...[7]

The offer of a radio programme with the BBC happened by chance, as a result of his friendship with Alice Head, the editor and managing director of *Good Housekeeping*, a magazine launched by William Randolph Hearst in 1923, in which Cronin's books and short stories had been successfully serialized. On Hearst's behalf, Alice Head had written to Sir John Reith, the Director General of the BBC, suggesting that Cronin be used in broadcasting, not only because he was one of the best authors of the day, but because he had a "speaking voice of rare quality".[8]

That approach led to the Talks Department offering Cronin the book-reviewing programme, a fortnightly series of talks entitled *Current Fiction*, commencing April 1934 to run until January 1935, at a fee of fifteen guineas a programme. It could not have come at a more awkward time, with Cronin working flat-out on *The Stars Look Down*, a book that was pivotal to the consolidation of his reputation, but he ended up accepting the offer.

A few months into the programme, somewhat ingratiatingly, he asked Charles Siepmann, the Director of Talks since 1932 and the executive responsible for hiring him, if he was giving satisfaction with his series. He wrote:

I hate bothering you... but I should be extremely glad if you would let me know whether or not I am giving you what you want in my "current fiction" series. As you originally suggested, I am trying to aim these talks at the average library subscriber, but it is purely a matter of adjustment to give you more considered literary essays if you want them.

Actually, these doubts assail me because of the fact that in the *Listener* on the last two occasions my talks have been cut down to a few half phrases isolated from their context. Mind you, I don't in the least object to my talks not being published in the *Listener* but I do rather resent their condensation to a form which I regard as being almost derisory...[9]

Siepmann supported Cronin's position and promised to take up the matter with the founder and editor of the *Listener*, Richard S. Lambert. Siepmann asked: "Can you accommodate him on a point which I think not unnaturally upsets him." There followed a mild wrangle among *Listener* staff about policy and working practices, in which Janet Adam Smith, the magazine's assistant editor, commented that she did not understand Cronin's problem: "As he has sold us the right to print his stuff in the first place, he cannot really complain when we decide to use only part of it..." She offered a way out: "If he feels that in any particular instance we have misrepresented him by not picking out the best extracts, we should of course be quite willing for him to mark on his script those passages which he considers the best for the purpose..."[10] In the end Lambert wrote a conciliatory letter to Cronin, explaining the *Listener*'s policy, but offering nothing. Cronin by that stage was probably fed up with the entire business and replied: "I realize however, on mature reflection, that whatever my own feelings in the matter, the question of policy is obviously for you alone, and as such I think we had better leave it."[11] Typically, the mischievous Cronin had made his presence felt, stirring things up and achieving nothing, but keeping an avenue for retreat. It was not the last time he was to put the BBC through the wringer for minor reasons.

Just before the episode with the *Listener*, an amusing incident occurred which typified another side to Cronin. For the preparation of his programme, he had to decide which books to review; he would then be sent copies from the BBC. Never one to miss an opportunity, he overstepped the mark on one occasion and had to be brought back into line when it was pointed out to him that *The Letters of John Galsworthy* and W.S. Percy's *Strolling Through Scotland* could in no way be construed as current fiction.

Cronin was serious when he told Gollancz that he intended isolating himself in the country in order to work on *The Stars Look Down*. From 1st April 1934, he and his wife hid themselves away at Waterloo House, a friend's private estate in Burford. Later that month he was able to report to Gollancz that he had "already written something like 40,000 words" and that "there never was a better place than this for the production of a really great book; an old Cotswold house in 500 acres, the quiet is absolute... that is what I am aiming at – a really great book – and if I hit the mark I shall expect you to do more than headline it. I am working eight or nine hours a day – hard."[12] Cronin left a detailed description of his writing habits at Waterloo House, Burford:

I rose at eight, wakened myself with a cold bath, went to breakfast in flannel trousers and a sweater, walked round the orchard for five minutes, and was at work by nine o'clock. I worked, with a break for tea at eleven, until lunchtime. After lunch I sat in the garden for half an hour, but by two o'clock I was again at the infernal desk. At four o'clock tea was brought up to me, and I must remark in passing that it is necessary to be an author to appreciate the miraculous qualities of this gentle but stimulating beverage. Five generous cups kept me going until six o'clock when I rose, stiffly, to take my walk. The word is perhaps misleading. It was no slathering exercise, but a quiet stroll round the Waterloo pastures, on which I was usually accompanied, not by the spectacular Great Dane which adorned the premises, but by one of the mangier farmyard cats. What this cat saw in me I do not know, but it solemnly attached itself to me during the entire period of my tribulation. After dinner I began again, usually about eight o'clock, and I worked on sustained by coffee, until midnight. Often, indeed, I did not stop until nearly one o'clock in the morning, when, in dazed fashion, I would get up, clutch the candle laid out for me – the house was not wired for electric light – and stagger upstairs. There I fell insensible upon the bed. Next morning I woke up to begin my gay gambols over again...[13]

As shown by the above passage, Cronin was totally absorbed in the writing of his new novel, and towards the end of April reported to Gollancz: "I have just finished Book 2 and can come up to breathe," adding that he honestly felt it was miles ahead of anything he had done before. He felt that "psychologically the drama is very intense and... when you consider that... I am running the lives of at least eight main characters over a period of twenty-five years you may have some vague idea of the scope of the thing".[14] The letter was hurriedly handwritten, and Cronin apologized for his scrawl, adding in a postscript: "But the book is bloody good."

The Stars Look Down was indeed a magnificent literary effort, delighting author and publisher alike. It was talked about as a classic, and comparisons with Dickens, Hardy and Balzac were trotted out again as they had been over *Hatter's Castle*. At the same time, the book signals a shift of power in the relationship between Cronin and Gollancz. Cronin's confidence soared. He knew the novel's worth even before completion, drawing from it a negotiating strength he previously lacked. Gollancz was eager for a December 1934 publication date, but Cronin, now firmly in the driving seat, would not oblige. Sheila Bush claimed that "he refused to surrender the manuscript until he had worked on it to his entire satisfaction, for in retrospect he felt that his last two books had both suffered because he had written them too hurriedly".[15] It would not be out of character for Cronin to blame outside pressures for his own failings, but in this instance it is far more likely that commercial considerations dictated events. In July he broke the news to Gollancz:

Much as I regret it I am afraid the date will have to be in 1935 – the spring, if you consider this suitable. The plain fact is that Dick Berlin [Richard Emmett Berlin, General Manager of all William Randolph Hearst's magazines] has made me such an offer for the serial rights on this side and in America that it would be sheer insanity on my part to refuse. At the same time I am deeply upset at missing the December publication. I know you wanted it and I had set my heart on it, too, chiefly because I am so carried away by the novel I have written that any prospect of delay in publication exasperates me quite frantically...[16]

Spring 1935 came and went with no date fixed for publication. It was not until June that details were hammered out. Gollancz played his usual hand – lavish advertising campaigns, hoping to recoup his outlay with huge sales and by trimming the author's royalties. But this time Cronin was ready, and countered his proposals in a letter dated 19th June:

Having thought over your proposition fully, I must reluctantly say no. You see, I feel that I have already made a generous gesture in respect of your advertising by accepting 20% instead of 25% on the first 10,000 copies – the more so when you consider this in the light of offers made to me by other publishers. Only two weeks ago one firm made, through an intermediary, an offer of £12,000 for a four-book contract with a 25 to 30% royalty rate and a solid advertising appropriation. I mention this not that I have the remotest idea of accepting but merely to indicate that I have very definitely not gone out for my pound of flesh from you over *The Stars Look Down*... I might point out that Little, Brown on their side have set apart nearly £2,000 for advertising purposes... but I cannot help feeling that on a point of principle alone the decision to spend or not to spend must be solely yours...[17]

Gollancz, who was no fool, might have been prepared for some resistance, even a rebuff to his proposals, but even he was probably surprised at the final paragraph of Cronin's response, which turned out to be more than simply a demonstration of Cronin's business acumen. The message bore all the hallmarks of a gambler confident of the future. It read:

I think I did say to you that I intended this book to be a kind of test case between us and that on the ultimate results our future relationship would largely depend. So far you have handled it magnificently. Whether this adjective may still be applicable is entirely up to you![18]

Gone were the expressions of gratitude for Gollancz's initial acceptance of *Hatter's Castle* and the excellent job he had done in promoting that book. The wheel had turned full circle, with Cronin now in full command. He closed that same letter with a postscript: "It may interest you to know I have just sold the film rights to the new Wolf combine for a really big British production."

The contract for *The Stars Look Down* differed from that for *Hatter's Castle* in that it gave Gollancz rights only in Britain and Ireland, its Dominions, Colonies and Dependencies, with the exception of Canada. Europe was now excluded. The obvious merit of the book boosted Cronin's negotiating power, enabling him to secure from Gollancz a royalty rate of 20% on the first 10,000 copies and 25% thereafter. In Britain alone, with a book selling at around eight shillings (40p) and modest sales, say 60,000, Cronin's earnings would have been around a million pounds in today's money.

Opening in 1911, *The Stars Look Down* is set in Sleescale, a fictional mining town in Northumberland, and focuses on four characters: Davey Fenwick, who is drawn to politics despite his mining background and who becomes an MP in order to campaign for the national ownership of the mines; Joe Gowlan, a miner who becomes a war profiteer; Richard Barras, the unprincipled owner of the Neptune Colliery, and Arthur Barras, his idealistic son. The first part of the book describes the events leading to a disaster at the mine that claims the lives of a hundred men, caused by a flood in the notoriously dangerous Scupper Flats – a disaster that Robert Fenwick, Davey's father, had predicted and had brought the men out on strike to avoid. In the second part the symbolic echo of that life-and-death tragedy is played out in the outbreak of the First World War. The repercussions of both the disaster and the war are brought to a conclusion in the third and final part, in which Davey's defeat at the polls stands for the Labour Party's annihilation in the general election.

Cronin's first-hand knowledge of mines and miners imbues the book with authority and realism, as the turbulent relations between the miners of Sleescale and the mine-owning Barras family are explored. It is a story of strikes, low wages, starvation, inhuman working conditions, dangerous working practices, lockouts and terrible tragedies, pitted against powerful, ruthless and deeply entrenched interests.

Cronin chose the period with care. Miners' wages at the time the novel is set were universally low – they were near the bottom of the wages league, an injustice that was the cause of most industrial disputes. Strangely, in those days, miners seemed resigned to the inhuman and unsafe working conditions, but persistently protested over wages. All over Britain the industry was in turmoil. In 1910, in Tonypandy in South Wales, 12,000 striking miners were locked out by Cambrian Collieries Limited, following a decision to cut wages. The government of the day sent in troops, who charged striking miners with fixed bayonets. After ten months on strike, starvation eventually forced them back to work. Less than a year later, a national strike brought out a million miners, and conflicts continued even in the war years, when Lloyd George was forced to place all coalfields under state control. After the war, "a land fit for heroes" never materialized for demobilized soldiers, and the hostility in the coalfields worsened.

Cronin never actually witnessed a strike in South Wales, a hotbed of dissent, but in 1921 his introduction to Treherbert, a typical valley village – one of hundreds of closed communities where the pit was the only source of employment – left a lasting impression on him. He tended the individual sick miner, but was powerless to improve the general health of the community. He said of his time there: "As a doctor I practised for four years in the valleys of South Wales, where every man is a pitman, predestined from birth. Life has few illusions for the overworked general practitioner; he sees his fellow man without their masks."[19]

There was no obvious place in *The Stars Look Down* for Cronin to express his concern for the general health of workers in the mining industry, and the matter was to be taken up at length in *The Citadel*. However, reference is made to the curse of all miners – pneumoconiosis – through Robert Fenwick, a key player in the mine disaster that is central to the story:

> Then he began to cough... it was not a racking cough, but a deep, gentle, experienced cough. It was an intimate cough. In fact the cough was himself... it filled his mouth with a vast quantity of phlegm. Raising himself upon his elbow he spat upon the square of *Tit-Bits*... he would spit upon the little square, contemplate the result, fold it and burn it... burn it with a sort of optimism...[20]

Like the tiny blue scars that pitted his face, arms and torso, a miner's cough symbolized his trade, and eventually consigned him to his grave.

Unlike his first three books, there is no single protagonist in *The Stars Look Down*. Centre stage is shared by Davey Fenwick, Joe Gowlan, Richard Barras and Arthur Barras – all deeply touched in different ways by prevailing conditions in the industry and specifically by the disaster in the Neptune pit. Cronin explores good and evil, and failure and reward, through the humanitarianism of Davey Fenwick and Arthur Barras on the one hand, and the unscrupulousness of Joe Gowlan and Richard Barras on the other, demonstrating that morality transcends the class system.

Davey, working-class hero – upright, genuine, full of the milk of human kindness, struggling for his degree on an inadequate scholarship – has one aim in life: "I'm not educating myself to teach... I

want to do something for my own kind, for the men who work in
the pits… I want to help to change things, to make things better."[21]
Arthur Barras, son of a tyrannical mine owner, shares Davey's
dream and, when he finally gets control of the Neptune, embarks
on a programme of occupational safety and modernization that is
years ahead of its time. Adam Todd, a consultant mining engineer
and old family friend, is overjoyed: "'It's a fine thing you're doing,
Arthur. You'll have a model pit if you go ahead with it.' The words
thrilled in Arthur's ears… that's what I've dreamt about… a model
pit."[22] But Cronin's realism precludes fairy-tale endings: Davey
and Arthur's dreams of selfless service fail dismally, destroyed by
political expediency and reactionary ignorance.

In his esteemed maiden speech in the House of Commons,
Davey's hopes of steering the nationalization bill through Parliament come to nothing when he is betrayed by his own party.
Downcast and desperate for release, he leaves the House and walks
round by the Mall:

> And here the noise of traffic broke through his far, fixed sadness. He
> stood for a moment staring at the rush of life, men and women hurry-
> ing… as though each one amongst them were trying desperately to be
> first. They cut in and squeezed past one another, and took to the last
> inch every advantage they could take, and they all went the same way.
> In a circle. He gazed, and the pain deepened in his sad eyes… the mad
> swift rush became for him the symbol of the life of men… on and on…
> always in the same direction; and each man for himself… man would
> sacrifice the happiness and the lives of other men, cheat and swindle,
> exterminate and annihilate, for the sake of his own welfare, his own
> interest, for the sake of himself…[23]

Cronin himself explained his intentions:

> I decided that David Fenwick… must, in his effort to advance the miners'
> cause, be elected to Parliament, and that, in Parliament, with ability and
> integrity and the best intention in the world, he must be ignominiously
> defeated. I wished, above everything, to be honest. A true hero of fiction
> would doubtless have secured justice for the men in a scene of wild and
> stormy triumph. But reality is a dog which follows closely at my heels. I
> realized that, in life, the idealist meets humiliation oftener than victory,

and that frequently such humiliation comes from his own side, from the very men to whom he has dedicated his service... moreover, I was well aware that, for all their heroic qualities, the miners as a body had often been fickle in the past, stubborn, reckless and stupid. Although my sympathies were with them I could not yield to this bias. I had no desire to produce a propaganda novel. And so, unhappy and unpalatable though it might be, I resolved to end the book in tragedy...[24]

Arthur Barras, an equally tragic figure, desperate to bring sanity into industrial relations in the coalfield, is paying good wages and is prepared to continue, but, by virtue of his membership of the Northern Mining Association, is forced into joining the other mine owners in a costly lockout, one he cannot afford after almost bankrupting himself with his modernization programme. By this stage of the novel the year is 1921, and after a three months' lockout, the men, beaten, humiliated and crushed, return to work for lower wages. Then comes the slump and lay-offs. Always misunderstood, Arthur's sympathetic nature is met with suspicion; the men eventually turn against him until, finally, his resolution cracks: "He caught sight of himself suddenly in the small square of mirror... he looked ten years more than his age of thirty-six... why was he wasting his life like this... chasing insane ideals... embracing the mad illusion of justice... For the first time he thought, God, what a fool I've been."[25]

Arthur meets Davey, the prospective parliamentary candidate, on polling day. Ironically, Arthur casts his vote for Davey:

> "Funny isn't it?" he said, "ending up like this"... Davey thanked him and continued on his way... [Arthur was] profoundly troubled by the encounter, where so little had been said and everything implied. It was like a warning: how terrible defeat could be. Arthur's ideals were shattered, he had stepped away from life, shrinking, with every fibre crying... I have suffered enough. I will suffer no more... the battle was over, the flame had gone out.[26]

Arthur eventually sells the pit, bringing to an end a hundred years of family ownership.

Cronin understood that opportunism was a far more potent force than idealism. It provided the flame that sustained Joe Gowlan's and Richard Barras's lives: their worship of money. Joe is unprincipled, utterly ruthless and streetwise. Life has taught him to lie, cheat and flatter, and from nothing Joe prospers: "He began by swindling Millington out of the foundry. He swindled his shareholders in the boom. He's never done an honest day's work in his life. Everything he's got has come crookedly – from sweating his workmen, corruption on contracts…"[27] He ends up, with his partner, owning a steelworks and the Neptune mine and – the jewel in the crown – defeating Davey himself in his attempt to be re-elected to Parliament. Joe is returned as Tory member for Sleescale, but, unlike Davey, does not intend to serve his constituents. The people who had voted for him "were his, all his, they belonged to him, for his use, to his purpose… he would go on, on… the fools beneath his feet would help him…"[28] Like weights on a balance, as Davey sinks, Joe rises, and the miners are left unrepresented.

Joe is a vital component in Cronin's moral canvas, his presence in the book illustrating that treachery is not confined to the upper classes. By contrast Richard Barras takes pride in his mining ancestry and the shrewd, hard-headed qualities he has inherited from his forebears, which have bestowed on him an almost unquestionable right to control the destinies of his employees – in effect the entire town. In the pursuit of profit he recklessly sacrifices a hundred lives, escaping public censure by concealing the truth. But retribution finally catches up with him when he suffers a stroke, is forced to retreat from public life and eventually dies in ignominy.

Despite his tremendous enthusiasm for the book, Cronin was never free of anxiety. This was the first, and possibly the only novel, in which the characters were almost entirely imagined. He confessed to knowing little about politicians or the House of Commons, having never been there. Although we are not told which one, he was also troubled by one of the major characters, which haunted him "as a phantom shape, mere shadow of the flesh and blood I longed to create. This single character alone nearly drove me crazy. I never saw him properly, nor heard him speak – yet I am told that a distinguished reviewer pronounced him afterwards to be the only real person in the book…"[29]

But Cronin's greatest concern was the dramatic structure of the story. He explained:

> I have always maintained that an essential quality of the novel should be to compel the reader's interest with a steadily increasing intensity... but in *The Stars Look Down*, the climax of dramatic action, the actual disaster in the Neptune pit – and one of the least unworthy chapters I have ever written – came, not on the final pages, as I would have wished it, but at a point half-way through the book. No amount of frenzied ingenuity could alter that melancholy fact, and I was, in consequence, faced with a backwash of reaction, a horrid flat spot, negative and hollow, in which I felt the reader's interest must certainly flag... [30]

His concern was unfounded. The early sections including the mine disaster are probably the most powerful, but there was no mention among the critics of the narrative dragging in subsequent sections.

Many would argue that *The Stars Look Down* was the worthy follow-up everyone expected to the early success of *Hatter's Castle*. But it was his next book, *The Citadel*, that became the most popular and successful of all Cronin's works. The author's enthusiasm for it rivalled that for *The Stars Look Down*. In a letter to Victor Gollancz, dated 10th February 1937, he said:

> A moment snatched from work to tell you I have finished Part 2 and am beginning Part 3. I am enraptured with the book! Writing morning till night, can't stop, the thing going swimmingly. Never had such compulsion except perhaps with Part 1 of *The Stars*. Oh boy this is going to be a whale of a novel...

The Citadel is a story of systemic failure and medical incompetence in the deprived valleys of South Wales as well as the marbled corridors of Harley Street where, paradoxically, the incompetence stems not from lack of resources but from an overabundance of wealth. No sooner has the hero, Andrew Manson – a newly qualified Scottish doctor fresh from medical school – unpacked his bag in his new home, "Bryngower", in the Welsh mining town of Drineffy, than he faces a microcosm of all the country's ills. His principal, Dr Page, had been "a damn good old doctor, but he's finished now, finished by overwork, and he'll never do a hand's turn again".[31] Therefore Manson is left to do the work of two, risking the same fate as his broken and bedridden principal.

Another principal, Dr Bramwell, accepting an invitation to view one of Manson's patients, typifies the apathy and ignorance then endemic in the profession:

> His entire conduct at the case betrayed his ignorance... to think that a qualified practitioner, in whose hands lay the lives of hundreds of human beings, did not know the difference between the pancreas and the thymus, when one lay in the belly and the other in the chest – why, it was nothing short of staggering![32]

Manson's greatest challenge is a typhoid epidemic. The District Medical Officer, Dr Griffiths, ignores his call for advice and help – or, as Annie the maid puts it: "You'll never find Dr Griffiths this hour of the day... he do go to golf at Swansea afternoons mostly... when he don't go to Swansea I've 'eard tell he do say 'e 'ave gone... I wouldn't waste my time on him if I was you."[33] It is left to Philip Denny, yet another underpaid assistant to a "list" doctor in the town, to acquaint him with the cause – the main sewer that leaks into the water supply at the bottom of the town – and the solution: "There's only one way to make them build a new sewer... blow up the old one!"[34] After an eventful six months, Manson resigns from his post, going on to become an assistant in a miners' Medical Aid Society in Aberalaw, a nearby colliery town, and marry Christine Barlow, a teacher.

Dedicated to improving the lives of his coal-miner patients, Manson researches extensively silicosis, a form of lung disease. He is granted the MRCP, and an MD on the strength of his research. As a result of his achievements, Manson gains a post with the Mines Fatigue Board in London, but abandons this after a short period and opens a private practice in the West End of London. And so from unscientific attitudes, useless remedies, ineffective medicines, poorly trained nurses, malingering workers and established doctors exploiting their juniors, Manson finds himself in an environment where the patients, not the doctors, are exploited. He joins a smart set, where even the method of administering medicines is calculated for profit:

> If I prescribed a veripon powder... it wouldn't cut one guinea's worth of ice... but if you give the same thing hypodermically, swabbing up the skin, sterilizing and all the rest of the game, your patient thinks,

scientifically, that you are the cat's pyjamas... take Charlie's case... suppose he'd prescribed manganese, the good old bottle of physic... all he knocks out is three guineas... instead of that he splits the medicine into twelve ampules and gets fifty... Andrew's head rocked. He took another swig of brandy to steady himself...[35]

Another patient, Mrs Raeburn – an elderly, wealthy hypochondriac with a non-existent lung condition – spends her time in West End nursing homes eagerly awaiting the visits of her saviours: "You've no idea what a gold mine that old woman has been to us... we've taken nuggets out of her."[36] The swindling champagne years of his London practice continue until a surgical disaster finally brings him to his senses:

> I've suddenly got sick of it... there are too many jackals in this square mile of country. There's a lot of good men, trying to do good work, practising honestly, but the rest of them are just jackals. It's the jackals who give all these unnecessary injections, whip out tonsils and appendices that aren't doing any harm... split fees, perform abortions... chase the guineas all the time...[37]

A surgeon's incompetence leads to the death of a patient, and the incident causes Manson to close his practice and return to his former ways. He rekindles his relationship with his wife, from whom he has become estranged, but she is killed in a road accident. He travels back to Wales to recover, and he is subsequently reported to the General Medical Council because the American tuberculosis specialist with whom he worked does not have a medical degree, but avoids being struck off the medical register as a result of the vigorous defence of his own actions that he presents at the hearing.

The reception of *The Citadel*, probably more than any other Cronin book, was dogged by confusion and misrepresentation. It was suggested that it represented an attack on the entire medical profession. The press over-emphasized its message with unwarranted and unsubstantiated claims, suggesting that Cronin was betraying his colleagues. The *Times Literary Supplement* wrote in condemnation:

As a novel Dr Cronin's book may be reckoned his best piece of work. As propaganda it is lopsided. Anyone familiar with the medical profession or with social work has met Dr Cronin's characters here and there. True, he has given us the picture of honest doctors; but not enough of them. All over the country today are county and municipal officers who care less for fees than for healing; in general practice are insignificant men and women living devoted, anxious lives with only fourteen days a year away from the clamorous telephone by day and night. In Harley Street are men who might stand beside Lister without shame. Above all, in the research departments of many a hospital are heroes and martyrs. These should have been made an offset to Dr Cronin's selected types...[38]

Even within the profession itself there was some adverse reaction, as described in a much overstated article from the *Glasgow Evening Times* of December 1984:

In modern jargon, Dr Cronin "grassed" on some of his erstwhile colleagues. The novel "lifted the lid" on some of the more unsavoury aspects of medicine... his target, as he was at pains to point out, was not the vast majority of hard-working doctors, but the unscrupulous consultants, who made vast sums out of exploiting rich, gullible patients... the ultra-conservative medical profession of the day were scandalized and outraged. They fiercely denounced the book... and they never forgave Cronin...

Cronin refuted such accusations, claiming his intention had only been to highlight the practice of overcharging by unscrupulous London consultants. Admittedly that message comes to the surface, but it is submerged by a tide of other medical exposés from which few doctors emerge with credit. In his study of Cronin, Dale Salwak reminds us that, across the Atlantic, the *Journal of the American Medical Association* referred to the novel as giving an unfair picture of medicine either in Great Britain or in the United States, and expressed surprise at Cronin's "overemphasizing the small percentage of evil that everybody knows about".[39]

Cronin attempted to answer the criticism at the *Sunday Times* Book Fair in November 1937. He showed profound support for the profession, admitting it to be the finest in the world, but his fear was that patient gratitude should not blind them to the shortcomings of the system. He was concerned that progress towards a more scientific approach in medicine was too slow, that commercialism, which he regarded as an enemy to medical ideals, was gaining ground, and that attitudes among doctors were generally too conservative. In fact, Cronin's views on medicine and the health of the nation were ahead of his time, more in line with Nye Bevan, the eventual architect of the National Health Service in Britain who, years later, found that "much the strongest bent in the medical mind was a non-political conservatism, a revulsion against all change".[40] Bevan also recognized that many of the revolutionary discoveries in medicine "were made by men and women whose work was inspired by values that have nothing to do with the rapacious bustle of the Stock Exchange".[41]

But Cronin's objection to the suggestion that he was guilty of sensationalism was perhaps slightly disingenuous. At that point in his writing career, Cronin was one of the rising stars of literary fiction, and behind his softly spoken, self-effacing manner lurked a shrewd businessman with a nose for the market. He knew that fiction, like newspaper articles, sold best when it was controversial. He had paid his dues to the medical profession and owed it nothing. He was now in the business of writing books, and before his new novel was even published he told Victor Gollancz: "It's the best you've ever read. Also don't forget it has a thesis. There's a purpose close behind me and it's treading on my tale."[42] He could scarcely have made it clearer when he added: "It ought to do the medical profession a hell of a lot of good." [43] He may have set out with mischievous intent, but his motives probably sprang from deeply held beliefs. There is no doubt that the book touched a nerve among British people from all walks of life. It stirred the passions of some doctors. Dr Edwin Davies, for example, who was the chief medical officer of the Tredegar Medical Aid Society during Cronin's tenure, portrayed in the book as Dr Llewellyn, "considered suing him for libel as he considered that the Medical Superintendent in the novel was a slur on himself".[44] Certainly, there were aspects of his character that Cronin might have had difficulty in defending, had he been sued, but after due consideration Davies dropped the matter.

In fact, there was nothing startling in the message of the book. Most doctors of the day would probably have agreed with Cronin, and Manson's impassioned speech at the hearing of the General Medical Council would hardly have found one dissenter among a profession of about twenty thousand practitioners. There is a campaigning zeal in the pages of *The Citadel*, but Cronin was not a political animal, and so the greatest medical scandal of the day, the lack of a universal system of affordable medical care, was ignored.

* * *

The Citadel presents us with a great interpretative challenge. Cronin had been a doctor in South Wales and later in West London. It was never likely, therefore, that the novel would be treated simply as a story about the early life and aspirations of a young, idealistic practitioner.

Since medicine was Cronin's chosen profession for fifteen years, it is tempting to assume that much of the narrative derived from his experiences, and that the views of the hero were Cronin's. However, just as an identification of the character of James Brodie in *Hatter's Castle* with Archibald Montgomerie has to be resisted, so any direct correspondence between Andrew Manson and Cronin should be avoided. Similarly, the events in the book should not be construed to be an accurate reflection of reality. During Cronin's South Wales period, for example, there was no typhoid epidemic, no dynamiting of the drains, no pit disaster, no amputations, no marriage to the local schoolteacher, no miraculous resuscitation of a dead child, no arguments in committee over vivisection and no research into dust inhalation.

The fact that Manson's experiences were not necessarily Cronin's does not diminish the value of the book or lessen its interest, but if misinterpreted – that is, if the autobiographical element is exaggerated – it could give the wrong impression of the author.

Perhaps the most significant difference between Manson and his creator concerns their respective attitudes to their profession: in essence, the former is an idealist and the latter a pragmatist. Dale Salwak claimed that the main interest in *The Citadel* "lay in the unmistakeable similarity between the hero's personal philosophy and Cronin's own opinions... There is the same integrity of character, the same effort to focus public attention on the social forces that are responsible for many of the ills of his patients."[45] The supposition is appealing but questionable.

Cronin seems to have lacked a bedside manner, and was certainly not a driven healer. He chose medicine mainly as a means of making a living – one that, seen in the context of his humble background, appeared to be a very good one. Although he never failed to lavish praise on the medical profession and described it once as "a profession of self-sacrifice and humanity",[46] he recognized his own lack of the altruistic temperament necessary for a medical career. Despite his reservations about his own suitability, he strove to gain higher qualifications in order to obtain the greater comfort and rewards of a successful London practice. If he had to practise medicine, he reasoned, then at least practise it as painlessly as possible. But it was not long before he became restless again, until he finally admitted to himself that he never truly wanted to be a doctor of either type – in pit boots scurrying around the terraced houses of an ugly, downtrodden town buried in the Welsh valleys, or a well-paid practitioner dressed in Savile Row suits and handmade shoes from Lobbs. Having battled with his conscience for years, he at last found himself able to confess that *Hatter's Castle*, his first novel, "was a rather fumbling attempt... to escape from the neat little pathways of the practice of medicine into the unconfined and, to my mind, infinitely more attractive pastures of literary art".[47] The book's success enabled him to justify postponing a return to medical work. In a speech to the Press Association he admitted that it had provided him with an opportunity "to leave my practice which I hated and take up the job of writing which I love".[48] At last the truth was out: he was not a born doctor, but had at last found a vocation that promised to endure.

Manson, on the other hand, is a passionate young man, a dedicated doctor who looks upon his chosen profession as a vocation and whose blood runs with humanitarian fervour. His motives in gaining higher qualifications, and hence gravitas in the medical world, are compassionate, the ultimate goals being the advancement of science and the health of his patients, not his own status in the medical profession. Despite a brief spell of money-making madness in London, Manson is consistently motivated by idealism:

he gains his MD for his work on dust inhalation and falls out with the committee as a result, resigning in a fit of anger; with his humanitarian passions rekindled, he sets up the practice of his dreams with two equally dedicated friends and colleagues – and presumably, in the fictional thereafter, tends the sick with devotion for the rest of his life.

Cronin and his creation also differ at other levels. Manson, for example, is not an intellectual: as long as he has enough money for his cigarettes and his work, he is happy. He has no social graces, and is undiplomatic to the point of rudeness. Cronin, in contrast, was quite the opposite: clever, articulate and capable of lighting up a room with sparkling, intelligent conversation. He was also cultured in music, art and literature, in later life building up a considerable art collection.

The typhoid outbreak at Drineffy represents another notable departure from the reality of Cronin's Welsh experience. In the novel, Dr Page, Manson's principal, informs him: "It's always been difficult. We've no hospital… if you should run into anything very nasty ring up Griffiths at Toniglan. That's fifteen miles down the valley…" There was, in fact, an isolation hospital at Tyntyla, founded in the previous century, about two to three miles from Treherbert (Drineffy). It had eighty beds split almost equally for cases of diphtheria, scarlet fever and typhoid. Cronin's decision to focus in the novel on typhoid fever is an interesting one, since there was no epidemic in Treherbert in 1921, when he was there. Between 1901 and 1921 there was only one death from this condition – in 1917 – in the whole Rhondda region, compared with 1,361 from measles, 353 from scarlet fever, 773 from whooping cough, 769 from diphtheria and 2,748 from diarrhoea – possibly as a result of cholera.[49] Indeed, Cronin chose to highlight the one disease that was under control. The typhoid mortality rate in England and Wales had fallen from thirty-two cases per 100,000 in the 1870s to just one per 100,000 in the late 1920s. Specifically, there were only fourteen cases in the entire Rhondda region in 1921 and no deaths, compared to the nine cases handled by Manson and Denny between them in the novel – one of which results in a death.[50]

Another important difference concerns the subject of Manson's research. Recognizing that "after he had made a complete clinical survey of the pulmonary conditions of all workmen in the district, and tabulating his findings, he had plain evidence of the marked preponderance of lung disease amongst the anthracite workers",[51] he embarks on an extensive programme of research over a three-year period that is of enormous social importance. The work, carried out in his spare time, takes its toll on his health, but gains him an MD, enhances his reputation and is instrumental in landing him a prestigious post with the Mines Fatigue Board. It is also the reason he leaves Aberalaw, since some members of the committee object that he has done research on animals without applying for a Home Office licence. Though exonerated, he decides to resign. The incident is central to Manson's time in Aberalaw, and an important indicator of his character.

Readers of *The Citadel* may have been led to believe that Cronin also carried out unpaid research for the same altruistic reasons. Many articles about Cronin, most notably the *Times* obituary and a recent 2008 paper in the *English Historical Review*[52] encourage that view, but the truth is that the author did not carry out any research in Tredegar. In fact, far from resigning in anger, Cronin left Tredegar peaceably in September 1924, and it was not until October 1925, during his time as Inspector of Mines, with spare time on his hands, that he was asked by the health-advisory committee of the mines department to investigate working conditions in iron-ore mines in Cumberland and North Lancashire – not coal mines in South Wales. It was a competent study, significant enough to be referred to in a more detailed forty-five-year study of pneumoconiosis in the haematite-mining industry carried out by John Craw and published in 1982, but it could hardly be described as a major report.[53] It was received for publication in February 1926 – that is, after only a few months' research – and it ran to only four pages.[54] As has been discussed, Cronin's MD was gained for his work 'The History of Aneurism' in 1925.

Cronin's use of real-life people and events as inspiration for his novels had previously caused difficulties, such as the accusations of plagiarism over *Hatter's Castle*. The publication of *The Citadel*, and the controversy surrounding it, now presented potential legal problems. Cronin had practised medicine from 1921 to 1930, so most, if not all, of his patients and colleagues were alive when the book was published. Gollancz was extremely worried about the possibility of libel, having been caught out in 1931 with a first novel, *Children Be Happy* by Rosalind Wade, which had turned out to be autobiographical. After a flood of solicitors' letters, the book was immediately withdrawn, while records "in the firm's accounts or catalogues... disappeared without trace, like a bad dream".[55] Victor Gollancz's company had only been in existence for four years, and he was so concerned that the episode might wreck his business that it left him with a "terror of legal proceedings" which at times inhibited him "from publishing books he felt to be both artistically worthy and capable of helping mankind".[56]

In reference to *The Citadel*, Harold Rubinstein, Victor Gollancz's solicitor and brother-in-law, wrote on 14th June 1937:

> As this novel makes a general attack on certain sections of the medical profession and in particular the fashionable West End practitioners, it is imperative that the author should satisfy you as far as possible that no doctor could claim to be identified with any character...

That same day Rubinstein's concerns were communicated to Cronin in a letter headed "LIBEL". The following day, 15th June, fresh from a motoring holiday in France, Switzerland, Austria and Hungary, Cronin responded confidently: "I have so mixed fiction with fact that no person is in my opinion represented as a recognizable entity." Sheila Bush commented many years later: "It is amazing how foolhardy otherwise sensible authors can be about libel; is this because they really don't understand the risks involved, or just for the hell of it?"[57]

Cronin's assurances satisfied Gollancz, and publication went ahead. But in October 1937 a communication – admittedly not un-friendly – was received from Emrys Hughes, the editor of *Forward*, a Scottish socialist journal, objecting to the use of his name in the book. A month later, ICI complained that the word "Rexine", if not spelt with a capital letter, was a misuse of a registered trademark. In subsequent editions Emrys was changed to Emlyn and a capital "R" was used for Rexine. Peace then reigned for almost a year, until it was shattered by a threatened libel action from Mrs Hinde-Arnold, widow of Dr William Hinde, Cronin's principal in Treherbert. Mrs Hinde-Arnold claimed that she was easily recognizable as Blodwen

Page, wife of Dr Page in the novel. On 27th October 1938, Victor
Gollancz called for his solicitor's intervention:

> Will you please take this over. I imagine from gossip I have heard in
> Wales that what is said is probably true... I have been told by Welsh
> people that a great number of the characters are easily identifiable. As
> you will see, they make very modest demands, but the real difficulty
> is – will Cronin on his side agree to them?

Rubinstein acquainted Cronin with the full details of the complaint. On 29th October the author replied:

> It was with feelings of absolute astonishment that I read the letter
> you have received from Mrs Hinde-Arnold's solicitors... though it is
> seventeen years since I saw Mrs Hinde my recollection of her extreme
> kindness and generosity... has left me with nothing but the deepest sense
> of gratitude and esteem towards her... the character of Blodwen Page is
> wholly and utterly fictitious and in no way resembles that of Mrs Hinde.

It clearly did not occur to Cronin that the Treherbert locals would
be unaware of his high regard for his ex-landlady. In an attempt at
mitigation, he suggested that some reference to the unintentional
slight be inserted in the leading Welsh newspapers and that as a
gesture of goodwill he was willing "to reimburse her for any reasonable amount she has incurred". That was not wholly acceptable,
and pressure on Gollancz's solicitors increased with the imminence
of the film based on the book, which was to be premiered in Britain
in December. Mrs Hinde-Arnold's solicitors were concerned that
further cheap editions of the book would be so widely read that,
in conjunction with the film, she would be identified on a wider
scale. For his part, Gollancz was anxious for a quick solution, as the
book was almost out of stock and he needed to rush out another
edition to catch the Christmas rush. On 5th December he wrote
to Rubinstein: "Is there still nothing from Cronin?"

A week later Rubinstein received a letter from Mrs Hinde-
Arnold's solicitors which contained the outline of a statement of
unqualified apology to which Cronin would have to agree and sign.
Typically, Cronin insisted on changing the wording of a sentence
or two in the solicitor's text, but once that and the alterations to

the subsequent editions of the book were agreed – Mrs Page the wife became Miss Page the sister – the matter was settled out of court. There was no discussion between Rubinstein, Gollancz and Cronin about resisting the claim in court, but Cronin's capitulation suggests that he knew he had overstepped the mark. In the first edition, Mrs Page is painted as an overfed, guzzling hypochondriac, a scheming, domineering, "mercenary bitch". Manson accuses her of "barefaced extortion". He says: "I know for a fact that you are making one thousand five hundred pounds a year because of the work I do for you here. Out of this you pay me a miserable two hundred and fifty, and in addition you've done your best to starve me." Subsequent editions of the book were considerably softened in tone, while still making the essential point that Manson and Blodwen did not, and never would, get on.

The Citadel, aided by a strong publicity campaign orchestrated by Gollancz, was a huge commercial success, "shattering every record in the nine years of the firm's existence".[58] It sold a hundred thousand copies in about three months, and was subsequently re-printed at the rate of about ten thousand copies a week. Together with Daphne du Maurier and Dorothy L. Sayers, Cronin became one of Gollancz's biggest sellers. *The Citadel* established him as one of the most popular novelists of the 1930s.

His contract with Gollancz, which extended to his next two books, paid an advance of £3,333 per title and a 25% royalty rate on the published price at home and 6d (2.5p) on every copy sold to the Colonies. In view of its enormous sales, greater than any other of his books, *The Citadel*, by today's standards, elevated Cronin to the multi-millionaire class.

The BBC ran a series of ten readings from *The Citadel* in August 1938, and in June of the following year the Programme Department in Newcastle upon Tyne investigated the possibility of a radio version of *The Stars Look Down*. There was no shortage of enthusiasm for the project, but it was dropped at the last minute because the government was unhappy about the prominence given to strikes in the book and the adverse effect it might have on the morale of the population. The project was revisited in 1952 for the small screen, only to be dropped a second time because it was felt that the novel was too vast to be compressed into a television series.

The film adaptation of *The Citadel* premiered in New York in November 1938 and in London the following month. As this was Cronin's most popular novel, it is not surprising that it was also a very successful film, with estimated earnings of around $2,500,000. Directed by King Vidor, with a budget of one million dollars, it starred Robert Donat as Andrew Manson, with a supporting cast that included Rosalind Russell, Ralph Richardson, Rex Harrison and Emlyn Williams, the latter also contributing to the script. Though an MGM film, it was shot on location in Abertillery, South Wales, and in London, giving it a more realistic feel. In 1939 the film received an Academy Award nomination for Best Picture. There are two big departures from the plot of the novel: Manson's wife, Christine, is not killed, allowing a happy ending, while his great friend, Phillip Denny, dies on the operating table and cannot, therefore, join Manson and Hope in the Stanborough group practice.

Despite the unsuccessful efforts at adaptation for the small screen, a film of *The Stars Look Down* was released in Britain in January 1940 and in America in July 1941. The first attempt to film the book, soon after its publication, failed through lack of funding, but later Grafton Films invested a huge sum, £100,000, in the venture, and the film was distributed by Grand National Pictures. Carol Reed, the director, called it a "gloomy little piece" and expected a box-office disaster, but was surprised how wartime audiences warmed to it. The cast included Michael Redgrave, Margaret Lockwood and, again, Emlyn Williams. Shooting took place at a mine in Workington in Cumbria, then transferred to the biggest exterior set ever constructed for a British film – an exact replica of the colliery used on location – in studios in Denham and Twickenham. The film was a commercial triumph. In more recent years, from September to November 1974, Granada TV ran a very successful thirteen-episode adaptation of the novel.

Life at 3 Eldon Road in Kensington suited Cronin, as he was close to people and places that were shaping his life. But according to his 1976 autobiography, May began to get restless, saying she was missing the countryside, and so Cronin started looking for a country house. He discovered Sullington Old Rectory in Storrington, Sussex, an eighteenth-century property, on the market because the rector (Sydney Le Mesurier, father of the actor John Le Mesurier) found it too expensive to run. Cronin conducted the negotiations himself, eventually agreeing a figure of £2,750, and signed the contract on 29th July 1935.

Returning to Eldon Road late one night, during the period when he was arranging to buy the property, May accused her husband of having been "out with the girls" all day: "Barefoot and in her nightdress, her hair dishevelled and such a look of devilish anger contorting her face, she screamed: 'What the hell do you mean coming in at this hour?'" In an attempt to calm her down, he told her about Sullington Court, whereupon she turned white and fell to the floor writhing. He picked her up and carried her back to bed, with her begging him: "For Christ's sake, darling, don't leave me... I implore you..." He gave her a strong sedative and eventually she fell asleep. The next morning she was back to normal.

After the move, life at Sullington Court passed smoothly. In a speech to an audience of American ladies many years later, May eulogized over the house, describing it as "a really lovely old place hidden in the sweep of the South Downs, with glorious country all around and adjacent to a little Norman church shaded by yews, five hundred years old and containing the tomb of a genuine Crusader. [*Crusader's Tomb* would be the title of Cronin's eleventh novel.] In reconditioning this eighteenth-century property we spent some of the happiest months of our lives..." May became pregnant again, and as always in that condition she was quiet and untroubled. In the same speech she continued: "When in 1937 I returned from the nursing home in London where our third child, Andrew, was born [27th October]... I could have sighed with happiness. This, at last, I thought to myself, is home..."

Before her confinement, May had interviewed and taken on as nanny a young woman who at the time was governess to two little girls in Lowndes Square in Belgravia. Margaret Jennings, later known as Nan, was a small lady, slightly over five feet tall, with brown hair and a clear complexion. A qualified nurse, her father had been the headmaster of a private school in Norfolk, and her mother had a flat in Streatham.

Cronin said of his wife's confinement: "Oddly enough I missed my wife. At times she might be a source of exasperation, provoking me beyond endurance, yet when she was not beside me I became anxious for her return." [59] Such late-flowering tenderness, however, was not to last. The ambivalence of Cronin's feelings for his wife seemed to suggest that he simply could not handle her bouts of abnormal behaviour. His first meeting with Margaret Jennings, at the nursing home, was not the most auspicious. He became irritated at being told that the reason the baby cried whenever he picked him up was that he was not holding him correctly. When Miss Jennings picked him up, he was always quiet and well behaved. Cronin even dubbed her "Miss Know-All". But things changed as they began to spend more and more time together, sharing a passion for long walks on the Downs near Sullington Court. He even taught her how to play golf. Before long the inevitable happened – they fell in love. There is no suggestion of a physical relationship at this stage, but the depth of feeling was such that they discussed how they were to live under the same roof and how they might continue to stay together when her duties as nanny expired. To obviate that eventuality, he suggested that at the appropriate time she should take a shorthand and typing course, so that she could become his full-time secretary. And so, for the second time in his married life, in close proximity to another woman, the sad realization of his stale marriage prompted him to reflect bitterly on his lot:

> One moment of weakness and stupidity had endowed me with a wife I have never wanted but who was now the mother of my three children, and herself so erratic in her conduct that she had become entirely dependent on me... I could not now desert my wife who had begun to lean heavily upon me in every aspect of our daily lives...[60]

Cronin could not have been clearer: what kept the marriage together was a sense of duty.

Chapter Five

On 29th July 1939, just before the outbreak of the Second World War, Cronin, his wife, their three sons and Margaret Jennings ("Nan") left Britain for America, embarking at Liverpool, bound for Boston, on the Cunard White Star liner *Samaria*. Mrs Cronin, in the previously quoted speech to a ladies' society in America, explained:

> Previous to 1939, A.J. had made several visits to the United States and been impressed not only by the warmth of his welcome but by the breadth, vigour and immense potentialities of this vast and splendid country. His American public was already large, he felt he must know more of a people who had been so good to him, he wanted to go fishing in Maine, sit in a drugstore in the Middle West, wander through the old missions of California. Besides, he suspected that we were getting into a rut at Sullington – fatal mistake for an author for whom travel and experience of life are as necessary as meat and drink.[1]

This explanation was repeated by Cronin himself in *Adventures in Two Worlds* – indeed, it is possible that he wrote Mrs Cronin's speech for her – in which he added that "this seems a smooth and simple undertaking, but in reality it took time to effect the transposition of roots long planted in European soil and to adjust both idioms and ideas to transatlantic standards".[2]

This notion of a writer desperate for fresh inspiration is plausible, but unconvincing in the light of subsequent events. The enthusiasm he carried with him across the ocean seemed to disappear after the publication of *The Keys of the Kingdom* in 1941. Most of Cronin's later works added little to his reputation and, more importantly, are devoid of American influences, leading to the inevitable conclusion that sitting in a drugstore in the Middle West and wandering through the old missions of California was not conducive to literary inspiration. In the sixteen years he spent in the United States, he only wrote five books, which include three works that might be termed "fictional reminiscences" and a fourth, *The Spanish Gardener* – initially envisaged as a magazine piece – that was little more than a novella. None of these books, except *Beyond This Place*, involved him in original research.

When Cronin moved to America, his reputation was at its highest. *The Citadel* had truly established him on the American scene. Its popularity was perhaps due to its crusading message, a point that his American publishers, Little, Brown, went to great lengths to publicize in their promotional material. On 4th March 1938, a delighted Cronin wrote to Alfred McIntyre, the head of Little, Brown & Co.: "I am overjoyed that the book goes so splendidly. Why don't we make it another *Gone with the Wind*?"

A letter to Alfred McIntyre, dated 20th December 1938 from Sullington Court, revealed the novelist's intention of starting a new work:

> We are going to Switzerland for two or three months as from the middle of January. I am taking a chalet there and amongst the snows I mean to write my next novel, not merely a successor to *The Citadel* but one which, when you read the manuscript, will make you throw your hat over the top of Beacon Hill. It will be real Olympian success (touch wood!). My present intention is that we might publish this in the second half of 1939...

He was wildly optimistic in his assessment, even allowing for his incredible speed of writing. Notably a slow starter, and easily sidetracked, nothing was done during that winter break, and by 14th May of the following year he informed Alfred McIntyre that the book was still only "fully formed in my mind. I am looking forward to having particulars of the Maine holiday resorts within the next few days as I am seriously planning to write the novel there." But there were other, not insignificant issues competing for his time: the move to America, the prospect of a new world war and two short stories, both with a medical theme and published in *Good Housekeeping*: 'Vigil in the Night' (1939) and 'The Valorous Years' (1940). No doubt Cronin had realized that medical stories were sure-fire successes with his readers. Indeed, an adaptation of the former story, about two nurses – one selfless and virtuous and the other greedy and selfish – appeared on the big screen early in the following year, 1940, starring Carole Lombard, at the time Hollywood's highest-paid star.

Cronin wrote again to McIntyre on 20th May 1939:

> I do not mind you choosing a place for me without having seen it. I think you have an idea of what our tastes are. As regards place, I think we should prefer a quiet spot provided it were not too isolated, somewhere up the Maine coast not far enough to get the fogs and yet distant enough from New York to avoid the crowds and be cool. I feel Long Island would be a little too sophisticated for us and probably very expensive. As regards the house, we should not want a large place nor have to bother with a lot of servants – one or two would be about the number. Also we should require about four or five bedrooms and two or three living rooms. You see I am not wanting anything elaborate provided it is nice.

Between then and the planned move towards the end of September, he was still confident he could get on with the novel. In the same letter Cronin said:

> Regarding your trip to Europe, we shall be delighted to welcome you to Sullington in June. I think the international situation is a little easier although living here in Europe is like being perched on a keg of gunpowder and one never knows when Hitler is going to apply the match.

In fact, the book was never started, but the move to America took place at the end of July 1939 – earlier than originally anticipated. The Cronin family moved into Laighton Cottage, in York Harbor, Maine, experiencing for the first time "the glory of a New England summer. Never had we known such blue skies, such continuous and brilliant sunshine."[3] Intense media speculation and innuendo about the reason for emigrating so close to the beginning of the war accompanied the move.

In the autobiographical fragment of 1976, the move to America is condensed to an extraordinary degree, as if it contained nothing of interest and took place overnight with no foresight or planning, suggesting that Cronin's main purpose in committing his thoughts to paper was an outpouring of his marital difficulties. Talking about May, he commented on the "tragic future, looming nearer and still nearer. She was practically in her first childhood, and I prayed that she would so remain." May did not even accompany him to settle the two older boys – Vincent, fifteen, and Patrick, thirteen – in their new school, the well-to-do (and Catholic) Portsmouth Abbey School on Rhode Island. That was left to Cronin and Nan, who became an integral part of the household after they left Britain. One of the boys' teachers even assumed that they were man and wife.

Nan's status was a matter of crucial importance to Cronin. Just as he was not prepared to be parted from her when the family left England (an American nanny would not have been hard to find), so her continued stay in America was equally necessary. For this, he relied heavily on the services of his US publisher, asking Raymond Everitt, the company's chief executive:

> If you would be so very kind as to get the immigration authorities to renew Nannie's passport. There will be no necessity to renew ours since we are acquiring residential status (please treat this as STRICTLY CONFIDENTIAL!)… naturally she will remain with us and will accept no employment in the USA…[4]

The matter dragged on until August, when Cronin asked Alfred McIntyre to intercede:

> Would you be so very kind as to take the matter up with the department. Must she still report every six months? I regard this matter of great importance since she is invaluable to us. Moreover she was assured by the authorities that she would be allowed to remain until hostilities had ceased…[5]

In 1939 Cronin was forty-three and Nan was thirty-one. Their relationship during this period, especially after they discovered and expressed their love for each other, became central to the life of the entire family.

No public scandal ever attached itself to Cronin's life, and so the views of family members are crucial at this point. Vincent, aged eighty-three when we met, possibly not the worldliest of men, avoided discussions of his parents' marriage. From his obituary of his father, in a somewhat unemotional appreciation of his mother, he was predictably guarded: "He was fortunate in his wife, a fellow student at Glasgow University. She created for him a series of happy homes... and kept his social life in repair, thus obviating one of the novelist's occupational hazards; protecting an imaginary world by keeping real-life's people at arm's length..."[6]

Andrew, the youngest son, on the other hand, who knew Nan better than anyone except his father, was more forthright, insisting initially – in letters he wrote to me – that there were no hints of impropriety in their conduct, and that their affection was platonic, although he also suggested that Nan may have been sexually molested by her father. This conjecture only came to light after Cronin's death in 1981, when Nan moved back to America to live with Andrew and his family, first in Potomac, Maryland and then Germantown. Nan was then seventy-one years old. On three occasions, Andrew and his two sons heard her scream in her sleep: "Get away, Daddy... Fuck you."

However, subsequent correspondence with Alexandra, Andrew's daughter, who has always taken a keen interest in her grandfather's life and work, reveals that when he was about ten years old, in 1947, Andrew walked into his father's study at Woodlea Hill to find Nan on his lap with his arms around her. Nan immediately stood up, as a shocked Andrew quickly closed the door. Nothing was said about the incident, but naturally, from that moment, Andrew suspected that they had an intimate relationship. Alexandra, born in 1973, was eight years old when Nan moved from Switzerland to join her family in America, and so much of her childhood was spent in Nan's company, whom she grew to know and love. She said that Nan once told her that she loved her grandfather very much, and that when she asked her if she loved her grandmother she said: "But of course. She was a lovely person." Her loyalty to both, Alexandra points out, was unwavering.

Alexandra disagrees with her father Andrew on the question of Nan's possible sexual molestation. Alexandra points out that Nan never used expletives or foul language, and while agreeing that she also heard Nan's nightmarish outbursts – she slept in a bedroom right next to Nan's, nearer than the rest of the family – she insists that her father was mistaken, not only in what he heard, but also in what he inferred. She heard neither "fuck you" nor "daddy" in

Nan's outbursts, simply her screaming "Get away from me", which is hardly proof of a past sexual molestation.

Cronin's 1976 autobiography is unambiguous on his feelings towards his wife and Nan. But the question remains unanswered: was it a classic *ménage à trois*, open and aboveboard, or secret, suspected perhaps, but never discussed? The individual personalities in this drama are, of course, material to the domestic situation. Cronin, as we know, was a self-made man who, according to Alexandra, was proud and demanding. She also refers to his quick temper, which also subsided quickly, but she stresses that nobody in the family ever crossed him. Right or wrong, he always had the last word. Clearly, there was something in his character that made his uncompromising attitude palatable, since not only were they in awe of him, but also they all professed to love him.

May, as portrayed in the 1976 autobiography, is unrecognizable to Andrew's family. Andrew insists that until she began to show signs of Alzheimer's she was not mentally ill. Alexandra, who never actually knew her grandmother, except when she was in the nursing home in Canada, derived her opinions from talking to her father and mother – who enjoyed a particularly close relationship with her mother-in-law – and Nan. She describes her as "extremely bright, stable, well-mannered and outgoing... she always dressed beautifully and was very fashionable... she read no less than five newspapers a day, golfed, played tennis (my grandparents regularly hosted tennis parties at their home) and had numerous friends throughout her life. She went into New York City every week to see plays, musicals, the ballet, the opera etc. – she was definitely not the confused, anxiety-ridden disaster of the 1976 autobiography... she loved people and loved being around them, so we are mystified by the diagnosis that she was depressed or had mental disturbances..."

But these expressions of respect and love for her miss an essential aspect of the story: that her relationship with her husband was flawed. It seems clear that May loved him more than he loved her – if he loved her at all – and it was that very emotion, which she could not renounce even when he deserted her, leaving her to live out her life in a nursing home, when he could easily have arranged care for her in her home, that tied her to him to the end.

Nan seems to have been the opposite of May: she dressed simply, loved walks and nature. She had soft blue-grey eyes, wore no make-up and hardly any jewellery, except for special occasions. She had greyish-white hair that she wore in a bob, which she allowed Alexandra, when young, to cut. She loved poetry and literature, and would sit in her room every evening with her cats and read, do crosswords or occasionally watch television. Interestingly, Alexandra thought that her grandfather liked women with a natural look. Contrary to Cronin's 1976 autobiography, Alexandra recalls that it was Nan "who had the nervous disposition – she made to-do lists every single day and had a hard time relaxing... in short she was a worrier..."

Whether May knew or even suspected her husband's feelings for Nan is impossible to say, but Andrew and his wife, Anne, are in no doubt that she was unhappy with Nan being in her home, after her duties as nanny had finished. She also found her presence on family holidays particularly irksome and awkward. Whether she made her feelings clear to her husband is not known. Nan was of course a paid employee; however, through her closeness to Cronin, she became such an essential part of the family that she occupied a unique position halfway between a trusted domestic and a family member. The two women never enjoyed a close relationship. Andrew recalls: "The relationship between my mother and Nan was a little strained. However, I only remember once when they got into a loud argument..." Nan regularly acted as chauffeur, because Mrs Cronin never took out an American driving licence, but they never shopped or socialized together. Mrs Cronin may well have treated Nan as an employee, but to Cronin and young Andrew she was clearly much more. During the summer months Cronin and his wife usually went to Europe, leaving Nan in control of affairs. Nan also looked after her own mother, who had a flat two miles away in the town. Occasionally, Mrs Cronin forced Nan to spend her nights with her mother in the village, much to Andrew's chagrin: "But this never was for long... much to my happiness... Dad and I liked having her around the house... I adored Nanny..." He even admitted that he loved Nan more than his mother, and was closer to his father.

Andrew's admission is perhaps not as startling as it first appears. His mother once told Anne, Andrew's wife and her favourite daughter-in-law, that "Andrew was not raised the way I would have wanted him to have been…" Her attempts at disciplining her son always came up against the united front of his father and Nan, who spoiled him. Nan even packed his bags for trips when he was an adult and could never break the habit of mothering him. Indeed, Alexandra recalls: "She loved to take care of us."

Under such circumstances it is difficult to see how Mrs Cronin could have avoided feeling demeaned by her obvious relegation in the pecking order of family affections.

* * *

In February 1940, Cronin learnt that Raymond Everitt was planning a trip to the west. Keen to repay some favours, he immediately wrote to him:

> I understand you are coming west shortly. I hope we shall see much of you. Are you going to one of the Arizona ranches? If so we'd like to motor out and see you for a couple of days. Also to entertain you if, and when, you are here…[7]

Everitt had been very kind to Cronin, his wife and baby on a trip they had made to America in 1937 for the promotion of *The Citadel*. He had written to him from RMS *Queen Mary* expressing his thanks: "For all your kindness to me in New York and especially for your most extraordinary taste and generosity in choosing such charming gifts for my wife and the new infant." He then mentioned that Alfred McIntyre, on the strength of the performance of *The Citadel*, had offered him $20,000 for each of his next three novels, commenting that "King Alfred" – or "the Old Man of the Sea", as he sometimes called him – was certainly a gambler in a big way. In the same letter he brought up the subject of his play, *Jupiter Laughs*, which was scheduled for production in London and Broadway. He informed Everitt that:

> Warners have bought the film rights, Gollancz is publishing it in London. Do you wish to publish it here? I imagine the Broadway production will be in March. You might let me know your decision soon, also the best terms you can offer since I have an offer to publish

from another quarter. The play is a first class piece of work – my very best writing...[8]

As it turned out, the play was not a great success: the show closed after just twenty-four performances. However, a film adaptation was indeed made, albeit under a different name: *Shining Victory* opened in New York in September 1940, starring James Stephenson, Geraldine Fitzgerald and Donald Crisp, with Bette Davis in a cameo appearance. Several years later, in February 1948, *Jupiter Laughs* was rejected as a radio play on the advice of the Corporation's head of drama Robert MacDermot, who considered it "futile, simply a sex drama set in an unconvincing clinic".

In November 1939 the Cronins had relocated from freezing Maine to spend the winter at 521 North Arden Drive, in Beverly Hills, California, a move they would repeat annually for many years. When he was there, he revealed to his publisher that he had not yet started on his new novel: "I now have the idea for my big novel fully in mind and propose to start it presently." [9] To Cronin, "presently" meant when he was in the mood. It is well known that he hated the "actual writing of the book":

> Beginning a novel troubles me enormously, and I am only driven to it through a kind of cumulative force, the tremendous and despairing pressure of dire necessity. I believe there are some writers who enjoy writing. For my part I loathe and abhor it...[10]

Months later, in April 1940, still in California, he began to think about researching material for the book. He wrote to Raymond Everitt, asking if there was "a really fine library in Boston from which I could have books of reference on loan when I am in York Harbor."[11] By July he was back in Maine, and though he was still searching for reference books in August – a descriptive book on the Chinese interior, a graphic account of the great epidemic of bubonic plague in China and a short travel book on Spain – he was at least able to inform Ray Everitt that "I am now really getting down to work and much enjoying it."[12] In October, about a quarter of the way into the book – some 25,000 words – he reported he was unbelievably thrilled with the work, and that it was worthwhile doing something real again. By December 1940 – another proof of how quickly he worked – the first draft of the book, some 90,000 words, was in typescript form, and Cronin was "deeply impressed with the result":

> While simple and moving, it is by far the most important thing I have ever done, and deeply significant to the world today... you might also let me know if our provisional arrangement re publication date still stands. I know you have other books on your 1941 list but since mine is the successor to *The Citadel* I am hoping that, when you have read it, you will give it the premier place... if you knew how I have worked you would appreciate how eager I am for a truly great success.[13]

That *The Keys of the Kingdom* should have been written at this point in Cronin's career is in some ways surprising. The alleged influence of doctrinal bigotry in the shaping of his character would point to a book on a religious theme early in his career, yet it took twelve years and three international best-sellers before *The Keys of the Kingdom* appeared. The novel can be regarded as the last part of a trilogy in which the conflict between the individual and the establishment is explored: idealism against materialism in the mining industry (*The Stars Look Down*), altruism versus apathy in medicine (*The Citadel*) and, finally, saintliness against dogma in the Roman Catholic Church. The lone voice against the system is a favourite Cronin theme, which imbues his work with heroic grandeur. The reason may be deep-rooted in his early life: an upbringing as an only child, with a natural tendency to solitariness, and teenage years on the fringe of his peer group, possibly fostered an introspective nature. Profound and thought-provoking, his trilogy reveals that intelligence is not the sole preserve of the well-off, that medical formulae are not immutable, that ownership of God's coal-filled earth is not vested in individuals and that the route to salvation is manifold.

Cronin was an observant Catholic all his life, but some of the views expressed by his characters appear to contradict the tenets of the Roman Church. In July 1933, a few years before writing *The Keys of the Kingdom*, he was asked, with other well-known figures, to contribute a short article for the *Daily Mirror* on the question: "Is religion a spent force?" Most contributors thought it was not, but there was a consensus that some change was necessary to accommodate shifting attitudes in the modern world. Cronin's judgement on modern society had a pessimistic flavour: "Religion – an all-pervading sense of reverence for, and responsibility to, a higher power. But, as the rising generation has neither responsibility nor reverence, how can it have religion?"[14] There was general agreement among the contributors on the falling off of congregations, but not on the reasons. The Bishop of Newcastle thought it was only a temporary phenomenon, although history has proven him wrong. Another commentator, on the subject of reverence, said:

> The youth of every generation has in its heart some secret, or open crusade. It is the day of frankness now. Youth has, as I see it, more real religion than ever before but does not respect so highly, as it was forced to do in the past, any religion which raises costly cathedrals and does not trouble about the slums...[15]

Cronin took up the point: "The question is much wider than that of elemental belief in God! It is a question of elemental conduct, of right thinking."[16] Was he, perhaps, remembering the rampant sectarianism he had witnessed in western Scotland at the turn of the century, all carried out in the name of God? That memory might have also led to his observation that "creed is such an accident of birth, of race and antecedents, even of latitude and longitude, that it cannot, surely, be the exclusive determinant of our salvation?"[17]

In approaching *The Keys of the Kingdom*, he intended that "the whole purpose of the book is to preach tolerance, humility, generosity and liberality of spirit as against the material values which are poisoning the world today".[18] Interviewed by *Time* magazine, he explained how on a visit to Rome for the anniversary of a famous saint, face to face with a life that had been blessed with an excess of achievement and goodness, he thought how much more appealing it would be to write about a completely opposite character: a humble man, a man of the people with human weaknesses. He kept the thought in his head for ten years or so, until the brutality of the Second World War convinced him that the time was right. Deeply troubled that the simple virtues of tolerance and brotherly love were being swept aside by the horror of armed conflict, he felt compelled to make a plea for the return of simple goodness, personified by his central character.

The title, *The Keys of the Kingdom*, is taken from Matthew 16:19, in which Jesus says to Peter: "And I will give unto thee the keys of the kingdom of heaven." The action of the novel takes place over six decades, recounting the life of Father Chisholm, an unorthodox Catholic priest who attempts to found a mission in China. He withstands many years of difficulty and privation, including famine, disease and war, in the province to which he is assigned. Nevertheless, thanks to his kindness, courage and tolerance, Chisholm succeeds, earning the respect both of the Chinese people and of his previously hostile fellow clergy.

Readers and critics were by now getting used to controversy from the Cronin pen, and his latest novel did not disappoint them. Cronin's liberal attitude to matters of deep religious significance, oscillating between humanist and Christian perspectives, generated strong criticism from several quarters. Before its publication in Britain, Cronin admitted to Gollancz that "the first Catholic reaction was mixed, some supporting, others condemning, but gradually the tide has turned and now I am overwhelmed by letters from prominent Catholic clergymen praising the book".[19] One of its most influential reviewers, J. Horton Davies, saw the theme of the book as "Blessed are the meek", and while he recognized Cronin's tolerant attitude to all faiths, he pointed out that "its chief defect is that while it is an ecclesiastical novel and a good one, it is in no sense a theological novel. It is concerned with integrity of morals, with compassion, and service. But it does not penetrate the mystery with the searching categories of grace and sin, as do Greene, Mauriac and Bernanos..."[20]

Critics are sometimes guilty of cavilling when a book does not quite fit the model of their expectations. If Cronin had intended an "ecclesiastical" novel, then it can only be judged on that basis – to do otherwise is like condemning a comedy because it is not a tragedy. Cronin had trodden the theological path in *Three Loves* – and was, therefore, no stranger to doctrinal controversy. In that novel, the proud and spirited Lucy's unfortunate reaction to the Order's rules of obedience, submission and lowliness and her eventual downfall are an exposé of some distinction, but the author's goal in creating the rascally Father Chisholm in *The Keys of the Kingdom* was significantly different. Some critics, Cronin once said, referred to him as "a born storyteller".[21] It is true that he told simple stories in which the *goodies* and the *baddies* are easily distinguishable – a fact that does not detract from the quality of the work or the enjoyment of the reader.

While Cronin's intimate knowledge of mining and medicine undoubtedly qualified him to take on those subjects in his two previous novels, his competence to handle doctrinal issues was questionable. His simplistic sentiments appealed to the average reader, but many devout Catholics, laymen and clerics, complained that the book presented the Church in a bad light and, more importantly, exposed Cronin's lack of understanding of Catholic doctrine. Father Meinrad Koester of Lacrosse, Wisconsin, took issue with him for not distinguishing between "tolerance of the individual and tolerance in doctrine. As Catholics we must always hold there is no compromising with error."[22] Cronin's statement that not all atheists go to hell, Koester insisted, missed the point: those who do not acknowledge God in their lifetime plainly have no wish to be with him in the life to come, and God will not deny people their free will. The priest further castigated him over his "flippant remark" that God would not make a person roast in eternity for eating a pork chop on a Friday, pointing out that it was not for eating the pork chop that a soul is condemned, but for "exercising disobedience to the Church in an important matter, and that important matter is penance. For Christ says we must all do penance or likewise perish. The absence of meat on a Friday is a portion of this penance."[23]

Father Koester pointed to at least eight statements attributed to Father Chisholm that he considered erroneous. He suggested, however, that Father Chisholm's apparent ignorance of doctrine might not mirror that of the author: "just as we say Shakespeare says when we really mean Shakespeare's character says".[24] But, just as readers of Dickens would expect him to be fully conversant with the provisions of the nineteenth-century Poor Laws, as well as being acutely aware of the true conditions in Victorian workhouses, so they had a right to expect Cronin to understand the complexities of Catholic doctrine.

Faced with his detractors, Cronin stubbornly maintained his position, never once offering doctrinal ignorance as an excuse. He was careful to avoid being drawn into a detailed discussion of the issues raised by his ecclesiastical opponents, preferring to argue that his widespread support somehow validated his assertions. Father Koester, however, was adamant that there was no defence. He insisted: "Let it be emphasized that no lay writer, man or woman, no matter how brilliant, can properly pry into the nature of a priestly mind consecrated by ordination. Dr Cronin together with others of his kind would have done well not to make a priest the hero of his story."[25]

Another Catholic priest, Bernard Weaver of St Gabriel's Monastery in Boston, Massachusetts, was so incensed at the book's "gross injustice to the priesthood, with its thousands of Christ-like, noble and generous members"[26] that not only did he write a scathing criticism to Cronin himself, but he also contacted Sister Mary Joseph of the Gallery of Living Catholic Authors – founded in 1932 as an exclusive academy of Catholic writers – expressing his dismay that Cronin had been chosen as a member of that august assembly. He also attacked the book's literary merits:

> As to the worth of *The Keys of the Kingdom* as literature, quite a few of us agree with Harry Sylvester, who wrote in the *Commonweal*: "The book is a sort of regurgitation of all the hack writers that Cronin has read and failed to digest." Jerome Weidman was only expressing the exasperation of many other critics when he wrote: "*The Keys of the Kingdom* is a classic of corn, bad taste, insufferable writing and public hoodwinking."[27]

Weaver ended by objecting to a sacrilegious passage in *The Stars Look Down*, where Joe Gowlan and Laura Millington have sex in a church, a scene described by *Time* magazine as "sizzling". For that alone, he suggested, Cronin should have his membership of the Gallery withdrawn. Sister Mary Joseph answered that she realized a large number of Catholics had been outraged by *The Keys of the Kingdom*, and assured him that the matter would be brought to the attention of the board.

Another clergyman to take exception to the book was the Reverend Edward Wuenschel. His article, running to about 10,000 words and to be found in the *Ecclesiastical Review* of January 1942, is a treatise of philosophical complexity, in which he contradicts almost every religious utterance made by Father Chisholm. His greatest complaint concerned what he termed the "loading of the dice". He pointed out that the book painted the established church in a bad light. Cronin's claim to impartiality in his work may have been impossible to live up to. His heroes were always so easily loveable that the "bad guys" never stood a chance in readers' affections. Was this inadvertent or purposeful? It is hard to believe that Cronin did not set out to create two distinct religious categories in *The Keys of the Kingdom*, and that his intention would ruffle feathers. Why else would he have accumulated such a rogue's gallery of Catholic clerics? Anselm Mealey is a suave, selfish opportunist; his secretary Monsignor Sleeth is proud, prejudiced, pedantic and cruel; Father Tarrant, a ruthless, sardonic martinet; Father Gomez, wily and obsequious; Father Kezer, surly and tyrannical – not to mention many more. Arranged against them are the loveable Father Chisholm himself; Father McNabb, the only other Catholic priest he presents in a favourable light; Holy Dan the Nonconformist preacher, the best man Father Chisholm ever knew, and the two brave; gracious Methodist missionaries.

Despite the criticism from these and other Catholic quarters, Cronin remained unrepentant. Commenting in *Life* magazine in October 1941, he noted the few "protesting wails" from members of the clergy, saying that though some were genuine, others were from publicity-seekers and trivial in the extreme. He likened their carping to the very intolerance highlighted in his book, and claimed to have support from a very important Catholic figure who, like him, felt that those few narrow-minded bigots did the Church more harm than good, especially in the eyes of liberal non-Catholics. He thought the book would promote respect for the Church, but that those who condemned it were in danger of defeating that end.

If the substance of Father Chisholm's views are truly the author's, then one could wonder what sort of a Catholic Cronin was and why, in his private life, he remained loyal to a faith that is arguably one of the most dogmatic and restrictive of all Western religions. From the age of sixteen, while he lived with his devout Catholic mother, he attended St Aloysius' College, a school with a strong Jesuit ethos, where religious education was a compulsory subject in the school curriculum. He attended Mass and gave Confession throughout his life, and even his scientific training and medical profession did not seem to weaken his faith. At the time of researching this biography, his two surviving sons told me that, even as a young man, he practised his religion seriously, and that throughout his life his religious perspective never changed. Indeed, Cronin brought up his children in the faith, without offering them freedom of choice: they were all baptized, taken to church from the age of four and educated in Catholic schools. Vincent was sent to Ampleforth College in Yorkshire, described as the "Catholic Eton", in September 1937, and in America both he and Patrick attended Portsmouth Abbey School, a prestigious Catholic institution in Rhode Island. Andrew attended St Luke's in New Canaan and then Canterbury School in New Milford, Connecticut, before going on to Yale.

Cronin claimed he was not without support from ordinary readers and members of the clergy. The pleasure his book had given them afforded him great pride. One clergyman from Florida urged him not to be downcast, suggesting that if the evangelists were writing today, they would be in worse trouble. But by far the most encouraging response came from an old parish priest in Maine, who confessed to being amused by the book and being reduced to tears. He also expressed surprise that anyone could write so well of the priesthood without being a member of it, and assured Cronin that he intended rereading the book during the long Maine winter and using it for meditation. He thought it might do him more good than so-called "pious books".

The American success of *The Keys of the Kingdom* should have been replicated in Britain. Early in 1941 Victor Gollancz had every reason to be excited about the book's potential impact on the British market, until he learnt that Cronin was not prepared to publish in Britain for financial reasons – tax anomalies between the two countries, unfavourable to the author, that could not be overcome. Gollancz's efforts at resolving the problem on the British side of the Atlantic were fruitless. However, as time went on, it emerged there was another stumbling block. In April Cronin wrote to Gollancz:

> Thank you for your letter of 13th March and for the enquiries which you made on my behalf. I have considered very carefully the matter

of the new novel. As you remark it is from every angle a difficult situation... But I have quite definitely made up my mind not to publish the book in England until the end of the war. It is not the question of money alone which prompts me to this resolution. I have a very strong premonition that the book will do much better in England if it is held over for some time.

Typically, he soon changed his mind, although he still believed that "there was some advantage in delay, since the mass effect of mounting American sales would launch the English edition admirably when this was brought out".[28]

Earlier that same year the Treasury in Washington had recognized the anomaly in the tax situation and reversed the previous legislation, leaving the way clear for publication to go ahead. On 17th November 1941, feeling the time was right, Cronin sounded out Gollancz on the subject. At that point he was unaware that three thousand miles away sections of the British press "had burst out with an entirely false and gravely damaging explanation of the situation".[29] The *Sunday Pictorial* on 2nd November had published the following on its front page, under the headline "WHAT IS CRONIN UP TO?"

A.J. Cronin, forty-five-year-old British doctor, now in Hollywood and making a fortune, has just written another best-seller. It is called *The Keys of the Kingdom*. But for some reason Cronin refuses to let Britain see the book.

Cronin's publisher, Mr Victor Gollancz, said yesterday, "He has imposed the ban for reasons best known to himself."

We asked John Walters, our New York staff correspondent, to make an investigation and this is what he cabled last night: "Cronin is staying at a secret address in Hollywood and your correspondent here cannot get him to say a word.

"I have examined the book, however, and am not surprised that he won't let Britain see it. The hero is a Catholic priest, and this is how he soliloquizes about war: 'We send millions of our faithful sons to be maimed and slaughtered... with a hypocritical smile and an apostolic blessing.'"

When the London blitz was at its height a call went out for more doctors. An appeal was made in America. Cronin, a brilliant surgeon, stayed in America while US doctors volunteered for Britain.

DOES CRONIN SUPPORT THE FIGHT AGAINST HITLER OR NOT? IF HE DOES, WHY DOESN'T HE COME HOME?

Press sniping continued. On 16th November 1941 the *Sunday Pictorial* again carried a front-page photograph of Cronin with Andrew, his youngest son, and his nephew Magregor Ritchie. The feature took up a third of the page with a headline "HERE'S DR CRONIN HAVING A LOVELY TIME... 3,000 MILES AWAY!" It went on:

A nice, peaceful, happy picture of Dr A.J. Cronin, novelist and playwright, at home with his two younger sons. Where was it taken? On the coast of Maine, USA, 3,000 miles away from Britain – and war! The war, it seems, is something that has no appeal for Dr Cronin, either as doctor or writer. Why doesn't he pay his own country a professional visit?

Cronin did not see the articles immediately, and it was not until 19th December, after he had made the decision to allow publication in Britain to go ahead, that he angrily wrote to Gollancz:

Every purported reason advanced therein is a malicious invention. I never at any time made any statement regarding English publication. Moreover, the statement that I declared the book would never be published in the British Empire is manifestly false since the book was produced in Canada six months ago, simultaneously with American publication... As plain evidence that the purpose behind the campaign was vindictive in the *Sunday Pictorial* article, one sentence was combed out of the entire novel so that the work should be odiously misrepresented as unpatriotic in its design. Following upon this, in the same article, as a kind of logical deduction my loyalty and patriotism were tacitly impugned.

Cronin was right. The *Sunday Pictorial* had taken the sentence out of context. The statement made by Father Chisholm in the novel, which does not necessarily represent Cronin's own view, results from an argument he overhears between the nuns under his care and protection. Two sisters on the Allied side of the war and the Mother Superior, a German, instead of maintaining a pious neutrality, are hotly disputing which side has the most righteous cause. Father Chisholm intervenes, chiding them, pointing out that irrespective of nationality and creed, the true path to follow is a pacifist one: "Throw down your weapons. Thou shalt not kill" – hardly a surprising response from a Jesuit missionary. In fact, Cronin was not a pacifist. He had served in the navy for a short spell at the beginning of the First World War, while his two older sons, as soon as they were old enough, served in the British Army during the Second World War.

For some reason the *Sunday Pictorial* at the time saw in Cronin a convenient target – even his earning power was unacceptable to them. Obviously Cronin's return to Britain would have made no difference to the outcome of the war, and the moral implications of his move to America were a matter for his own conscience. It is undeniable that he and his family avoided the austerities of wartime Britain, but he was not the only author to leave Britain's shores before the war. There were a host of other British writers in America at the same time, such as James Hilton, William Golding, W. Somerset Maugham, R.C. Sherriff, Alfred Noyes, C.S. Forester and W.H. Auden. Besides, leaving or staying was only one aspect of the debate. Would the *Sunday Pictorial* have its readers believe that the rich people who remained in Britain suffered the same extremes as the average Londoner from the East End? Were British aristocrats in their remote estates in the same danger as the average factory worker on the outskirts of a major manufacturing city? But the timing of Cronin's move was certainly inopportune, and the resultant criticism hurt. Vincent, his son, who was fifteen at the time, was aware of the distress it caused – "through listening to my parents' chagrin" – and he doubted whether the wound ever healed.[30]

Cronin was too old for active service, but through the British Embassy in Washington he worked for the Ministry of Information. His words show the unfairness he felt:

I have already supplied Brooks (of Heath and Co.) with an account of what I am doing... all my work, all my articles here have been motivated towards the preservation of democracy and the destruction of totalitarianism. I have hundreds of letters in my files testifying to the help and encouragement I have given people in this struggle to preserve our freedom. For the past two years I've used all the little talent I possess to promote that Anglo-American unity on which the future of the world depends. God knows I have no claims to heroics... but that is a different matter from being misrepresented and utterly maligned...[31]

Before his move to America in 1939 Cronin had dispensed with the services of A.D. Peters, engaging those of A.M. Heath & Co., a well-known firm of literary agents, which still represents the Cronin estate today. Cyrus Brooks became his contact in Britain, and it was to him, therefore, that he appealed for help in the matter of possible legal action over his reputation. Cronin was prone to react impulsively to criticism, and he was sensitive to unfair treatment, but he was not one to wallow in self-pity. He empowered A.M. Heath & Co. and Victor Gollancz to engage whatever legal advice was necessary, at his expense, to refute future articles of a similar nature. Then he turned his attention to the more important business of British publication, acquainting Gollancz with a few details that could help him in the book's promotion:

As you may know it was the Book of the Month Club choice for August. It has been for the past six months (and still remains) top of the best-seller list. Apart from a few unfavourable notices the reviews were excellent. Number of copies to date 527,000... I think I mentioned that it was the Canadian No. 1 best-seller. Also, David Selznick will produce the motion picture... I know you will keep me in touch with the progress of events and I do rely on you to establish the truth...[32]

Written entirely in the US, *The Keys of the Kingdom* brought Cronin's British period to an end. Published in America in 1941 and a year later in Britain, it was a huge success on both sides of the Atlantic. According to *Time* magazine it became a best-seller in America even before reaching the bookshelves, with advance sales to the Book Club and bookshops of over 250,000 copies – the highest since Hemingway's *For Whom the Bell Tolls*. Vincent Cronin felt that this novel was less admired in Britain than the famous trio – *Hatter's Castle*, *The Stars Look Down* and *The Citadel* – but that on the Continent it became his best-loved and most influential work. The film adaptation of the book was shown on French television in 1980, and the novel's message was discussed by a panel that included Mother Teresa.

David Selznick of Twentieth Century Fox paid $100,000 for the film rights and allocated a budget of $3,000,000 to make the film, one of the most expensive pictures of the year. It was directed by John M. Stahl, with a screenplay by Joseph Mankiewicz, and shot on location in Malibu and Laguna, California, and at the Fox studios in Hollywood. The lead role was played by Gregory Peck, then a newcomer, later to become one of Hollywood's matinee idols, physically the most unlikely Father Chisholm, standing 6' 3" tall, lean, wiry, dark and handsome – in stark contrast to the stout, balding little man Cronin envisaged as his hero. Peck was nominated for Best Actor, but failed to win the award. At first, the author was strangely pessimistic about the film: "From the outset I had been dubious about the chances of this novel in Hollywood. I wrote to my friend Hedda Hopper that no one would have the courage to make a picture of a story which aroused so much controversy, and in this she agreed with me. So I am wrong in the right company..."[33] Also starring Vincent Price, Thomas Mitchell and Edmund Gwenn, it was a huge success, starting Peck on the road to becoming an international star. The script kept reasonably close to the book's storyline, and Cronin, who had met Gregory Peck on one of his trips to California and liked him, was happy with his performance. A few weeks after the film's release, Cronin wrote to McIntyre: "The press notices have been extremely favourable and just five minutes ago Jules Fields of 20th Century phoned me to say that the box-office records of 'Bernadette', the previous best, are being smashed..."

Cronin dealt directly with Alfred McIntyre in America and Victor Gollancz in Britain over contracts and royalty rates, and proved to be a hard bargainer. Long before he left Britain for America, Cronin's improved "selling status", as he called it, was a major factor in those negotiations, and was further enhanced by *The Keys of the Kingdom*. His reputation, and the subsequent demand for his books, meant that he could hold out for terms that suited him, safe in the knowledge that, provided he was not being unreasonable, he could always find some publisher to meet his demands. This strength was no better exemplified than over the question of paperbacks.

At first Cronin seemed reluctant to embrace this innovation. Paperbacks started in Germany with Albatross Books, founded by Kurt Enoch in 1931. They proved to be a great success, and the idea was copied in Britain by Allen Lane, who started Penguin in 1935, the books selling at sixpence, the price of a packet of cigarettes. In America Robert de Graff followed with Pocket Books in 1939. Traditional publishers and a great number of authors were naturally suspicious, and it was some time before Cronin had to face the prospect of seeing his titles in paperback.

In America Cronin and McIntyre first discussed the subject in 1941, without reaching an agreement. The following year, in a letter dated 7th March, McIntyre brought it up again. Cronin replied: "As regards the Pocket Books offer, if my memory serves me our personal negotiations upon this matter last winter were not productive, and we agreed to shelve it indefinitely. In the interests of harmony perhaps we had better leave it so." It was partly a point of principle that decided Cronin's attitude, as he explained in a letter to McIntyre a couple of years later:

> Regarding the Pocket Books edition of *The Citadel* I have tried awfully hard to bring myself to give my consent, because of our friendship and the extremely good relations now existing between us. But, alas, the invisible partner is obdurate. Honestly, Alfred, I don't think my ultimate percentage on such an edition would be a fair one. Lately I have gone into the question of these paperbacks – there is a considerable profit to the publisher and a minute one to the author. Also the one rate of royalty policy which makes no distinction between authors is, in my opinion, inequitable. There are many more arguments which I could bring to bear on the subject but I don't wish to do so. I think the best solution is that we should amiably forget about it as we did before.[34]

The subject of paperbacks was briefly revisited on 4th December 1944, when Cronin replied to a note from McIntyre: "I am so glad you understand my feelings about the Pocket edition of *The Citadel*. I am sure we can get together on this at a later date." In Britain at this time paperbacks were not an issue between Cronin and Gollancz, but he agreed to the New English Library (founded in 1961) publishing all his books in paperback much later in his career.

Cronin was not so much against cheap books as against the unfavourable economics of paperbacks. In fact, he had earlier agreed to *The Citadel* being published by Grosset & Dunlap, another publisher of affordable editions in competition with paperbacks. The company had started out by producing hardback copies of books already in print – pirating them, according to some, and avoiding the payment of royalties – but eventually became the pre-eminent reprint publisher of the first half of the twentieth century by changing their policy to purchasing reprint rights from publishers. Cronin had agreed with Alfred McIntyre a five-cents-per-book royalty for *The Citadel*, but regretted it later. He was prepared to accept the same terms for the cheap *The Keys of the Kingdom*, but when the time came for drawing up the contract for *The Green Years* he wrote to McIntyre: "I am agreeable that you should proceed with the 'cheap editions' negotiations with Grosset & Dunlap provided the payments thereby accruing be dealt with under the new contract."[35] In other words, Cronin was looking for an increase in his share. On 29th September 1945 he wrote again to McIntyre:

> Do not misunderstand me, Alfred, I am not being hoggish but I feel that as Little, Brown & Co. is now a one-third owner of Grosset & Dunlap you would, to a certain extent, be participating in their cut of the "three-way split" and for this reason, being the fairest man I know, might wish to give me a proportional increase in my share...

* * *

From 1939 to 1947, as the drama of war was being played out in Europe, the Cronins moved around the United States, coast to coast, and holidayed abroad. They never spent longer than a year in one place. This nomadic existence finally came to an end in June 1947 with the purchase of Woodlea Hill, in New Canaan, Connecticut. On 22nd April 1947 Cronin wrote to McIntyre: "You may be interested to hear that we have finally bought a property in New Canaan. It belonged to a Mr Hutchins who owned the *Washington*

Post and is rather an antediluvian shack, but the grounds are very charming and the location is central and convenient…" During most of this period Vincent and Patrick were away at school and university. Andrew, Cronin's youngest son, said of this time:

> When we moved into our huge house in New Canaan things settled down. I actually got to go to the same school for four years. My parents went to Europe most of the summers and I had a lot of friends to play with. Nanny usually took me to Maine for a two-week vacation.[36]

Serious literary ambition and a compulsive wanderlust do not easily coexist, especially when hampered by a restless temperament. In America, juggling his literary ambition with a roaming lifestyle proved to be a major problem, every change of venue providing yet another excuse for delay. Cronin must have been only too well aware that time away from his desk was time lost. We have seen evidence of his idiosyncratic writing habits and his preference for "stony silence and a solicitude best described as sepulchral". "I am insufficiently organized to be able to write at home," he said once. "I have tried to write in hotel bedrooms, in steamship cabins, in American Pullmans, on a bench in Hyde Park, in a sleeper on the Rome Express, and I have every time been foiled by the twin harpy of modern progress – noise."[37]

The adventurous atmosphere of his adopted country was not the only drain on his time. His involvement in the war effort, with the Ministry of Information – articles, foreign radio broadcasts and similar engagements – was a further distraction. Another major event at this time was the making of the *Hatter's Castle* film, produced by Paramount British Pictures at Denham Studios, Buckinghamshire, which opened in Britain on 2nd February 1942. It starred Robert Newton as James Brodie, James Mason as Dr Renwick, Deborah Kerr as Mary Brodie and Emlyn Williams as Denis. It was released in America only after the war, on 19th April 1948. The film departed from the original story in many ways. The bullying egotist James Brodie is literally destroyed in the film, perishing in a house fire started by him. His son chooses to commit suicide after being caught cheating in the examination for the Latta scholarship, whereas in the book it is Brodie's daughter who takes her own life. Several of the remaining characters are portrayed differently, most notably Dr Renwick, who is given a more prominent role than in the novel, and Denis Foyle, cast as the brother of Brodie's mistress, Nancy, and transformed into a thoroughly objectionable character. Overall, Cronin's motivation in writing the book is overlooked, and significant underlying themes are ignored.

As a result of his itinerant ways and his war work, it was not until 26th November 1942 that Cronin wrote to Alfred McIntyre about his next novel, *The Green Years*:

> I have a truly striking theme, quite the finest and most original that has ever come my way... I am quite carried away by what I have done of it. However, I fear it would be a mistake for me to attempt to complete the work at an early date. This would mean giving up my job in the national emergency (which I think neither of us would wish) and also sacrificing the quality of the book – for it is a work I venture to consider far more important than my other novels...

A year later, on 4th December 1943, another letter to McIntyre explained:

> I have been meaning to write to you for quite some time but have been terribly busy on a job for the Ministry of Information. They gave me a new assignment rather suddenly... I have been for several weeks on the move – in Washington, New York, Norfolk and Wilmington amongst other places – and am back now in Greenwich which is central for my activities... I have almost completed the new novel in its first draft – some 90,000 words, and I am altogether enchanted with it... if I could get the time and liberty to recapture its particular mood I believe I could finish it in a couple of months.

The point he makes is valid. No writer can be expected to give his best under such trying circumstances. In the same letter he said:

> I'm sure you understand that we are none of us our own masters in these wartime days. Moreover, normal and ordinary events have become wholly unpredictable, and only a very rash man would care to make forecasts. The best I can do is to explain my present situation and leave you to deduce the probabilities...

Cronin's protestations must be accepted as genuine, but there is little doubt that his perspective had changed since the halcyon days of the 1930s, when a book of about 250,000 words, *The Stars Look Down*, was completed in close to four months. The reason is plain. In Britain at that time his enthusiasm was fresh and, more importantly, his reputation was not yet secure. The two books that followed *Hatter's Castle* never approached the popularity of the first, leaving Cronin with the unpalatable fear of being branded a one-book author. The reassurance he longed for, and gained, was a major success with his fourth novel. By contrast, in America in 1943 his literary reputation was assured and his popularity invulnerable. It is far more likely, therefore, that lack of motivation was a bigger factor in his dilatoriness than his wartime activities.

Not only that, his name alone now assured him financial security. The serialization offer from *Redbook*, the American women's magazine, was, Cronin told both McIntyre and Gollancz, the highest ever made in the history of the magazine, though he did not disclose the amount. At the same time he broke the news that Metro-Goldwyn-Mayer had paid $200,000 for the film rights of the as-yet-unpublished novel, the highest price ever in the industry for the film rights, he claimed. The Cronin brand had been strong in Britain, but it was now impregnable. He was now bigger than any individual publisher and could afford to dictate terms and timings. He had always controlled serialization rights in Britain and America, and on this occasion, decided to delay publication of *The Green Years* until 1944.

McIntyre was far from happy, not only with the delay, but also because he felt he had been misled, and his response sparked the first dispute between them. Cronin's reply is illuminating:

> As you persist in your aggrieved attitude, assuming yourself to be the victim of conflicting statements, I have no alternative but to correct you... if you will read carefully my original letter of 4th December, you will find there NO statement that I do not intend to serialize my new novel. In fact the question of serialization was raised with the clear intention of showing you that it might delay publication...[38]

Cronin continued with other contentious issues and concluded with a very unpleasant parting shot: "In brief, I most thoroughly resent this kind of treatment. Nor for that matter shall I readily forget it."[39] In January 1944 he wrote again with more concrete news, offering McIntyre little comfort:

> I promised to let you know about the new novel, now entitled *The Green Years*, whenever I had definite light on the subject... I have now decided to serialize... The intention is to run the novel in six or seven instalments beginning in the May, and ending, possibly, in the November issue... This brings us practically to the end of 1944... I feel that book publication will not be possible this year... while this delay is probably irksome to both of us it will permit me to polish the novel further and may prove advantageous in the long run.[40]

During the next few months Cronin was heavily involved in drawing up contracts with MGM for the film adaptation of the new book and with McIntyre for the publication in book form, flexing his muscles even further in discussing the details of his contract with Little, Brown:

> I certainly hoped we might reach a compromise – say, an agreement of 20% straight with some adjustment, at least, of the discount clause – which would not have deprived you wholly of your profits and would at the same time have seemed to me commensurate with the prospects of the new novel and the improvement in my "selling status" since the publication of *The Keys of the Kingdom*... However, your letter, which concedes nothing... appears to close the door on that hope... I have weighed carefully the two alternatives... and I have decided, entirely without resentment, that there is no point in my entering into a new commitment with you for a further book. I prefer that our existing contract should run to its close... Under the circumstances I cannot at present say when it will be possible for me to bring my new novel to its final form, but as I have given no undertaking in any quarter to publish by a specific date I shall have ample time to complete the work to my satisfaction.[41]

The most significant aspect of that letter was the reference to Cronin's improved "selling status". Gollancz had been confronted with a similar ultimatum after the publication of *The Stars Look Down*. There was no denying that his last three novels had raised him to a level he might never have dreamt possible but, ironically, at that point in his career, there was a real need to reaffirm his priorities. His ambition for literary greatness was not served by *Redbook*, *Reader's Digest* or Hollywood. They bolstered his fame and fortune, but only published novels on major issues warranted consideration by serious literary critics and thereby the recognition as a major author that he still yearned for.

Returning to the question of the balance of his life and work, the situation remained unchanged even after the war. In a letter to Alfred McIntyre, dated 9th September 1945, from the Carlyle Hotel on Madison Avenue in New York City, Cronin regretted that "I shall be unable to lunch with you on that day. I'm sorry, for I had some points to discuss with you, but I must do so by letter, later on. At present, as you may imagine, I am terribly rushed." On 29th September, he wrote: "As to the new novel, this is shaped out – and it is magnificent. When I shall get down to the writing of it I cannot quite predict… maybe I shall take the winter in solitude in Ireland to do it." Five more letters passed between them before the book was mentioned again, and by then it was April 1947. This hectic situation was typical of his time in America, and continued until 1955 when the Cronins returned to Europe.

By contrast, in Britain in the 1930s, even when his relatively stable existence was threatened by his new-found celebrity status, his letters suggest that his fierce determination to fulfil his literary destiny was such that he would allow nothing to interfere with that ambition. His early books possessed, in his own words "an emotional impulse, a sense of communicative ardour in respect of some particular phase of life".[42] With no regard for reputation or reward, he felt compelled to uncover the iniquities of an unjust society, one that he understood, felt part of, suffered in and was confident in exposing. But in America he no longer tilted at windmills, and his once peerless social commentaries suddenly stopped. He appears to have allowed himself to be wooed into thinking that he could maintain his status by writing to suit his public, instead of drawing from his heart and conscience. He plied them with huge doses of Cronin – fictional reminiscences – rather than the profound humanitarian panorama at which he excelled. His readers, hooked on his reputation, remained loyal to whatever he served up, unlike the British public, which he himself recognized was "more discriminating than the one we have on this side of the Atlantic".[43] It was possibly at this point in his career that the mantle of greatness began to slip away from his shoulders. In the end, he discovered too late that while his earning potential seemed limitless, surpassing almost all contemporary writers, the price he was paying was high.

The enrichment was financial, not spiritual. There was almost a sense of destiny in Cronin's early books. In them, the correlation between the themes and Cronin's background rendered him, unintentionally, the champion of the oppressed. And though the characters in his first six novels were uniquely British, the subject matter was universal: sectarianism and social injustice were not the sole preserves of Scotland, any more than the conflict between capital and labour was specific to the north-east of England. Cronin never seemed able to decipher the American social milieu. He was bowled over by the geniality of his New World cousins, but his fame and wealth insulated him from true empathy with his adopted culture. American society, though obviously very different from Britain, was equally flawed and equally ripe for exposure, but Cronin's perfunctory involvement created an emotional vacuum that probably explains the absence of a real American novel.

Almost five years into his transatlantic experience, and following three major international best-sellers, Cronin's new book, *The Green Years*, returned to the familiar setting – which some found tedious – of sectarian Scotland at the turn of the twentieth century, giving the lie to the author's earlier claim that he had left Britain for fresh inspiration. The novel traces the development to maturity of a young Catholic orphan in the Protestant household of his grandparents in Levenford. Dale Salwak suggested that "for the creation of Alexander Gow, Cronin drew upon his own great grandfather".[44] However, little in the book resembles Cronin's childhood: for instance, his real-life mother was alive and remained the dominant influence in his development. Also, Cronin did not have to work in a factory, and the only male great-grandparent who lived in the household, together with his wife, was Francis Perry – dark and serious-minded, not red-haired and irreverent like the character Gow. A distinct feeling of déjà vu permeates some sections of the book: elements of *Hatter's Castle*, *Three Loves* and especially

The Keys of the Kingdom – which would have been still fresh in readers' minds – are presented again, albeit from a different angle.

The Americans in particular loved it. Advance orders from bookshops approached 200,000 copies, almost equalling Little, Brown's previous record of 250,000 for *The Keys of the Kingdom*, and the book went on to top both the American and Canadian best-seller lists.

No assessment of *The Green Years* should overlook the fact that it came directly after *The Keys of the Kingdom*, following which nothing was likely to fail. On 21st July 1944, Cronin assured Alfred McIntyre that he was "very happy that the advance news of the book continues favourable. I hope we have a great success and that, if we do, the paper shortage won't cramp our style." Two months later, on 14th August, responding to a note from Ray Everitt, he wrote: "I'm thrilled that the first copy of *The Green Years* gave you a thrill though I am so cursedly modest and sceptical I can scarcely believe it. I do hope we have a bit of luck with the book however and that not all the critics spit on it." How different from the infectious excitement caused by his greatest British books, when failure was never contemplated...

Cronin received his first copy of *The Green Years* in August 1944, months ahead of its launch date in November, and was "heart-broken". The wartime paper shortage was forcing publishers to cut corners, and he reacted angrily: "Naturally I realize that this insignificant format must be due to the paper shortage but I did not anticipate such a blow, especially as you told me it was your intention to give the book as much bulk as possible. I find the piling of chapters, one on top of another, particularly displeasing and had I known that you proposed to do this I should have objected most strenuously..."

Then Cronin's paranoia surfaced: "I've gone through a number of current novels, including several published by Little, Brown and in not one do I find this crushed concertina effect. (After all there is no point in making chapters if they are not properly spaced)." This was followed by a slightly more reasoned disappointment: "You have made such fine and noble-looking books for me in the past that this present let-down is all the more of a shock. (Even the cover is such a sickly green it makes me almost ill.) I know you have to contend with war conditions... nevertheless I hope you have not defeated your object for frankly, if I were a member of the reading public approaching this very tenuous volume I should feel that it was not a full-length novel at all… and also that it was poor value for any man's money."[45] Cronin had always been fussy over the appearance of his books. He liked the famous Gollancz yellow dust jacket and complained to John Bush, a key Gollancz employee, when it was dropped. In typical fashion, a week later he recanted and wrote to McIntyre:

> I do see your difficulties very clearly and I'm sorry for having added to them. It's just that you have spoiled me in the past by making such lovely books for me… really I regretted my letter after I had written it and I am so glad you met it in so reasonable a spirit. It's an odd thing – small disappointments are sometimes harder to bear than big ones. But the Scots have a saying: "What canna be cured maun be endured"…[46]

Reviews of the book were complimentary, but it was not generally seen as a profound work. A minority of discerning critics – in the *Boston Sunday Post*, the *Dallas Times Herald* and the *Philadelphia Record* among others – was not swept along in the euphoric tide, yet even they were forced to concede that Cronin's conservative philosophies and his easy, gracious style would override its dubious literary merit and guarantee success among the "bustle-bound" women's clubs across America.

The novel was later adapted as a major Hollywood film, which was shot in the MGM studios in California and had its premiere on 4th July 1946. The *New York Times* thought that its British-bred director, Victor Saville, had done his job honourably, and that he and producer Leon Gordon had given Metro another high-minded hit. Charles Coburn as Alexander Gow was nominated for an Oscar as best actor in a supporting role, but did not win.

Cronin had kept Gollancz informed of the progress of *The Green Years* by telegram. The first one, dated 30th November 1944, read as follows: "Green Years has had wonderful reception here. Reviews almost unanimously eulogistic. Breaking all Little, Brown records." The second, dated 5th April 1945, said: "Green Years still top best-seller. Now chosen August Premium Selection Book of Month Club. Estimate total American and Canadian printing that date just under one million copies." Despite the book's popularity Cronin's statistics are debatable.

On 15th June 1944 he had written to Gollancz about publication of *The Green Years* in Britain and their existing contract:

> How will the paper shortage affect your plans to publish? I definitely don't want to publish in England in 1944 but would be glad to agree with you upon any subsequent year... you may remember that this is the last book called for under our present contract. If you wish to continue to sponsor my works I should like to make a new contract now (superseding our existing agreement) embodying *The Green Years* and one further book. I don't ask for any better terms. The new contract would be in every essential similar to the existing one...

Gollancz naturally went along with Cronin's wishes and made his plans for a 1945 publication, but was still worried about the possibility of libel suits. The firm's lawyer, Rubinstein, saw *The Green Years* as semi-autobiographical, assuming that Cronin had drawn on memories of his own childhood and youth, and suggested that Gollancz should question whether any of the characters – in particular Adam Leckie, an unsavoury insurance agent in the novel – could be identified with real people. When Gollancz sought assurances, he felt the lash of Cronin's tongue. The author cabled Gollancz from a holiday resort on Nantucket Island:

> Deeply annoyed and resentful your persistence this bogey of libel. *Green Years* the most utterly inoffensive novel I have ever written. On point of principle I refuse give blanket assurances on what your solicitor elects to call unsympathetic characters. I offer you this book in good faith. If you do not wish to publish you are perfectly at liberty to refuse it...[47]

This was not the first, and would not be the last time Gollancz faced the petulant trait in Cronin's character.

A letter sent to Alfred McIntyre in April 1944 suggests that Cronin's literary ambitions may have undergone something of a transformation during this period, from the pursuit of critical recognition to a more popular, commercial approach to writing. Referring to *The Green Years* he had said: "If it succeeds I am hoping it will be the first book of a trilogy – but more of that later."

Then, having had time to digest the book's impact on the American market, he had written to McIntyre again: "I am pleased at your figures for *The Green Years* and I trust you will continue to push this book as you have done, so splendidly, in the case of all my other works – not only because a large sale will work advantageously for a sequel, but also because, as you must know, authors are solicitous for their offspring and having laboured to bring them forth, dread to see them prematurely interred."[48] However, a note of caution had soon crept into Cronin's references to a sequel. In January 1945 he wrote to Alfred McIntyre: "I have sounded out a couple of the critics on a sequel to *The Green Years* and they are enthusiastic. But maybe we'd better wait and see what the 1945 sales shape like before finally deciding." It is striking that Cronin, a writer with an established international reputation, should consult critics and wait on the results of sales figures before proceeding with a new novel.

In September 1945, on his way to Britain for a long holiday, he acquainted Alfred McIntyre of his progress on the sequel, entitled *Shannon's Way*: "As to the new novel, this is all shaped out – and it is magnificent... We hope to return to the USA in 1946 and I would love to have the manuscript in my bag, though I cannot promise." The book, however, was only half-finished by April 1947, and would not be published until 1948.

Cronin's youngest son, Andrew, is convinced that his father had never intended to remain in America after the war, and that the family holiday in the autumn of 1945, first to a flat in Hove and then to a rented estate in Ireland, was partly a reconnaissance trip for a return to Britain. But the harsh realities of life there – rationing and shortages in Britain continued for many years after the end of hostilities – had weighed heavily against a change. This was perhaps accentuated by the social and political transformation that Cronin saw taking place, as he confided to Alfred McIntyre: "I will give you all the news when we meet. Sufficient to say here that the Europe you and I knew is gone and will not return in our time."[49] Socialist Britain – in thrall, as he saw it, to "the creeping paralysis of the modern age – regimentation by the state"[50] – was anathema to Cronin who, of course, had the means to make his choice much simpler. As mentioned earlier, in 1947 he bought Woodlea Hill, a huge villa in New Canaan, Connecticut, thereby opting for America and comfort and rejecting his homeland – perhaps with some regret – for a second time. To millions of fellow Britons, what he described as "this present unhappy age"[51] was the dawning of opportunity, a social revolution – maybe not to Cronin's liking; but even supposing he preferred the social injustice and the class divisions of pre-war Britain, it is difficult to see how their disappearance would have affected the lifestyle his wealth and status now guaranteed.

According to the 1976 autobiography, the subject of May's health remained paramount during the Cronins' years in America. Cronin reports that her physical condition was deteriorating to the point where he had to help her up steps. At some stage he claims to have consulted a famous psychiatrist in Hollywood, who was not identified, with the hope of getting a prognosis that would help shape their future. The professional diagnosis was that "her condition is an open-and-shut case of advanced premature degeneration of the brain cortex. Undoubtedly there was early brain damage... the circumstances and strain of your enforced marriage, above all the persistent sense of guilt which has endlessly tormented her thereafter... I must add it would be better if she had a settled home..." The same treatment was recommended – patience and forbearance in the light of the progressive condition. The settled home came in 1947 with the purchase of Woodlea Hill. However, although his wife showed him tenderness, she still had an aversion to physical contact – "so violent that even the gentlest attempt to caress her produced a repulsion so acute one knew at once the danger of proceeding".

When the cold New England winters began to prey on May's mind, Cronin bought a Mediterranean property – Villa La Meluitza, near Monte Carlo – to which they retired every year. Unfortunately, the property was damaged by a powerful storm in 1956, and so it was sold. The 1976 narrative ends there.

References to Cronin's private life cannot be challenged, but the testimony from his family raises doubts as to whether the Hollywood psychiatrist was real or imaginary. Quite apart from their refusal to believe that May's mental state was anything but normal, all family members affirm that physically she was in fine shape. The alleged psychiatric examination took place before the purchase of Woodlea Hill in 1947, so May was not yet fifty, and on the evidence of several family members she was still very active, playing golf and tennis and travelling the world. Cronin's claims in the 1976 autobiography have to be reassessed in the context of these observations. Later in this book other testimonies will shed further light on that controversial document.

At the first opportunity in 1947, Cronin persuaded his mother to join them permanently in Woodlea Hill. The two had been estranged, although the reason for this is not clear. It may have been her son's choice of partner that she objected to; it could have been her disappointment at his decision to abandon a medical career in his native Scotland; another possibility is that, like Lucy Moore in *Three Loves*, she expected him to establish himself as a physician first – in which undertaking she would have been more than ready to play a prominent role – before taking on the responsibilities of marriage and a family. Whatever the reason, time and Cronin's conciliatory overtures eventually healed the breach, although her estrangement from May continued for the rest of their lives. She had not accompanied the family to America in 1939, but from 1941 to 1944 she made the crossing to join them in Blue Hill, Maine, where they spent their summer vacations. Later, in 1945, she joined them in Ireland, and is fondly remembered by both her surviving grandsons. Vincent remembers her seated in an armchair, always busy, knitting something for them to wear. He said she always seemed to be knitting. Andrew, the youngest, who was eight in 1945, remembers his grandmother – whom he referred to as Mandy – with great affection, recalling how he liked talking with her. He saw more of her than his brothers, because he was not away at school. His memory of her is of a sweet old lady who always had time for him. He remembers a church in Dublin, in the winter of 1945, that had a Mass every half an hour on Sundays. Mandy would take him there early so that they could get the blessing from the Mass that was just ending and the blessing for the next one. Like Andrew's memories of Nan, the children's recollections of their grandmother – as indeed of their father – are full of warmth. Remembrances of their mother, on the other hand, do not give off the same glow.

It is implausible that Cronin would have invited his mother to join them in New Canaan in 1947 without the agreement of his wife, but Jessie's presence in the family would not have been well accepted by May: "Having her in the house didn't please my mother,"[52] Andrew recalls. The clash of personalities which the older woman had recognized at the time of her son's wedding had not softened over time. Two years after her move to America, she retired from the world, entering a convent near Boston. Andrew put it rather more crudely: "She was sent off after a couple of years to live in a convent." Whether the move would have taken place had domestic relations been different is unknown, but it is clear that her Catholic faith was strong and the move was no hardship for Jessie. Her relationship with her son had always been close, and he made sure she lacked for nothing. Vincent is convinced that it was her influence that kept Cronin devout. She continued to live in convents until her death in Switzerland in 1962.

Shannon's Way was finally published in Britain and America in 1948. As we saw above from his letter to McIntyre of September 1945, Cronin initially thought that his new novel was "magnificent". But the book's reception brought him to his senses, and he came to acknowledge that it was not magnificent, but "only a light and simple story". Critical reception widely echoed Cronin's final assessment of the book. There was a general consensus that this was not Cronin at his best and that the novel added nothing to his stature as a writer. One reviewer said: "Cronin has been sliding downhill rapidly since *The Keys of the Kingdom*."[53] But perhaps the most telling criticism came from the *Times Literary Supplement*: "Dr Cronin's competent new novel is reminiscent of nothing so much as the act of a once-promising variety artist whose performance has staled with repetition."[54] Nevertheless, Cronin fans ensured that *Shannon's Way* found its way into the top-ten best-sellers' list issued by *Publishers Weekly* in America. In a sense, history was repeating itself, and Cronin was again in need – as he had been after the poor reception of *Grand Canary* – of a new book to strengthen his literary reputation.

Cronin wrote to Gollancz in September 1949, on his return from a two-month break in France, which included his son Vincent's wedding and an emergency operation for appendicitis on his wife:

I have done two short novels of about 50,000 words each: *Gracie Lindsay* and *The Spanish Gardener*... while I think that these two together would make a most popular book which would command a large sale, I feel that I want, first of all, to publish a more important novel which is already in my mind, something with a definitely major theme and of much deeper significance in its relation to the trend of humanity in the world today... this could really be my best book and I think I am due it after *Shannon's Way*...[55]

Cronin had intended to publish the two short books after the magnum opus on which he was pinning his hopes, but something made him change his mind, and by mutual agreement with both publishers *The Spanish Gardener* – the story of a British diplomat in Catalonia and his jealousy over his son's friendship with a gardener, José – was published in 1950. Cronin told his son, Andrew, and his daughter-in-law, Anne, that the idea behind *The Spanish Gardener* came from his son's friendship with a gardener at Woodlea Hill, an Italian-American who had served in the navy in the Second World War.

The book received some recognition as a piece of popular fiction, but reviews were generally lukewarm. The hero of the book, Consul Harrington Brande, seeks help from his old friend, Professor Halevy, a quack psychiatrist, to explain what he considers to be the "abnormal behaviour" of his son with José, the gardener. Their subsequent conversation seems to insinuate feelings beyond mere admiration. Halevy's comments to Brande are pointed: "You know that filth exists even in the most unsuspected places"[56] and: "Are we not all the servants of our bodies, victims of the terrors and disgusts of our desires?"[57] There follows a grilling of the young boy, Nico, by the psychiatrist, that at times borders on the manic: "And because you wished him to be near you... to touch you... that is why you went home with him."[58] In the America of the early Fifties homosexuality was regarded as a mental illness in some sections of society, most notably in the armed forces. At the height of the McCarthy era – Cronin incidentally detested Joseph McCarthy – President Eisenhower signed an order allowing the dismissal of federal employees on the grounds of sexual orientation. In Britain homosexuality was still illegal, though resistance to the law was growing in the aftermath of the first post-war Labour government's liberalizing agenda. It's not clear whether Cronin was trying to highlight the highly sensitive subject, but whatever his intentions, the subject met with widespread silence among book critics at the time.

Despite being a mediocre novel, several years later *The Spanish Gardener* was filmed, in a production that boasted a solid cast of well-known British actors, including Dirk Bogarde, Jon Whiteley, Michael Hordern, Cyril Cusack, Maureen Swanson and Bernard Lee. The Rank Organisation released the film in London on 25th December 1956 and in America in September 1957. Directed by Philip Leacock, the film was shot at Pinewood Studios in Buckinghamshire and in Catalonia. The film was more widely acclaimed than the book, no doubt due to the presence of Dirk Bogarde, one of Britain's most popular actors at the time.

Cronin's return to the familiar themes of the destructive power of egotism and possessive love – explored earlier in *Hatter's Castle* and *Three Loves* – appears to be a withdrawal into his comfort zone, and another signal of his shifting attitude, away from a desire for greatness to a slick formula for success and high rewards.

Sheila Bush, who had worked for Victor Gollancz from 1936 to 1954, visited Cronin in America in 1951 and said of him:

> When I was with Gollancz and went to the USA on a book-hunting expedition, Cronin invited me to lunch at the beautiful house he owned in New Canaan. He then took me for a ride in his car (I don't think it was a Rolls!), ostensibly to show me the beauties of New England but in reality to pump me about the firm's intentions regarding his new novel. He talked at length about all the money and pictures and oil wells he owned, and at the end of it all I felt immensely sorry for him, for his money seemed to have brought him nothing that he valued...[59]

Ignoring the inaccuracies – such as oil wells, which can be put down to journalistic licence – Sheila Bush's observation of Cronin's financial preoccupation is significant. It is a shame she did not expand on what she felt Cronin valued above material wealth. Might she have been referring to literary recognition, and had she perhaps recognized the formula that was allowing second-rate work to pass as acceptable? Challenge, once Cronin's lifeblood, seems to have disappeared from his life, replaced, possibly, by self-delusion. Some years before, Kenneth Horan, a journalist with the *Dallas Times Herald*, reported a not dissimilar experience. He met Cronin at a book-signing luncheon in Chicago in 1948, and described him as a very dour doctor. Cronin had refused to sign any books until after he had had his cup of tea, and then went on to explain how he hated America.[60] It was a strange time to express such feelings, having just bought a new house and persuaded his seventy-two-year-old mother to uproot from Britain and join them in America.

By the end of December 1950, Cronin's earlier promise of an important novel with a major theme began to recede. He found himself sidetracked by Broadway's interest in adapting *The Spanish Gardener* for the stage, something that would take Cronin "a good three months' hard work and the various out of town try-outs will take up a further amount of time".[61] As a result, he anticipated a delay for his "big novel" of at least a year, possibly into 1952. About three weeks later, responding to a Gollancz letter outlining the precarious state of the publishing business, he commented:

Believe me, I fully appreciate and sympathize with your difficulties for, in some degree, we are suffering from the same thing over here. For example, the mania for television has cut the sale of most novels to the vanishing point. Only the big names are selling at all and several publishers I have talked with lately are at their wits' end as to how to make ends meet. On top of this, as you say, the world situation is perfectly terrible. I get the gloomiest reports from my European correspondents in Switzerland, Belgium and Holland. One friend in Amsterdam, who is president of a large oil concern, has advised me that he is convinced Russia will invade Western Europe when the spring rains are over... What depresses me most, apart from the great issues involved, is the loss of all the little things that you and I enjoyed so much in those gracious days when we planned our projects together in an atmosphere of peace...

...Because of the world situation and because, also, there is much work to be done upon it, I have put away my big novel for the time being and have decided to do, instead, a book which I have long wanted to do...[62]

Blaming a hectic lifestyle and the world situation for the change of mind and the consequent delay of his big novel suggests not only fading ambition, but also a failing grip on reality: the works in question were a feeble echo of his greatest works.

The book he referred to in his letter to Gollancz was *Adventures in Two Worlds*, a work defying a simple categorization. It is not a novel, yet it is more than a collection of short stories. The earlier point regarding Cronin's failing literary energies is relevant here. A large section of the book is a reworking of *The Citadel*, while several chapters had already appeared as articles in *Reader's Digest* between 1939 and 1952 – a fact that did not go unnoticed among reviewers.

Since he chose to write *Adventures in Two Worlds* in the first person, the idea to promote it as an autobiography – given the appeal of Cronin's name – made sound commercial sense, even though he had told Gollancz: "It will *not* be an autobiography but will be full of incident, tender, moving and dramatic, with just that medical flavour which readers love, a really warm and interesting book."[63]

It is a work of reminiscences and reflections divided into four parts, roughly following the main events in the author's life. The first three parts ("the first world") provide the medical flavour referred to in his letter to Gollancz. They cover student days in Scotland, early experiences in the Lochlea mental hospital and midwifery duties at the Rotunda hospital in Dublin. The action then moves to the Highlands, and an assistantship with a Dr Cameron of Tannochbrae and his housekeeper, Janet, both of whom would go on to be portrayed successfully in the 1960s television series *Dr Finlay's Casebook*. The medical journey continues to the valleys of Wales and finally to London – a reworking of *The Citadel*. The fourth part ("the second world") deals with the life of a novelist, followed by a collection of short parables that explore the dignity of the human spirit in adversity through observations of Europe after the Second World War. The book ends with a commentary on the importance of religion to individuals and society, and some personal reflections on life.

In the last two chapters of *Adventures in Two Worlds* Cronin indulges his passion for sermonizing, advocating religion as the only force capable of ensuring world peace and stability. His emotional outpourings lack the blinding clarity usually associated with his writings. The sincerity of feeling is clear, but his competence as a theologian is again questionable. In these final chapters he roams widely: condemning the modern obsessions of materialism and pleasure at the expense of all other considerations, railing against atheism, ruling out a scientific explanation of creation, entering the political arena with his references to the two halves of the world – one atheistic (the USSR), the other apathetic (the USA) – while promoting the notion of a Supreme Intelligence and offering faith as proof of such an existence.

An autobiographical analysis of *Adventures in Two Worlds* is not very constructive, but if the book is interpreted allegorically – i.e. with "I" representing Everyman – then the thrust of Cronin's argument in the last part of the book can be more easily understood: that the worship of materialism alone, with no reference to spiritual values, can only cause disillusion among individuals and "an avalanche of horror and destruction... total war" among nations.[64]

Published in America and Britain in 1952, the book was widely reviewed and well received. Many critics were not convinced by its alleged autobiographical content, and some complained that they had learnt no more about Cronin than they had from his previous works, while the *Saturday Review* saw "the emergence of a more mature, more philosophical talent, which... may yet herald A.J. Cronin's most important field of work".

Adventures in Two Worlds was in some ways a pivotal book. When it was published, Cronin had been fourteen years in America, having lived through a world war and its subsequent upheaval. He made no secret of his discomfort at what he perceived as a threat to the long-established social order on both sides of the Atlantic. The Britain he had deserted was on the point of disappearing, while America in the 1950s compared unfavourably to his pre-war vision of a land of virginal opportunity and was no longer the refuge he had once sought. During this turbulent period, his literary aspirations had become disconnected from the world around him. His choice of subject matter – Scottish reminiscences and nostalgic sketches – appeared almost to deny the contemporary scene. Why his surroundings had failed to evoke a seminal literary response is unclear, but there can be little doubt that Cronin was experiencing some form of moral crisis.

In the previously quoted speech to an American ladies' society, May said:

> He is sustained by the hope, which is doubtless the pet illusion of all authors, that he will one day write a really fine book, something that will live. Studying him as he goes into one of his baleful trances I sometimes wonder, cold-bloodedly, if he will ever succeed in this supreme endeavour...[65]

Had May simply been referring to his American novels, few would have disagreed with her, but including all his work was perhaps too harsh. It was only in America that he failed to maintain the standards many had come to expect from him. Life in America had started as one grand merry-go-round. He had regularly wintered in Los Angeles, savoured the delights of Hollywood, rubbed shoulders with the stars, been feted by his adoring readership, pursued by the press, publishers and periodicals, and had moved in exalted circles – in the winter of 1944–45 living next door to Senator Prescott Bush, the father and grandfather of two future presidents – but he was losing ground as a literary force, and he must have wondered if he had passed the point of resurrection. His next book, he knew, had to be different. Even his patient fan base would not support another fictional reminiscence.

Beyond This Place, the last novel to be published while he was living in America, in 1953, represented a long overdue departure from the previous Cronin brand. However, it lacked the freshness of a new novel, having been serialized earlier by *Collier's Weekly*, in a shortened version entitled *To Live Again*. The story concerns Paul Burgess, a young man about to begin a career in teaching, who discovers that his mother has hidden from him the fact that his father is a convicted murderer. Paul devotes himself to investigating the case in an attempt to have his father's conviction quashed and, eventually, Rees Mathry, Paul's father, is granted an appeal and is freed. The novel expresses the concern that the centuries-old system of trial by jury might yield the wrong result, particularly in cases where the prosecutor happens to be stronger than the defence counsel, and sets out a hypothetical case of a miscarriage of justice. It is a whodunit of sorts – an unlikely genre for Cronin.

But perhaps his venture into crime literature was not so surprising. He had explored social causes in several of his early books, and he would have been aware of the growing movement in Britain for the abolition of hanging, in which Victor Gollancz himself was closely involved. In *Beyond This Place* both sides of the argument are articulated in a conversation between a Member of Parliament and Paul Burgess:

> "You forget that we need the common hangman."
> "Why?"
> "Hell and damnation!" Birley exploded. "To hang our murderers of course."
> "Must we hang them?"
> "Of course we must. We have to protect the community. If it wasn't for the fear of the rope any blackguard would cut your throat on a dark night for a five-pound note."
> "In countries that have abolished the death penalty, statistics show that there has been no increase in crime."[66]

The shortcomings of the jury system may have been Cronin's inspiration, but it was not the only social issue he raised in this book:

> Crime is the product of a country's social order. Those who make that social order are often more guilty than the so-called criminals... there's no justice. So long as people are comfortable themselves, with plenty to eat and drink, spending money in their pockets and a roof over their heads, they don't care a damn about right and wrong. The whole world's rotten to the core... it's time for a newer, better system...[67]

This outburst by Paul Burgess is reminiscent of Cronin's work in the 1930s. Echoing the questions of contemporary liberal thinkers, he goes on:

> As the silence continued, Paul gazed almost with panic at the grotesque and brooding figure of his father. How could this man, so gentle and elegant, who had led him by the hand to sail boats on Jesmond Dean, taken infinite trouble to amuse him by sketching and cutting out silhouettes, who never failed at the weekend to bring him some little toy, whose every action had bespoken love and consideration... What

frightful process of brutalization had changed him, brought him to this state?[68]

There is, in that single paragraph, enough raw material for a full-scale exposé of another major British institution – the closed, influential, class-dominated legal profession – which could have rivalled his earlier excursions into the mining industry, medicine and the Church. The complex seminal issues such as the callous promotion of personal careers before justice, police corruption, political intrigue and penal reform offered Cronin an opportunity to return to his best form. However, such an enterprise would have demanded a huge commitment in time and effort, something he had not attempted for years. *Beyond This Place* is very readable but, perhaps inevitably, in a book of this kind the characters tend to become submerged by the plot and lack substance. Compared with enduring characters like Father Chisholm in *The Keys of the Kingdom* or Richard Barras in *The Stars Look Down*, the players in *Beyond This Place* are cursorily introduced and lack any depth. Lena, the one female character with the potential to reach the heights of the great Cronin heroines, disappears from the narrative too soon and never comes to full bloom. The concept of trial by jury could have been relegated to a subordinate position to allow an expansion of the major characters within a broader framework.

Published in Britain and America in 1953, *Beyond This Place* was later adapted for the screen by Georgefield Productions. It was released in Britain by Renown Pictures Corporation in April 1959, and in America, under the title *Web of Evidence*, by Allied Artists Pictures in October 1959. Earlier than the film, however, CBS in America screened a television adaptation of the novel, directed by Sidney Lumet and starring Farley Granger as Paul Burgess. When the film was released, Cronin was living in Switzerland, and his interest was financial rather than artistic. Nevertheless, the combination of a universally popular genre – a whodunit – an American lead, Van Johnson, a British director of some repute, Jack Cardiff, and a cast of accomplished British stars, produced a film of considerable appeal.

After *Beyond This Place*, Cronin revived the idea of a "big novel". When this took shape in his mind, a sense of enthusiasm, reminiscent of the old days, can be felt in his letters, such as the following to Victor Gollancz:

> I had meant to write to you at this season partly because of our friendship which, as you know, I value, and partly to let you know about the new book which is approaching completion... It's a long novel... in the neighbourhood of 120,000... I regard the book as one of the most important I have done in recent years. Some of the action, though not all, takes place in Spain, also in Paris, provincial France, Sussex and London. So you see the canvas is a large one...[69]

The significance of the novel, *Crusader's Tomb* (*A Thing of Beauty* in America), is not that it was to be the last one he wrote in America, but that it was written from the heart, not to a formula, and with no regard for a particular audience. It was as if the pre-war Cronin was back, and he fussed over detail:

> Because of my feelings for this novel, I don't want to turn it into you before I have completely revised and polished it... As regards title, I have discarded my original idea: *The Crusader's Tomb*, and now feel that *The Price of Beauty* is better. What do you think? I am particularly anxious to get hold of something really arresting this time...[70]

On 9th March 1955 he was able to tell Gollancz that:

> Following my cable of last week I should like to tell you that I have just read through the first typescript in its entirety and, in all modesty, I'm completely thrilled with the book ... I consider it far and away ahead of anything I have done in recent years, extremely moving in parts and absolutely compelling in its interest, besides having that controversial quality which a good Cronin ought to have. Since I think so well of this particular novel, I want to work on it and polish it thoroughly... as you probably know, I am always tempted to send in my manuscripts too soon, and for this reason alone, and because of other rather important matters which now preoccupy me and which I will tell you about when we meet, I think it would be perhaps three or four months before I shall finally be satisfied...

And he continued dithering over the title:

I have thought a great deal about the title, and it seems to me that *Stephen Desmonde*, the name of the principal character, is both simple and effective. What do you think of this yourself?

When he met Gollancz in America later that month, Cronin broke the news – the "rather important matters" referred to in his letter – that he had decided to leave America for Switzerland. The plan was to depart on 15th June, spend a month in Le Touquet and then go on to his new home, Villa Allwinden, Kastanienbaum, near Lucerne.

About a month later he informed Gollancz that he had sold the serial rights to *Woman's Home Companion*, which would further delay publication, adding: "As you know, I was not terribly keen to serialize, but their offer was so very tempting I felt it would be stupid to turn it down."[71] He softened the blow by explaining that "this time there has been more than usual interest on the part of the magazines. Add to this the fact that I still want to make a few changes in the book, the upset that we are at present enduring in moving back to Europe, and also the minor detail that I have just been in the Harkness Pavilion for ten days having an unromantic and painful operation for the removal of varicose veins, and you may sympathize a little with the plight of your most loyal author. However, be this as it may, I promise that you shall have the manuscript first of all the publishers who are importuning me, and at the earliest possible date…"[72]

In another letter to Gollancz in October, he said: "We are delighted with our new home – after years of being stifled in American suburbia, it is a change which has refreshed and re-invigorated me, and given me a new incentive for my work." The word "stifled" is an interesting choice. Only three years before he had claimed to feel a curious affinity towards the United States, and had characterized Americans as having "a genial tolerance of others… large-heartedness, a supreme generosity of heart and spirit".[73] However, there seemed now to be a suggestion that for sixteen years he had somehow been prevented from pursuing a lifestyle of his choice or from achieving his literary ambitions.

Later that year, Cronin was able to tell Gollancz: "I hear wonderful reports of the serialization in the USA – an immense success for the *Woman's Home Companion.*"[74] Indeed, when *Crusader's Tomb* was finally published in May 1956, it received universal acclaim, some critics hailing it as one of his greatest books, or at least his best novel since *The Citadel.*

The book – which tells the story an English painter, Stephen Desmonde, who sacrifices everything for the sake of art in a conventional world – betrays Cronin's fascination with people's artistic and spiritual struggles. Many years later, Cronin offered a brief insight into his own individual heroes and his view on the vicissitudes of life in general. In a series of unpublished notes he urged people to take control of their own lives: not to live in a rut, but to be prepared to face the dangers of change and never give up hope. Cronin was a great admirer of John Bunyan, who wrote *Pilgrim's Progress* from a prison cell, and Wilkie Collins, who, wracked with pain, still managed to write. But his greatest hero was Paul Gauguin, the Parisian accountant who gave up the comfort of an easy life in order to become an artist.[75] Cronin's admiration for the spiritual rewards of sacrifice permeate the pages of *Crusader's Tomb.*

His reaction to the book was similar to the enthusiasm of his early years. New books had always excited him – especially when things were going well – invariably producing a wave of bonhomie towards his publisher. Just prior to the move to Switzerland in 1955, he wrote to Victor Gollancz: "The strengthening of our friendship in these recent years has been a source of joy to me."[76]

But that mood never lasted for long. By March of the following year Cronin had decided to bring up a subject that had been bothering him for some time. It concerned the share of the advance from Reader's Digest Condensed Books, the Companion Book Club and others. According to Gollancz, in Britain and America it had always been a 50–50 split. But that did not suit Cronin. On 29th March 1956 he wrote to Gollancz:

> Bearing all the circumstances in mind, which I will not bore you by enumerating, I feel very strongly that, in the case of the Digest Condensed Books, a 50–50 division is not equitable to me as the author, and I propose (using the mildest word possible) a 60–40 split. If I chose to write you three pages (but as aforesaid I won't) I think I could make a very convincing argument. I will say, however, that it's not the cash, which is inconsequential, but the principle that matters... I have in

recent years been very cooperative in accepting, without question, all the royalty rates, and changes in rates, which you have put up to me. I hope, therefore, that you will reciprocate with good feeling in this instance so that the tranquility of our relationship may be preserved.

Gollancz countered by pointing out that "in a world of violently rising costs and far less wildly rising prices",[77] he was getting less profit from Cronin's books by virtue of paying him a 22½% royalty on first publication and 10% on cheap editions when all other authors were accepting 20% and 10%, including Daphne du Maurier, his biggest seller. He, therefore, needed a 50–50 split "to make ends meet",[78] and pointed out that Cronin had accepted the arrangement in the past. But Cronin would not budge, and it says much for his standing as a writer that on 12th April 1956 Gollancz sent him a postcard saying: "OK my dear A.J. – you win."

As publication of *Crusader's Tomb* approached, Cronin as usual began to behave like a nervous parent. From his new home in Switzerland, anxious over the marketing of *Crusader's Tomb*, he wrote to Gollancz:

> Your bare announcement of my new novel in today's *Sunday Times*, thrown in with Mr Farson's superb autobiography (an adjective which certainly invites invidious comparisons) is so unlike your earlier promotion of my books which (again to quote the *Times*) bubbled over with enthusiasm that I hope your defeat in our recent set-to over *Crusader's Tomb* does not mean that you are going to take it out on the book… I'm sure I must be wrong in this supposition – if not, it would be a sad ending to a relationship which perhaps we both now feel has lasted too long.[79]

Cronin was probably making a mountain out of a molehill, but he might reasonably have expected a superlative in the advertisement of his book, because Gollancz always dealt in superlatives: "Gollancz splashed the literary pages of the *Observer* and the *Sunday Times* with enormous spreads which shouted to the rooftops the merits of his wares…"[80] Gollancz replied that he was advertising *Crusader's Tomb* and *A Mirror for Narcissus* – the second autobiography of Negley Farson, the American adventurer and author – more in advance of publication than any book since the war. He also pointed out that in the *Observer* and the *Daily Telegraph* Cronin would "see *Crusader's Tomb* described as 'his finest in years'". Neither point fully placated Cronin, whose last words on the subject were:

> I shall not venture to interfere in what is obviously your business. But over two years I've put a lot of sweat into *Crusader's Tomb*... I therefore hope that your promotion of this book will be more along the lines of what you used to (and it was quite magnificent) rather than what you've been recently doing...[81]

It would be simplistic to suggest that, immediately on his arrival in America, Cronin jettisoned his ambition for greatness in pursuit of wealth. When he crossed the Atlantic he was already rich and famous, but a gradual change in outlook is undeniable, none more so than in the letters to his publishers. An almost amateurish ebullience, a single-minded excitement for the coming book lit up his early correspondence. This was gradually replaced by an unemotional, business-like posture, in which the projected reception of the book almost relegated its literary value to second place. In terms of his literary career, therefore, it is hard to understand why he made the journey in the first place. Cronin appreciated the finer things of life: the top schools and universities for his children, first-class travel, period furniture, vintage wines and Impressionist paintings. His art collection, mostly accumulated during the war when prices were low, included works of Degas, Gauguin, Matisse, Renoir, Vuillard and Mary Cassatt. Yet there was nothing ostentatious about him. He never possessed a plush study, and preferred to write in any odd corner of the house, demanding only seclusion and quiet. Nor did he ever master the typewriter, favouring instead a simple fountain pen. His wife once recalled that he could be "extremely generous or preposterously stingy".[82] In London, before the war, he bought her a fur coat, but minutes later insisted that they walk to their destination, in the rain, all of two miles, to save the taxi fare. She added that she had seen him take, with the utmost calm, a decision which meant the loss of $20,000, yet "let him mislay his half-dollar penknife and he moans about it for weeks".[83] May expressed the view that it was not uncommon for successful men from a poor background to develop "a vague dread of the workhouse".[84]

In America, unlike Britain, balancing his ambition for greatness with financial prosperity proved to be beyond him, and his American legacy probably fell short of his aspirations. Even when he decided to leave America, money was the overriding influence in his choice of domicile. Britain, possibly Scotland, was the obvious option, but the cost of living there was high, so he chose to become a tax exile in Switzerland. He claimed that his heart belonged to Dumbarton, but his life was ruled by his head, not his heart. Always a canny Scot, he got more for his money by living outside Britain.

Chapter Six

Cronin was sixty years old when *Crusader's Tomb* was published in Britain in 1956 and, invigorated by the move from America, his new life in Switzerland promised a return to former glories. But the book's reception in Britain was a painful reminder of how the post-war world had moved on. Booksellers now faced stiff competition from other sources. Cronin seemed to be out of touch with contemporary Britain – or else refused to acknowledge the changes that had taken place – and his disappointment at the book's poor performance in his country prompted an angry response: "The reception has been particularly poisonous... in contradistinction to the general reception elsewhere, where the reviews have been extremely good and the sales extraordinary."[1] As he hit out at the critics – never his favourite breed – and the book trade in general, he missed the essential truth. It took the cool head of Victor Gollancz to bring him back to reality:

I was very distressed by your letter... With very few exceptions, established novelists of pre-war vintage have been getting either very bad presses, or virtually no press at all... All this is exceedingly disagreeable, but, of course, quite understandable: a new type of young novelist and critic is emerging, and they think they know everything. At critical periods this sort of thing has always happened... The sales of *Crusader's Tomb* must have seemed to you disappointing. But I doubt whether you would think this if you were on the spot and knew what was happening with sales generally... all established novelists have been down these last couple of years... Compton Mackenzie, whose sales have been absolutely steady for years told me... the sales of his last novel were over 25% down... yours are down less than most...

He urged the author not to be too disappointed:

The reasons are manifold. Television is one of them: the paperbacks are another: the general change of climate is a third: the frightful rise in prices (owing to the rise in the cost of production) is a fourth: the drying up of middle-class incomes under taxation, which is now beginning to take its full effect, is a fifth: and the virtual collapse of the circulating libraries is a sixth... I am speaking confidentially when I tell you that the "Times Book Club" which used to repeat anything up to a thousand copies in the week of publication if a book had a good press, now normally repeats 25: and that Smith's library... has now definitely and finally abandoned repeat orders altogether... It is altogether a very bad situation indeed... [2]

Cronin had not yet taken paperbacks on board. As mentioned before, he eventually agreed for his books to be published by the New English Library, which was created in 1961. WH Smith's lending libraries, which had been established in many of their larger stores, closed the same year.

It was clear that Cronin had to get to grips with the unpalatable truth that the record sales he had come to take for granted were now virtually unattainable. Gollancz was not unduly pessimistic, pointing out that – with British sales of around 43,000, added to 25,000 from Australasia – there was a total of 68,000 in Commonwealth sales alone, placing *Crusader's Tomb* in the top six of eighteen thousand published books.

As Gollancz hinted, readers' tastes were changing, reflecting the new vogue of "realism", which extended beyond literature to films, theatre and television. Reform was the byword of the 1950s. Probably the most significant breakthrough was Penguin's successful challenge to the Obscene Publications Act 1959, with *Lady Chatterley's Lover*. At a stroke, the path to permissiveness was opened up. Even the least cynical reader would have been hard put to explain the sudden interest in the book (two million sales within a year) without reference to its sexual explicitness. A new expression entered the English language – "angry young men" – referring to a loose-knit movement which included writers like Kingsley Amis, John Braine, Alan Sillitoe and John Osborne, all disillusioned with traditional British society, who emerged to claim their inheritance.

The result was that, for the second time in his life, Cronin had changed continents and found himself at a crossroads. With the benefit of over fifty years of hindsight there is little doubt that by 1956 his position in the forefront of British writers was at best under threat and at worst usurped. In America he had lost ground. Now the question was how to regain it. The main problem was how, or whether, to compete with the younger writers of the day – but Cronin did not see the situation in that light. Still smarting over the performance of *Crusader's Tomb*, he was prepared to blame everybody but himself, failing to see that the book he had placed such faith in could never have been a trailblazer, because of its conventional subject matter and its limited appeal. Traditionalists loved it, but it was never likely to attract the new breed of readers. In this context his next book, *The Northern Light*, was to be pivotal to the next phase of his career. Written, by Cronin's own admission, with a renewed sense of optimism, passion and energy, the book was almost completed by October 1957.

There were some writers who found success with a singular style, regardless of trends and world conditions. In the Gollancz camp, Daphne du Maurier comes to mind, while the prolific Nevil Shute managed one of his characteristic romantic adventures every year for Heinemann from 1940 to 1960. Also, at Gollancz "a stream of interesting books was beginning to come from across the Atlantic... the proportion of American books... by 1951 formed half the total output..."[3] Regarding Cronin's place in the literary world, as much depended on his attitude as on the tastes of the reading public. It was as if there were two Cronins: the author who produced the incisive and thought-provoking social commentaries of the 1930s, and the one who had penned smug reminiscences in the 1940s and 1950s. It is unlikely that he saw the distinction so clearly, but his letters suggest that he understood that the choice facing him was either a return to the style of his early novels, against the trend of the best-sellers of the day, or a continuation of the kind of work that had served him well in America.

The Northern Light concerns a respected local newspaper which, having recently resisted a takeover bid from a huge newspaper conglomerate based in London, is forced to compete with a sensationalist rival publication set up by the London company in a bid to put it out of business. The book can be seen as yet another psychological study, an examination of a man's moral courage against the unscrupulous activities of big-business executives, whose deviousness represents the cynicism of a changing world.

Controversy surrounded the book from the start. In fact, its appearance in Britain at one point was uncertain. An out-of-sorts Cronin wrote to Gollancz:

> As regards *The Northern Light*, I don't know what rumours have reached you or from what source – I should be interested to know... it is true that I am very excited about this book, but less so over the matter of publication in England. The reception of my last two novels there has been particularly poisonous, and they have not sold terribly well... it seems obvious that the present literary climate in Britain, which is so favourable to books of the type of *Lucky Jim*... is highly unfavourable to the Cronin novels. In brief, I am getting a little tired of being expectorated on by these ex-barrow boys and angry young men... As of this moment, therefore, I have no definite plans for the English edition.[4]

Cronin's threat, however, was bluster. He simply could not afford to relinquish such an important market as Britain. Even before he moved to Switzerland, in a discussion with Gollancz over a reduced royalty rate for the cheap edition of *Shannon's Way*, he had said: "I therefore agree in this instance, but I do trust that this royalty squeeze will not continue, especially since, when I am resident in Switzerland, my English income will be of much greater importance to me."[5] Victor Gollancz went out of his way to keep Cronin on board, purely on the strength of his reputation. He had to wait another eight months before actually reading the book, but that did not diminish his enthusiasm:

> Whatever the critics may like to say, your novels – as you know from my constant letters to you about royalties! – have an astonishing vitality. Nark though the critics may, the public go on buying your books month after month: and surely this is, in the long run, what really matters – I don't mean in terms merely of money, but from a wider point of view. I doubt whether any other English-speaking writer sells with such absolute steadiness as you... I do beg of you, therefore, to reconsider any half-decision you may have come to, if you have come to it, not to publish in Britain...

Gollancz's view to some degree was selfish, as he acknowledged himself:

> You would think me less than honest if I did not add that, apart from the more intangible considerations above... the matter is one of real business importance to me. The making of a new best-seller on any sort of scale is virtually impossible nowadays... and the only way in which one can hope to "come through" is to have on one's list as many books as possible with a big assured sale. While unexpected things come up, of course, from time to time, we have only a few "big" items for next year that we can look forward to with real confidence: and consequently the loss of the turnover on *The Northern Light* would worry me a good deal... I recognize, of course, that my own business interests cannot (and rightly) begin to outweigh... your point of view as an author: but I dare to hope that, in view of our long association, they may come in as a sort of subsidiary...[6]

Gollancz's entreaty almost implies that he was not expecting best-sellers from Cronin, as in the past, but was content with work that satisfied the faithful and went some way to fulfilling his commercial aspirations; possibly a similar trap to the one Cronin had fallen into on reaching America in 1939.

Cronin took his usual winter break in December 1957, and from Cap-Martin in the south of France he kept Gollancz informed of the progress of the book:

> As regards *The Northern Light*, the question of when, or for that matter whether, I shall publish in England must still remain in abeyance, and you will, of course, treat the situation in complete confidence as between you and me. You are the only person to whom I have mentioned my feelings on the subject, and if these should be "leaked" it would certainly determine me not to publish... As a matter of interest, you might care to know that I sent the manuscript... to Little, Brown only a couple of weeks ago. The reaction is exceptionally [sic] favourable and already the book has been chosen by the Literary Guild and by Reader's Digest Condensed Books – I had a personal note of congratulation from Ralph Henderson only this morning...[7]

By March 1958, back in Switzerland, Cronin's attitude was softening: "I propose to await American publication on 22nd May before deciding as to the English release. The time lag involved is not great and I shall be better able to judge the possible reaction to the book after that date. I may say in confidence that my present feeling lies towards an English publication, but I would like to discuss with you certain of the suggestions which you yourself have raised in respect of a special kind of promotion."[8] He followed this with another letter to Gollancz in June:

> The Northern Light has been published in America and Canada and will soon appear in Australia. There was rather a nice review in the New York Sunday Times and several excellent ones in the Canadian papers, so the general reception seems to have been favourable, and my Continental publishers, Zsolnay, Bompiani et al, are unusually optimistic. Nevertheless I am still disinclined to publish in England, not only for the reasons I gave you in my previous letter but because the gutter press will certainly treat it venomously. My life nowadays has fallen into such a pleasant pattern that I am loath to subject myself to this kind of vituperation... The only thing which might induce me to change my mind would be a real regret at the thought of breaking our long association... You did hint some months ago at a method of promoting the book which might spare it at least some of the abuse which I anticipate... I won't therefore say no finally until I hear from you again...[9]

At that time Gollancz had still not read the book, but when he finally received his copy he raved about it:

> I read The Northern Light last evening. Let me say immediately that, apart altogether from my commercial interest in the book, I consider it would be a thousand pities if it were not published here... its theme is of crucial importance, and one that ought imperatively to be ventilated... and how astonishing this narrative power of yours is! I remember very well how it struck me all of a heap when you sent me Hatter's Castle: and here it is again, as fresh as ever...[10]

Gollancz also came up with a cunning plan, suggesting that no review copies be sent to the newspapers, at a stroke removing the possibility of adverse advance criticism, and that this reduced exposure be compensated for by "splash" advertising in the major British cities and in the *Bookseller*. He still thought it probable that "hostile reviews would in fact appear in one or two papers such as the *Daily Mirror* and the *Daily Express*, and in one or two of the mass circulation Sunday newspapers. I think that, if anything, these would increase rather than diminish the sale of the book... and I also think, quite apart from the question of sales, that they would enhance your reputation, rather than diminish it..." He kept the biggest carrot till last:

> John Bush [who had joined Gollancz as company secretary in 1947 and then became general sales manager and director in 1950] tells me that, since the appearance of the book in America, he has been bombarded with letters and telephone enquiries from booksellers here, asking why we are not subscribing the book, when it is going to be published, and even insisting on giving their orders over the phone...[11]

Cronin was hooked and duly relented. The very next day, in longhand, he replied:

> Your good letter, and the policy you outline therein, have finally convinced me. We will publish (and God be with us!). I daresay a fresh batch of lies will be propagated about me, possibly even about you; yet, as I wrote this book because I felt it must be written, and as you are good enough to believe in it, it would be weakness not to go ahead. What we must try for, of course, is a crashing success. And you are the man to do it...

In the final paragraph of the same letter he added: "And do understand... my regard for you, and for our longstanding relationship, has done much to influence my decision."[12]

The correspondence relating to the eventual publication of *The Northern Light* demonstrates the strengths and weaknesses of both men. Gollancz's over-enthusiastic reaction betrayed his commercial interest. Bracketing *The Northern Light* with *Hatter's Castle* is almost fanciful. There was nothing in *The Northern Light* to compare to the drive and passion that made *Hatter's Castle* an overnight sensation. For his part, Cronin now seemed to be more concerned with the question of publication than literary worth, as exemplified by the following reaction: "I understand there was a really fine review in the *Chicago Herald Tribune* and the book, after one week, is halfway up the best-seller list..."[13]

In fact, the expectations of both publisher and author were disappointed. The book's almost antiseptic treatment of the newspaper industry ruffled no feathers, and the anticipated backlash from the British press never happened. Its publication in Britain in 1958 was almost a non-event. Most critics accepted *The Northern Light* with forbearance, neither praising nor damning it. Cronin claimed to have directed his venom against the gutter press, but the book's background turned out to be irrelevant to its underlying message.

In America critics were unenthusiastic. The most complimentary review, while claiming that the book was no masterpiece, averred that even a second-rate Cronin was better than most other writers.[14] In Britain the *Times Literary Supplement* was equally unimpressed:

> Cronin's novel is readable and the northern industrial background is plausible. However, the characters are cardboard cut-outs, crudely black and white. Page's wife and daughter are too stupid and frivolous to come alive and his daughter-in-law, with her golden heart and her guilty past, is a figure of melodrama...[15]

The *Manchester Guardian*'s assessment most accurately summed up the direction Cronin was travelling, and his disconnection with current trends and taste: "Because of its excessive readability, this novel will fail to interest many readers. All the same it is admirably done in its way and will make large numbers of the more passive sort of reader, not to mention the booksellers, happy enough."[16]

Significantly, while the setting of the novel is contemporary, pre-war values and an acute sense of impending loss prevail in the nostalgic references to the simple pleasures of Henry Page, the virtuous newspaperman and the novel's hero:

> Above all, he did enjoy getting down to the sea occasionally, especially at Sleedon... the charm of the village was spiritualized for him by the fact that here survived a part of the real old England... the England that was, and must one day be again. With quiet sincerity he loved his country, the texture of its earth, the very salt of the sea that washed it.

He was not blind to the deterioration which, since the war, had changed the structure of the national life. Yet this could only be, must only be, a temporary aftermath of that Homeric struggle...[17]

Henry Page's character was intended as a metaphor for an earlier age whose standards of propriety were rapidly being replaced, much to Cronin's growing disillusion, by the coarse, cheap sensationalism of Nye and Smith, the representatives of change and opportunism in modern society.

It is possible, of course, that *The Northern Light* was a considered response to the literary climate of the time. Cronin may have felt that Britain had not completely surrendered to cynicism, and that his softer, old-fashioned approach was still marketable, offering an alternative to the brash realism of many contemporary writers. Or perhaps Switzerland, like America, was turning into an emotional desert, and life was too comfortable for him to undertake the rigours of another big novel, involving research and the handling of a wide cast of characters, with all the attendant difficulties of structure and balance. He had always found writing a frenzied business. "I do not enjoy writing long novels,"[18] he had said – and, quite simply, *psychological* novels were easier to write than *sociological* ones. Age, too, may have been a factor. He was sixty-two when *The Northern Light* was published in 1958, an age when, perhaps, reflectiveness replaces passion.

When he was writing *The Northern Light*, Cronin declared that there was nothing new to write about, only new ways to write about old things.[19] From his mountain retreat, cut off from a rich source of literary inspiration, it is not surprising he felt that way. He had spent too long on the sidelines of life now, and the vital spark that had deserted him in America was not rekindled in Switzerland. His final domicile was a place for reflection and reminiscence. His enthusiasm for writing, however, remained strong.

The first mention of a new novel was in a letter to Gollancz, dated 6th August 1959: "After debating three separate themes, I have decided to start work on my next full-length effort... I am quite excited about it but, as I shall try to do a really good job, it will be some time in the works..."

With reference to Cronin's observed lack of new things to write about, there seems to be a supreme irony in the setting of his next novel, *The Judas Tree*. The time in history is clearly recognizable as the 1950s in the hero's musings on settling in Switzerland after years in America:

> Presently he came to the outer suburbs: streets which seemed to have been scrubbed, green-shuttered white houses with their front plots of asters and begonias, their window boxes filled with blooming geraniums and petunias. Such flowers – he had never seen the like! And over all such a clean quiet air of neatness and efficiency, as if everything were ordered, and would never break down – and indeed nothing did – as if honesty, civility and politeness were the watchwords of these people... how wise to settle here... away from the vulgarity of the present age: the hipsters and the beatniks, the striptease, the rock and roll, the ridiculous mouthings of angry young men, the lunatic abstractions of modern art, and all the other horrors and obscenities of a world gone mad...[20]

If Cronin bore any resemblance to his hero, David Moray, it is not surprising that the past was the only source of inspiration for his work. He seemed to have no desire to understand the new world or challenge it. Yet, before emigrating to America in 1939, he had declared it was a "fatal mistake for an author for whom travel and experience of life are as necessary as meat and drink".

Cronin's point of view was not unique. His publisher, Victor Gollancz, had similar problems in readjusting to modern society. He complained about the new breed of authors, "the flood of literary ordure"[21] and the constant erosion of moral standards. Like Cronin, he left himself open to accusations of being out of touch. John Calder – another publisher, at loggerheads with Gollancz – accused him and others like him of not being "interested in examining the very real literary and intellectual values that exist in the work of those schools of writing that have developed since the war, because they are too far removed from the movements that they pioneered in their youth. They also do not like to admit how out of date their attitudes are and abuse takes the place of rational analysis..."[22]

The issue of the generation gap raised by Calder is valid, and it applies equally to Gollancz and Cronin. But whereas Gollancz's need to publish, to some extent, forced him to acquiesce, Cronin was free to do as he saw fit, and he stayed firmly in the conservative camp.

In 1961, as he was working on his new book, Cronin turned sixty-five and, whether or not age was catching up with him, there was a discernible change in his approach. He told Gollancz on 20th March:

> I have lived with this book, off and on, for the past two years and now I want to leave it, for probably six weeks or two months, before a final re-reading. You see, I haven't your capacity for intensive activity and have made up my mind never to be rushed or to work to a deadline... besides something quite important has come up in the interim in the shape of the BBC's intention to do a televised series... on my life... taken from *Adventures in Two Worlds*.

In fact, this was not a programme about Cronin's life, but a reference to what eventually became *Dr Finlay's Casebook*. However, it seems that, at last, he was slowing down. He also added that his new novel was "regarded by the few who have read it as early vintage Cronin" and that "one reader has said that I have done for the central character what I did with Brodie in *Hatter's Castle*, though in a different way".[23] Cronin fretted again over the title. He even circularized his publishers, eighteen in all, asking for their opinion on a list of thirteen titles. In the end it came down to a choice between *The Judas Tree* and *Man of Distinction*. In March 1961 he told Gollancz that he felt that the fomer seemed "terribly obvious" and that "the entire tone of the book is ironic and for this reason I like the title *Man of Distinction*". By June he had changed his mind.

The Judas Tree tells the story of David Moray, a wealthy middle-aged doctor who lives in retirement in a villa in the Swiss Alps, surrounded by his art collection and other trappings of material wealth. At a party in the company of the sophisticated but poor countess Frida von Altishofer, his equilibrium is unexpectedly shattered by a poignant reminder of his time as a romantic medical student, when he had planned to marry his first love, Mary Douglas, an ordinary girl from his Scottish home. However, on a sea voyage, aimed at restoring his health after an illness, he had abandoned Mary and all thoughts of a medical career, in favour of the alluring Doris Holbrook and the prospect of a wealthy future offered by her father if he joined his thriving drug company. At first things went well, until his new wife began to show symptoms of mental illness. Within a short time she was committed to an asylum, where she later died.

Years later, still subconsciously suffering from suppressed guilt, and convinced that he might resurrect his relationship with Mary, whom he foolishly thought would never have married, Moray returns to Scotland, only to discover that Mary is dead. There he meets and falls in love with her daughter Kathy, who bears a strong resemblance to her mother. Kathy agrees to marry him if he returns to medical practice and travels with her as a missionary to Africa. He agrees, without telling Kathy about what had happened between him and her mother. However, becoming afraid of the dangerous nature of missionary work, he abandons Kathy, resolving to marry Frida instead. When Kathy follows him home, she is told bluntly by Frida of the marriage and of her mother's past, and as a result she drowns herself. After identifying her body, Moray hangs himself from a Judas tree.

Cronin described *The Judas Tree* as "a different kind of book, not particularly dramatic (or melodramatic) but an analytical study, a complete dissection of a supreme egoist – a well-intentioned man who, through psychological and sociological influences, develops into a weak and self-indulgent heel who brings disaster on three different women and is himself destroyed by the fourth..."[24]

The reference to sociological influences implies that some new experience overwhelms David Moray's previous good sense, setting him on a downward spiral to eventual destruction. In fact he succumbs to the two oldest temptations in human history: sex and money, specifically an attractive temptress (Doris) and fifteen hundred a year, with bonuses and the prospect of a partnership.

Moray's path to affluence and social status is not unlike that of Joe Lampton in John Braine's iconic novel *Room at the Top* – which, though rejected by Gollancz, became a best-seller, and which to-gether with its 1959 film adaptation epitomized 1950s society. On the surface the books seem to be poles apart, but the similarities are obvious. Joe and David are different in background, intelligence and refinement – Joe is a lowly civil servant from a working-class background, happy with beer, cigarettes and women, waiting to step into dead men's shoes, while grafting, middle-class David, a newly graduated doctor, a lover of the arts, looks forward to a conventional and rewarding medical career. What binds them irrevocably is that they are both social climbers who marry the boss's daughter, with sex – not love – providing the path to social and economic elevation. Joe seduces the virginal Susan, while David is seduced by the worldly Doris. Joe ditches Alice Aisgill to marry Susan, while David deserts his first sweetheart Mary Douglas to marry Doris, then both are set up in business by their respective fathers-in-law. Both later regret their marriages, and retribution is played out in typical Faustian fashion. Having sold their souls for riches and success, the two men pay a terrible price: for Joe it is the death of Alice, and allegorically the death of his true self, while David pays with his own life.

To couple *The Judas Tree* with what was regarded at the time as a kitchen-sink drama from one of Britain's post-war angry young men illustrates how close to "modernizing" his books and thereby competing with younger novelists Cronin was. Braine, of course, intended his novel to be a social document, openly challenging sexual and class attitudes of the 1950s. By contrast, Cronin had given up writing social commentaries years before, intending his latest book to be simply a psychological study of a vain man, although there is an unmistakable atmosphere of disenchantment with modern life in its opening pages.

The Judas Tree was published in Britain and America in 1961. Its reception was mixed: as with *The Northern Light*, there was a lack of real enthusiasm, and the word "contrived" began to appear in more and more critical appraisals. The saintly Henry Page in *The Northern Light*, almost too good to be true, is ultimately believable, but Cronin blurs the boundaries of morality in *The Judas Tree* with his over-compassionate treatment of David Moray.

On 15th September 1962 Cronin's peaceful existence was rocked by the death of his mother. In a letter to her friend, the writer and translator Maria Shrady (the wife of Frederick Shrady, the sculptor), dated 6th November, May broke the news: "A.J.'s mother passed away here on 15th September. We buried her in a dear little churchyard at the head of the lake – she was eighty-seven. It has upset A.J. very much but he has absorbed himself in a new book – the best thing to do…" The significance of her death went far beyond personal grief, possibly influencing the direction of the final chapter of his career. Gripped by nostalgia, his thoughts returned to Scotland – Cardross, Helensburgh and Glasgow – and for his next novel he went back over familiar ground.

In *A Song of Sixpence*, published in Britain and America in 1964, the narrator Laurence Carroll recounts the story of his life from his early childhood in the Scottish Highlands to the beginning of his medical career. It is the story of a young Catholic boy's progress to manhood sustained by his hard-pressed widowed mother. The novel roughly parallels Cronin's early years, but many of the events and situations in it – as discussed before – are fictional. No doubt Cronin tried to inject a measure of freshness into *A Song of Sixpence*, but he must have known that resemblances to previous works were obvious. To readers discovering Cronin for the first time it is a thoroughly professional work, readable and moving, but there was only faint praise from the critics who, rightly, saw it as trite and commonplace. Despite its limitations, even the *Times Literary Supplement* did not condemn it completely. They found it "sluggish" but, nevertheless, "a pleasant, competent book, and only slightly dull".[25]

Besides his mother's death, other changes were taking place at that time. Cronin's hot-and-cold relationship with Victor Gollancz finally boiled over in 1961, ostensibly over a remark Gollancz made about *The Judas Tree*. Cronin had threatened more than once to end their association and, once that thought had taken root, he had to see it through, simply to prove a point. He had a fearsome reputation among Gollancz's executives – he was often referred to as Victor's "old adversary" – but the stubborn determination that had won him that name was probably far easier to handle than his sudden hot-headedness. His mood was prone to change at any moment. On 20th March 1961 he was full of sympathy for Gollancz: "I was disturbed by your letter of 17th March, so full of your woes and present difficulties, and I hasten to send you my sympathy... now, please, don't take life too seriously, look after your health and devil take the paperbacks." Two months later, in June, responding to an apparently innocent description of his latest novel he blasted him with the following: "Yours of 9th June to hand. Have you really read the novel? I doubt it. To dismiss *The Judas Tree* joyously as a 'spellbinder' when it is actually a devastating and tragic study of a vain and irresponsible egoist is the sort of insult one expects from the English critics, though not from one's publisher. But I suppose you are now too obsessed by your own preoccupations to devote yourself to your business and to the consideration of your author's feelings…" Whether the term "spellbinder" was apt or not, Cronin's response was certainly disproportionate. And Cronin added in a postcript: "Please don't trouble to acknowledge or answer this – I felt I must say it but further correspondence can only worsen the matter. I'll see how you promote the book."

That proved to be the last straw. In the end the relentless pressure told and their long association was terminated. Many years later, somewhat wistfully, Cronin admitted to John Bush, who took over the running of the firm after Gollancz's death, that his next two books "were taken from Gollancz because we had a row and I wanted to punish him".[26] After *The Judas Tree*, another fourteen years were to pass before Victor Gollancz Ltd published another Cronin book. Sadly, Gollancz passed away in 1967, so he was never aware of Cronin's return to the fold.

Ruth Dudley Edwards's claim in her biography of Gollancz that Cronin quit his publisher "because he said he was fed up with Victor's elevation of money wrangles to points of principle"[27] is slightly puzzling. She may have heard that from people who had known Gollancz, but the correspondence suggests that it was Cronin who always got on his high horse to state that it was not the money but the principle.

Since their relationship began, we have seen many clashes between Cronin and his publisher, two essentially different characters who paradoxically shared many similar personality traits. They were both moody, sensitive, tenacious, quick-tempered and capable of extremes – all qualities which endangered peaceful relations. Ruth Dudley Edwards is convinced that "neither man really liked the other and despite their ostensibly sincere exchanges, they had good reason for mutual distrust. Certainly Victor was unenthusiastic about Cronin's books. They stayed together for decades for commercial reasons; Victor in particular could not afford a rupture…"[28]

There is, of course, no rule that forces writers and publishers to like each other, and it is perfectly understandable that commercial considerations may at times outweigh personal inclinations: business is business. However, if both men really disliked each other deep down, then their level of concealment and dissimulation was extraordinary.

For instance, in 1935, in a postscript to a letter in which he was outlining the advertising campaign he had planned for *The Stars Look Down*, Gollancz said:

> If you will forgive a personal note, I still have that slightly uneasy feeling about which I wrote to you before that somehow or other the friendliness which I liked to think you felt for me (apart altogether from the business relation) has suffered some change. All the other authors on our list seem to be happy to meet me and talk things over at fairly frequent intervals, but it seems ages since I saw you. I console myself with the thought that a man who can write a book as big as *The Stars Look Down* must go his own way. But can't we meet soon?

From Cronin's side, there are many instances in his letters of what might be taken to be warm expressions of genuine friendship. Just to give one example, a letter written in May 1955, following a visit to America by Gollancz and his wife, says: "We did so much enjoy seeing Ruth and you and look forward to an early reunion. The strengthening of our friendship in these recent years has been a real source of joy to me."

Cronin and Gollancz were both great men in their chosen professions, endowed with all the strengths and weaknesses that characterize greatness. A fight can draw the contestants together in mutual respect. The contention that they stayed together purely for commercial reasons may be true to some extent, but it is hardly the whole truth. Gollancz was sought after as a publisher, just as Cronin was a prized author, but they could have survived apart. Indeed, as we have seen they split for several years, and the effects were not irrevocable. Nevertheless, there is personal warmth in many of the letters between them, which strongly suggest a genuine regard for one another.

A Song of Sixpence was published by Heinemann in Britain and Little, Brown in America in 1964. William Heinemann Ltd had been founded in 1890 in Covent Garden, London. On Heinemann's death in 1920, the company was taken over by Doubleday, Page & Co., the New York publishers, who later became Doubleday & Co., one of the largest publishing businesses in the English-speaking world. It boasted an impressive list of leading authors of the early twentieth century: H.G. Wells, Rudyard Kipling, John Galsworthy, Joseph Conrad, D.H. Lawrence and W. Somerset Maugham among them. Heinemann had, in fact, been publishing Cronin's books for years, but not in Britain. Paul Zsolnay, an Austrian Jew who had been an affluent property owner and successful publisher before the war, fled with his elderly mother from Hitler's regime to London where, almost penniless, he accepted a modest position at Heinemann's. A shrewd entrepreneur, he went on to sell French and German translations, mostly of English fiction, as he had done successfully with Galsworthy's novels before the hostilities. After the war he returned to Vienna and formed a new company, Heinemann & Zsolnay Verlag – with offices in Vienna and Hamburg – which included Cronin in its lists many years before *A Song of Sixpence* came under the Heinemann banner in Britain.[29]

The Second World War had devastated every country in Europe, and it was thanks to people like Paul Zsolnay that the publishing industry had started to flourish again. On 12th January 1948, he wrote to Cronin acquainting him with his activities:

> During 1947 we have published, jointly with the Artemis Verlag in Zurich, *Hatter's Castle*, *Three Loves*, *The Stars Look Down* and *The Citadel*. I think that the production of these books is remarkably good and I am sending you a copy of each, hoping you will like them. I enclose a prospectus of my Viennese firm from which you will see that we are publishing *Three Loves* and *Grand Canary*. We are contemplating printing 8,000 copies of each and are furthermore reprinting, jointly with Erasmus Verlag in Vienna, 20,000 copies of *The Citadel*. In Switzerland we are now printing 10,000 copies of *The Adventures of a Black Bag*... I can hardly tell you how pleased I am to find myself publishing your works again – it reminds me of the happy days when I started the publication of your books and when I first met you in Vienna...[30]

But Cronin's relationship with Zsolnay was not without problems. Towards the end of 1949, Cronin convinced himself that Zsolnay was not doing his best on his behalf, particularly at the time when the Austrian schilling had been devalued, thus reducing the value of Cronin's royalties held in Vienna. Cronin did not ask for an explanation of the position, but indirectly accused Zsolnay of lacking the will to tackle it. Zsolnay, in a well-argued response, was able to show that he had done everything possible, even accepting lower profits himself in an effort to protect Cronin's interests, and pointed out that in his opinion, in the near future, the best market for books in the German language would be Austria and Germany, published by old, established firms with a sound reputation like his own. Cronin was suitably appeased.

Charles Pick, the head of Heinemann in Britain, was delighted to have enlisted such an illustrious author as Cronin, even though past his best. In March 1964 he reported that "we have had an excellent response from our overseas managers and the orders for *A Song of Sixpence* are coming in very satisfactorily".[31] Cronin was pleased, but his return letter a week later – "I am glad to know that the omens appear favourable so far and, as much for your sake (since this is our first venture) as mine, I hope we shall have a success"[32] – contained a veiled insinuation that if the book was not successful it would be down to deficiencies somewhere on the publishing side. That was followed by more intimidatory pressure in December of the same year:

> I trust that *A Song of Sixpence* will continue in demand over the holiday season. The more popular of my later novels have always managed to get within close sight of 40,000 in Britain and I am hopeful that *A Song of Sixpence* will reach this level too. As you may know, it's been wonderfully successful elsewhere – for instance, Bompiani sold 35,000 in Italy in the first five days after publication, and only yesterday I had a letter from Jack McClelland in Canada saying that the book still tops the best-seller list… and Canada is always a very difficult country…[33]

That such a figure – 40,000 in Britain – had become a benchmark for success demonstrates the extent to which reading tastes had changed and how far his popularity had fallen. By January 1965 sales of *A Song of Sixpence* totalled 32,000, well short of Cronin's expectations. In April that same year Cyrus Brooks of A.M. Heath & Co., Cronin's agents, acquainted Pick with Cronin's feelings. In a letter marked "Private and Personal" he wrote:

I thought you would like me to mention the following points which have been raised incidentally by Cronin. He says that Heinemann sales don't yet quite match up to the normal Gollancz total... he adds that Gollancz had the commercial virtue of always paying on the nail, which I am sure Heinemann will equally do, and A.J. also seems to have some allergy against air-mail forms or, as he calls them "6d. letter cards"... no doubt you will know how to humour him...

Then, in his own handwriting, Brooks added: "Sorry this is so trivial."[34] It is unclear, incidentally, how much faith Cronin had in Brooks's judgement, since it was Cyrus Brooks who first advised him to leave Gollancz for Heinemann. It was a move that he never fully came to terms with, and he later admitted to John Bush of Gollancz that "it was the worst bit of advice I ever had in my entire life".[35]

It took five years for another Cronin novel to emerge, a short book of about fifty thousand words, again published by Heinemann: *A Pocketful of Rye*, a sequel to *A Song of Sixpence*. Evidently, even allowing for the perceived righteousness of his position, parting from Gollancz after thirty years had not sat well with Cronin, and though it took such a long time for his next book to be ready for publication, he almost immediately began angling for a return. In January 1968 he wrote to John Bush, now joint managing director of Gollancz with Livia, the founder's daughter, as follows:

I have finished my new novel, *A Pocketful of Rye* and am in the process of deciding whether to give it to Heinemann, who did a thoroughly excellent job on *A Song of Sixpence*, or to return to the Gollancz fold... while I would not ask any more money i.e. increased royalties, I should expect very much more than the usual promotion. I should also expect a better and more attractive format than usual. (Pick's job in this respect was delightful.) Finally, I would want you to make every effort to buy the tapes of *A Song of Sixpence* and bring it into line with my other titles in your excellent cheap editions. I don't think Pick would obstruct this since the book has been extremely profitable to him and in the usual Heinemann fashion he won't probably want to exploit it further as you would do, I am sure, and with profit... Well, turn this over in your mind and let me hear from you fairly soon...[36]

This letter features Cronin at his most presumptuous. There had been a time in his career when a click of his fingers would have brought publishers running, but in 1968 he was seventy-two years old, no longer in the best-seller category, and his future, if there was one, was at best limited. More importantly, *A Pocketful of Rye* was not as worthy an effort as *A Song of Sixpence*, and not surprisingly Bush rejected Cronin's offer, and in so doing laid down the ground rules for a very different relationship, if he ever decided to take Cronin back. In March 1969, therefore, Cronin cut his losses and contacted Charles Pick: "Certainly, I would be pleased for you to publish *A Pocketful of Rye*, despite very tempting promotional offers from another quarter." It is unlikely that he had any offers other than Heinemann's.

Cronin explained to Charles Pick that the book was "further, and thoroughly discreditable, adventures of Laurence Carroll." Later, in April, he explained:

> The theme of the novel, Carroll pursued by his Catholic conscience, was not easy and had to be treated in a very off-beat manner. Also, there were horrors of sentiment to be avoided in his relationship with the boy. Finally, sympathy had to be maintained for Carroll despite the fact that he was an absolute no-hero...[37]

In the same letter he suggested that on the flyleaf of the book, to indicate continuity with the previous novel, should be a reminder of the old nursery rhyme: "Sing a song of sixpence, a pocketful of rye" – the rye being the liquid, not the cereal variety.

In America, where the book was published by Little, Brown in 1969, reaction to it was a resigned acceptance, with some references to the lightweight nature of the book and an odd nostalgic mention of his past triumphs. In Italy, however, Cronin told Pick, Bompiani had gone crazy about it, and was rushing it out in July. One American critic wryly commented that Cronin was trying to breathe new life into his usual pious offerings by featuring a bit of sex.[38] It was certainly not the usual Cronin fare, hardly recognizable as a sequel to the sober reflections of *A Song of Sixpence*. Again written in the first person, in contemporary vernacular (with definite American influences), it differs considerably from its predecessor by virtue of its racy, ironic, sometimes humorous style, on occasions resembling a Hollywood script:

> Hulda Muller was a short thick woman of about sixty, her architecture late Victorian, with a magnificent portico... She was at her desk, sitting up straight, waiting on me. This office was smaller than mine and furnished with her own things, surprisingly feminine – strange, I never thought of her as a woman; to me, despite the milk bars, she was sexless...[39]

This passage might have come straight out of a Raymond Chandler movie. Equally unusual is how sex is dealt with – not obliquely, as in earlier books, but openly:

> Lying back with her knees up and apart and her thin wrapper flung open, she gazed up at me with such a look of silent pleading and half-frightened appeal, it hit me like a bomb. Everything seemed to happen instinctively and at once, and we were in bed under the blanket, her arms locked around me...[40]

But it is not simply the many references to sex that modernize this novel: there is also the hero's use of soliloquy as a means of accessing the character's mind:

> I took a third slug... with more positive results – this vodka might be unhealthy, but it had an Iron Curtain kick. The old Carroll morale began to assert itself... yes, I could bring myself, decently, to forget it, wipe out the entire complex mess, and get myself set for the future. Life was full of mistakes, everyone made them, why should I be the exception to the rule? We were all sinners, humanity was frail. Why mourn, why shed crocodile tears? No use crying over spilt milk... wipe the slate clean and start afresh... [41]

The book is full of staccato passages and slick, abbreviated dialogue that move the action along at a great speed. As a result it is not an easy novel to categorize or explain. Cronin tried to convince reviewers that it was a sequel to *A Song of Sixpence*, but it is not obviously so. His first attempt at a sequel was far more successful. *Shannon's Way* was a straightforward continuation of *The Green*

Years, with the two Robert Shannons, junior and senior, sharing similar temperaments, both quiet, introverted and determined characters, unworldly even, committed to the cause of science. That same bond is not found between *A Song of Sixpence* and *A Pocketful of Rye*. Apart from a shared name, it is hard to see how Laurence Carroll's flippant character and devil-may-care approach to life – in harmony with the changed writing style – evolved from such a serious nature and restricted childhood. Also, the Scottish setting and the early life of the hero in *A Song of Sixpence* distinguish it as a fictional reminiscence, whereas *A Pocketful of Rye* is so different from Cronin's own life that it is best viewed apart from its predecessor and judged on its own merit.

Cronin had no illusions of greatness with this novel, his only comment being that it "runs to about 50,000 words and reads, at least to me, like a very good seller".[42] Yet it is, arguably, one of his most distinctive works, and one of the most illuminating. It demonstrated that Cronin, in his early seventies, was not stuck in a time warp and that, from choice, he could adapt his writing style and subject matter as he saw fit. It is tempting to wonder how a modern theme in that style would have turned out.

Cronin was upbeat about *A Pocketful of Rye*, writing to Charles Pick: "Your continued enthusiasm for the novel has touched my lonely heart… They are actually paying more money in Norway, and they wanted to send a film unit from Holland where it is being serialized. Naturally I refused…"[43]

Pick informed Cronin that they would publish the book on 6th October 1969, with a print run of 25,000 and 5,000 for the Book of the Month Club.[44] It seems he was expecting lower sales than for *A Song of Sixpence* – and, in fact, it did not sell as well as hoped. Letters from Cronin to Pick indicate that he was happy with the presentation of the Heinemann books but, in an oblique reference to Heinemann not matching up to Gollancz, it was obvious he was not satisfied with sales. Cronin possibly blamed Pick for the book's poor showing, and by the time he embarked on his last novel, he had returned to Gollancz.

In 1967 the Cronins and Nan had moved from Villa Allwinden, Lucerne to Champ-Riond near Montreux, where *A Pocketful of Rye* was written. Allwinden was a huge property, with tennis courts, a swimming pool, a chalet for visitors and extensive formal gardens, overlooking Lake Lucerne. Cronin blamed the move on the foggy winters, during which you could not see the sun for weeks, and hoped that the reputedly sunnier Montreux would suit him better. However, Champ-Riond, a much smaller house, failed to live up to his expectations. He had allowed himself to be talked into buying it by Nan, who did the house-hunting with him, at a time when the real-estate market was tight. It is significant that Nan thought it a more practical, cosy house, and her view prevailed.

In the summer of 1968, during a holiday in Bermuda, May's illness had begun to worsen. Andrew, Cronin's youngest son – now living in an apartment in Bladensburg, Maryland, with his wife and two sons – recalls that he was sent a cheque for fifty dollars by his mother. When he called to thank them for the money, he discovered that his father knew nothing about it, and he overheard him berating his wife, explaining to Andrew later that she was beginning to show signs of Alzheimer's disease. At the time Andrew felt strongly that "this was the start of his plan to get rid of her" and that his father simply did not want the bother or the responsibility of looking after her, preferring to live out the rest of his life in an untroubled atmosphere with Nan.

A few months later, in a letter dated 6th March 1969, Cronin, possibly using May's illness as an excuse to discourage a visit, acquainted Charles Pick of the problem: "I don't think there is any necessity for you to put yourself about by making a one-day double flight to Switzerland. Actually, I am rather incommunicado at present since, unhappily, my wife is quite ill…" Early in the following year, 1970, Cronin arranged for his wife's admission to Pierrefonds, a nursing home in Montreal recommended by Patrick, his doctor son. From that time, Patrick, who was Dean of the Medical Faculty at McGill University, and who himself suffered from Alzheimer's later in his life, assumed responsibility for his mother's welfare.

Andrew is convinced that his father overreacted, and that his mother was sent to Pierrefonds too soon. Not long after her admission, he and his family visited her and found her in good heart. She recognized everybody, discussed things lucidly and thanked them all for coming. Somewhat poignantly, he said that he could not help feeling sorry for his mother, especially as Montreal had such a horrible climate in the winter months. Cronin, of course, could have afforded round-the-clock care for his wife in their home in Switzerland, but chose instead to entrust her to the hands of professionals under the watchful eye of Patrick and his family. Alexandra, Andrew's daughter, makes the point more forcibly, describing her grandfather's decision as selfish, but at the same time stressing that nobody dared cross him. And so from 1970 until his death, eleven years later, Cronin and Nan lived out their lives together at Champ-Riond, thousands of miles away from his wife, who also died in 1981. They had been married sixty years.

After May's departure for Montreal, there followed a long period of literary inactivity as Cronin and Nan forged a cosy, peaceful existence together in the idyllic surroundings of his Swiss home, spending their winters in Bermuda and later in Madeira. His wife's illness at last had provided him with the opportunity he had hoped for most of his life: time alone with Nan, free of family interference and the prying eyes of the press – whose interest in Cronin, by then, was lukewarm. Nan was no longer treated as an employee – she stopped receiving wages – but assumed the role, to which she was well suited, of wife, housekeeper and secretary.

The conduct of their life together is one of the most intriguing and mysterious aspects of the Cronin story. The precise nature of their relationship, platonic or sexual, was touched on earlier. However, soon after his wife's admission to the nursing home, at a time when he and Nan were finally on their own, aged seventy-four and sixty-two respectively, an event took place that would bring speculation to an end. On a visit to Montreal to see his wife and family, after drinking champagne, Cronin began to experience urinary difficulties, which led him to seek medical advice. He was diagnosed with prostate problems. Patrick arranged for him to have his prostate removed – which, in those days, was a very intrusive operation, almost certainly leading to impotency. During his time alone with Nan in Switzerland, therefore, regardless of desire, or age, the likelihood of a sexual relation with her was remote.

As far as his relationship with his British publisher was concerned, it was now left to Cronin to promote himself, and indeed the tone of his letters illustrates that the changing circumstances were not lost on him. On 18th March 1971, he wrote to John Bush:

You know how pleased I am that you continue bringing out edition after edition of all my books, and because of this I have been bending over backwards to accommodate you on the matter of royalties – rather different from my previous attitude when poor Victor and I fought this question out tooth and nail and I, to my deep regret, won, receiving a 30/70 split in my favour in respect of N.E.L.'s sales... You will by this time have received my letter accepting my 50/50 split on *The Stars Look Down*. It was, of course, my row with Victor that sent me to Heinemann...

In the 1960s and 1970s Cronin's books continued to sell moderately well, and the author kept a sharp eye on the pennies. The New English Library, which did a wonderful job in keeping Cronin's novels alive, offered John Bush £2,000 each for seven titles which, though flattering, Cronin felt obliged to turn down – at least temporarily – fearing that "British and super tax plus my other obligations would take practically the lot".[45] But, undeterred, he pushed Bush for an increase in royalty rates to 17½ per cent for *Shannon's Way*, "just to keep my morale up",[46] and he continued fighting his corner as vigorously as he had done with Victor Gollancz:

I think you'll agree I have bent over backwards to all your previous requests to take a reduced royalty on reprints of my books, but things are not quite so flourishing for me now, and really the poor old British pound has become worth so little in Switzerland... so let it be my way this time, and if you ask again I will try to let it be yours...[47]

He also suggested that Bush try to buy back the rights of *A Song of Sixpence* and *A Pocketful of Rye* from Heinemann so that all his books would return to the Gollancz imprint, pointing out that both titles had done well, particularly in Germany. He told Bush that Bertelsmann, Germany's major publisher, "have just made *A Pocketful of Rye* their big book for the Buchergilde [a German book club] spring issue and have guaranteed me 500,000 copies"[48] – an enormous act of faith on the publisher's part.

A.J. Cronin and May with their dog
Sally at Sullington Court, *c*.1938

A.J. Cronin with his son Andrew
at Sullington Court, 1938

A.J. Cronin with his three sons
at York Harbor, Maine, 1939

A.J. Cronin with his wife, mother
and sons Patrick and Andrew in
Blue Hill, Maine, 1943

A.J. Cronin with his sons Patrick
and Andrew in Greenwich,
Connecticut, 1943–44

A.J. Cronin with his son Andrew
in Ireland in 1946–47

A.J. Cronin with his wife May
at Woodlea Hill, New Canaan,
Connecticut, early 1950s

Nan in the garden of Villa Allwinden,
Lucerne, late 1950s

A.J. Cronin playing tennis with his
sons Vincent and Andrew at
Villa Allwinden in 1956

A.J. Cronin fishing in Scotland
in the late 1960s

A.J. Cronin at Villa Allwinden in the 1960s

Nan with A.J. Cronin's daughter-in-law Anne in the early 1970s

Alexandra, A.J. Cronin's granddaughter, in 1977

Alexandra and her mother Anne, shortly before A.J. Cronin's death in January 1981

Chapter Seven

Cronin's career throughout the 1960s received an unexpected boost from the television series *Dr Finlay's Casebook*. Many people of a certain age in Britain who were not regular readers became aware of A.J. Cronin through this series. Television was still in its infancy – the Television Act, allowing the establishment of a commercial service, breaking the monopoly of the BBC, only became law in 1954 – when in 1957 ITV began screening a twice-weekly hospital-based drama, *Emergency Ward 10*. It soon became obvious to all programme-makers that medical dramas captivated viewers' imaginations and guaranteed faithful audiences. In 1962, therefore, the BBC followed suit with its own version, though with a different format. *Dr Finlay's Casebook* was initially based on *Adventures in Two Worlds* and later on short stories which had been published in magazines and eventually brought together in a paperback form under the title *Adventures of a Black Bag*, published by the New English Library in 1969. The series was set in the 1920s in the fictional town of Tannochbrae in western Scotland.

The history of the programme is as fascinating as any of Cronin's own stories. According to the journalist Alasdair Marshall in the *Glasgow Evening Times*, "the creative spark which led to *Dr Finlay's Casebook* came from an unlikely source. Cronin himself could not have dreamt up a better story..."[1] That source was Graham Stewart, an enterprising young actor out of work, whose imagination had been fired by reading *Adventures in Two Worlds*, in which the characters of Dr Cameron and Janet appear. Seeing the opportunity for a film or television series, Stewart phoned Cronin, convinced him of the book's potential, and was invited to go and see the author's agents, A.M. Heath & Co. At that meeting it was agreed that Stewart had two years in which to come up with a concrete proposal. Familiar with both the television and film industries, he took the idea to Joseph Janni, an Italian film producer. With Henry Cass, the director of his 1949 film *The Glass Mountain*, Janni opened negotiations with the BBC, but to no avail, and their interest lapsed. The matter was next taken up by Robin Lowe of Christopher Mann Ltd, a London firm of literary and theatrical agents. Lowe wrote to Donald Wilson, head of the Script Department of the BBC, outlining the situation:

> I am aware of the discussions and negotiations that took place between the BBC and Joseph Janni together with Henry Cass about the proposed television series... I am now in a position to inform you that the rights acquired by Messrs Janni and Cass have reverted to Graham Stewart... Mr Stewart has asked us to represent him in connection with this project...[2]

Robin Lowe's letter seems to have spurred the BBC executives into action. An internal memo dated 18th January 1961 suggested that there might be "sufficient material in the books for a long series", and that thirteen fifty-three-minute programmes might be possible with an option for thirteen more. There was general agreement on the suitability of the Cronin material, and while both the BBC and Robin Lowe were anxious to proceed, they were unaware at that time of Cronin's state of mind. In March 1961 Cronin instructed his agent, Cyrus Brooks of A.M. Heath & Company Ltd, to suspend proceedings:

> Since my letter... I have had some further reflections, I won't as yet say misgivings, on the present situation of the proposed TV production of *Adventures in Two Worlds*, and it does seem that I am going in blind to a project which is likely to involve me in immense publicity and this in a very personal manner. In other words, unless some sort of stipulations are made I shall be almost completely in the hands of the scriptwriter and the producer. Now I am sure Mr Cross has the best intentions, but I have suffered a good deal in my life from misrepresentation and I have no wish to be put in an invidious position at this late stage of the game, and for a sum which is to me quite trivial...

Cronin had a disingenuous habit of ultimately relating all moral and personal issues to money, implying almost that he might be prepared to be misrepresented if the price was right, as happened with some of his plots at the hands of Hollywood moguls. But, for all his protestations, he was not uninterested:

> I am afraid, therefore, that in any contract which I sign there must be a clause giving me advance access to the script with powers to alter or veto any part thereof. I would also want to know how my name is going to be used in the production, if at all, or whether a substitute name, such as Finlay Hyslop, which I used in the *Black Bag* series, would be preferred...[3]

In the light of subsequent problems between Cronin and the BBC, this stipulation by Cronin is important. He went on:

> I don't want you to imagine that I am in any way obstructing what is and could be a most interesting and successful project, I only want to ensure contractually that it is treated in a thoroughly sympathetic manner, one which could not possibly prove offensive to me... [4]

By now the BBC was caught up in the idea, and they acted quickly. Donald Wilson suggested an immediate meeting in Switzerland with Cronin himself and John Keir Cross, one of the most experienced BBC scriptwriters. As it happened, it was a bad time for Cronin:

> I feel sure that our conferences will present no difficulties whatsoever and that any questions in my mind will be easily resolved. My one regret, and it is a serious one, is that owing to domestic circumstances I shall be debarred from offering you the hospitality which normally I should have been most happy to extend to you and Mr Cross. My mother is acutely ill, dying in fact, and we are altogether deranged domestically... however, I am sure you will be very comfortable at either the Hotel National or the Schweizerhof, where I will place myself at your disposal when you telephone me...[5]

The meeting was fruitful, so much so that Robin Lowe, who had been the original driving force of the project, thought it was a done deal and became anxious that Graham Stewart's part should not be overlooked. He wrote to Donald Wilson on 12th April 1961:

> I am glad that you have had a talk with Graham Stewart and I sincerely hope that you will be able to make use of his services in connection with the forthcoming Cronin series… Please bear in mind that without his energetic promotional efforts this series might never have seen the light…

He went on to point out that Stewart's initial outlay on options and the pilot script would never be recouped, owing to the meagre rewards from his share of the royalties, and he expressed the hope that the BBC might be able to improve his lot. At first the BBC was reluctant to recognize the full extent of Stewart's contribution, either with fees or credits, but Cronin's intervention possibly helped his cause. He wrote to Cyrus Brooks:

> I do not profess to understand the inner workings of the BBC nor do I imagine I have much influence with that organization. Certainly they have made their dealings with me unnecessarily complex. Nevertheless, I do feel that Graham Stewart deserves every credit for realizing, and furthering, the TV possibilities of the Finlay series and I think it would be most unjust if he failed to receive credit for this…[6]

Cronin knew full well the weight his influence would carry, even at such an early stage, and so after much deliberation and not without some misgivings among BBC personnel, it was agreed that the credits would read "Created by A.J. Cronin" followed by "The series produced by arrangement with Graham Stewart".

With the contractual business settled, the BBC finally turned to the programme itself. At that point, nobody appears to have had a clear idea of how to approach the task. Donald Wilson seemed to be fixated with Cronin's own life as a doctor, but Cronin wrote to him on 8th May 1961:

> The idea that the series should be autobiographical was never mine – this was the form in which the project was originally submitted to me. You may remember also that at our discussion in Lucerne I proposed that the central character should be named Finlay Hyslop already identified with the *Black Bag* series. Your present suggestion that… Finlay Hyslop should be transposed to Alec Finlay is therefore perfectly acceptable to me…

It was not until the script editor Donald Bull became involved that things began to take shape. In August Bull put his thoughts on paper:

> The idea of a series about a young Scottish doctor's first struggles, set (I take it) in the Twenties, is obviously first-rate. Cronin's writings seem to me pulp of a fairly low order, sentimental and insipid for the most part, and containing every cliché known to medical science, and written in a style reminiscent of Hollywood background music... a direct translation of such material is out of key with the alertness of present-day audiences. This does not affect the value of the idea, but puts a heavy burden on the scriptwriters, who have to make the stuff acceptable...
>
> There seems to me no question that these tales must be in their period; all the relations between doctor and patient have so utterly changed in the last thirty-five years, also the technical methods of treatment. Anyway, the period is to me three-quarters of their charm... but it does imply a finite extension to the series. One can't go on for ever in an illimitable past tense, when time itself is always hurrying on...[7]

Donald Bull stressed the point that scriptwriters should not be limited by Cronin's texts. At the same time Donald Wilson was adamant that while Cronin's original stories should form the basis of the plots and the continuity of Finlay's life, it was important that each episode should stand as a fifty-three-minute play in its own right. By March 1962, however, no acceptable scripts had yet been produced. The problem seemed to be finding the right balance between the source material and scriptwriters' input. John Keir Cross finally came to the conclusion that the only way forward was to stick closely to the original Cronin material. In a letter to John Bull he explained: "Whichever way I turn I come back to old Cronin. Read anything he writes and the instantaneous impact is effective. His cunning as a writer lies in a kind of alchemy of sheer immediacy. It doesn't bear analysis – but it isn't meant to. For all the rubbish that we, in our bones, know the stuff ought to be, it still commands a worldwide sale..."[8] That approach worked, and within a few months, on 16th August 1962, the BBC was ready to launch the first twelve-episode series of *Dr Finlay's Casebook*. The programme was introduced by its now famous theme tune: the march from *A Little Suite* by the British composer Trevor Duncan.

Still remembered by millions, this piece of music became as integral a part of the *Dr Finlay* experience as the central characters themselves: the indomitable trio of Finlay, played by Bill Simpson, Dr Cameron, the senior partner at the Arden House practice, played by Andrew Cruickshank, and Janet, their housekeeper and receptionist, played by Barbara Mullen. All three appeared in every one of the one hundred and ninety-one episodes. The programme attracted audiences of up to twelve million, and since then medical dramas, both British-made and American imports, have never been absent from our screens.

The BBC provided the basic ingredients of inspired casting and consistently good scripts, but underpinning those essentials was the unique synthesis of reality and morality that Cronin never failed to deliver in his writing. Cameron, in the first of the *Adventures in Two Worlds* stories, explains to his young assistant on Finlay's first acquaintance with the practice in Tannochbrae:

> I can't be hard on a poor devil like that. It's a weakness I never seem to get over. He owes me for his wife's last confinement – he'll never pay it. But I'll get out the gig, drive seven miles, see the child, drive seven miles back. And what do you think I'll mark against him in the book? One and six – if I don't forget. And what does it matter if I do forget? He'll never pay me a red bawbee in any case...⁹

Cronin's own performance as a doctor fell far short of the ideal personified in Finlay and Cameron, whose non-denominational Christian actions were endowed with the certainty and moral force of the Ten Commandments. At times the Hippocratic oath plays second fiddle to the almost pastoral requirements of the two doctors, who dispense integrity as well as medicine from their practice at Arden House. It is to the credit of the scriptwriters that by design or accident they were able to maintain that unique Cronin chemistry.

By October 1962 Donald Wilson, sure of *Dr Finlay*'s future, informed Cronin that he was ready to exercise his option for more programmes. Cronin was delighted, replying:

> I had felt, not only from press notices, but from my Scottish relations (a highly critical lot) that the programmes had gone well. I therefore

congratulate you on getting such good scripts and I trust that the new
series will be in the same vein, getting over the personality of the doctor
and holding the line between humour and sentiment. If you do this I
am sure you will have a permanent winner on your hands…[10]

His one reservation was that, according to his relations in Scotland,
there were not enough outdoor shots, the last thing struggling
BBC programme-makers, constrained by the high costs of outdoor
filming, wanted to hear.

Wilson was keen for Cronin's continued close association with
Finlay, even suggesting, in early 1963, a serial for the *Radio Times*.
Cronin was happy to cooperate, but foresaw a potential problem:

> I do fear that some of the proposals… are not really feasible… as regards
> the serial I don't think Mr Williams realizes how much he would have
> to pay… my serials usually go to *Woman's Own*, and for the last they
> paid me 7,000 guineas. I am quite positive *Radio Times* would never
> go to that figure…[11]

Wilson was also forgetting that Cronin was still actively writing,
and that early in 1963 he was halfway through his "new Scottish
novel", *A Song of Sixpence*, and "knee deep in heather and enjoying every minute of it".[12]

By the end of 1963 Donald Wilson had been replaced at the BBC
by Andrew Osborn, who had achieved great success with *Maigret*,
a detective series based on the stories of Georges Simenon – a
benchmark in television history. Osborn, like Wilson, was eager for
Cronin to be involved with the fourth series, a suggestion originally
made by Cronin himself, yet Cronin seemed unenthusiastic when
pressed on the point:

> I was most pleased… to know that you are proposing to give your at-
> tention to the fourth series… from what I have heard of your work on
> *Maigret* I feel sure that Finlay will welcome your intervention on his
> behalf… I am also flattered that you should recollect my suggestion
> that I might produce some ideas if I happened to be free… but I fear
> that my situation here in Bermuda, where I shall remain till the end of
> February, does preclude any idea of our cooperation…[13]

Cronin continued by pointing out that he had not seen any of the episodes and was, therefore, totally out of touch, contradicting an earlier claim that he was being kept informed by his observant Scottish relatives and also through press notices. This detail is important in understanding what happened next. Only three months later, with the BBC gearing up for a fifth series, Cronin, quite unexpectedly, withheld his permission. In a letter to Cyrus Brooks, he said:

> The financial question apart, I feel very strongly that this programme has been so far removed from my control and the original characters which I created and which are identified in the public mind with me are now so involved in episodes which I have neither approved nor seen, that in my own interests I am not disposed to sanction a further exploitation of my work... I think it wise to end on this note rather than run it on to a lingering death...[14]

Not for the first time in his life Cronin's behaviour is inexplicable and full of contradictions. One moment he professes that he is out of touch, the next he makes a judgement on the quality of programmes he has never seen. More to the point, Cronin had always possessed the right of veto over all Finlay scripts, but had steadfastly refused to become involved. In trying to understand his decision it is difficult to see beyond his capricious temperament, his sense of the dramatic and his love of the grand gesture.

On this occasion, any possibility of a swift retraction was thwarted by a newspaper article, dated 18th March. Within two days of the appearance of the article, Cyrus Brooks received the author's instructions:

> My attention has been drawn to an article in the *Daily Mail* in which someone by the name of Harry Green, photographed, visually at least, in the attitude of Rodin's *Thinker*, has assumed the right to pontificate on *Dr Finlay*, raising such abysmal issues as Finlay's girlfriend, announcing that the programme will run for ever, and taking the liberty of revealing my full private address in Switzerland. To what purpose this was permitted by the BBC I can only guess, but I wish you to protest to whoever is responsible on my behalf in the strongest possible terms,

and to indicate that it has served to confirm my decision not to permit the continuation of the series...[15]

Before blasting the BBC, Cronin had not even taken the trouble to discover the identity of the pontificator in question. The offending piece, by columnist Olga Franklin, was in fact an interview with Harry Green, one of the first scriptwriters of the *Finlay* series. Green had been responsible with Donald Bull for more episodes than any other writer, twenty-two in all, and ironically was the recipient of Cronin's earlier praise. In the interview, Green was simply explaining some of the reasons for the programme's success: realistic flavour, deliberate absence of glamour, exotic diseases and romance – Finlay did not even have a girlfriend – which Green rightly felt should be left to programmes such as *Dr Kildare*. Those sentiments, encapsulating the essence of Cronin's Scottish stories, might have been expressed by Cronin himself. The article ended in a resounding tribute to Cronin, with Green forecasting further success for the series and suggesting there was no reason why *Dr Finlay* shouldn't go on for ever, as there was never a shortage of stories real or fictional dealing with illness. Green's views merely confirmed what programme-makers had discovered early in the development of television: that the viewing public could not get enough of medical drama. As for the Rodin pose, the picture shows Green with his chin in his right hand, two fingers distorting his upper lip, smoking a cigarette. It is not even remotely reminiscent of Rodin's statue.

Andrew Osborn tried to get the author to change his mind, but Cronin offered a stout defence:

Alas, my decision on *Dr Finlay* remains unchanged... since the first series, taken directly from my book, it is apparent that the incidents have progressively departed from the sympathetic feeling and essential humanity of my original conception... some indeed are so "cooked up" they could be regarded as absurd. This I know from having read the scripts and also from reliable informants who have viewed the programme. As such it represents a decline which, with its fundamental association with my name, I must regard as damaging, the more so since I have an important novel due for publication in July. The popularity rating to which you refer and which in my view is due to the excellent beginnings of *Finlay*, will undoubtedly lapse as the stories continue to slump – already letters commenting on the deterioration of the material are appearing in the press. Of course, there is always a wide audience of sorts for soap opera, but who wants this?

Financial considerations are not of ultimate importance, but weighing the above arguments against the inadequate monetary return... I cannot see any immediate future... the poor fellow has been badly handled and needs a rest...[16]

If the level of fees was an issue, it is surprising that in view of the BBC's dependency on the series there was no sudden offer of an increase, even though their hands may have been tied by the Labour government's prices and incomes policy – at a time of economic difficulty in Britain companies were only allowed to increase wages and prices by predetermined percentages. In 1965 Cronin was paid £325 per programme, or £8,450 for a series. This was increased to £9,100 in 1967 and £9,750 in 1968. In addition, he received money from overseas sales of the programme. In 1965, for instance, Cronin accepted fifteen per cent per episode for a three-year licence in Sweden, Norway, Holland, Belgium and Denmark, which amounted to over £6,000. To put these figures in perspective, at that time, a four-bedroom house on a typical British housing estate could be bought for around £4,500. By his own admission Cronin could command 7,000 guineas (£7,350) for a serial in a well-known magazine, but for that he had the burden of writing the story, unlike the Finlay series, where his input was non-existent. As for his indispensability, there was no solution, except to hope that the scripts suited him, since he was simply not prepared to write anything, nor was he inclined to involve himself in the detail of the programmes.

Yet, miraculously, within six weeks the BBC were authorized to proceed with a further thirteen episodes. Cronin wrote to Cyrus Brooks to explain his change of heart:

I have had such a flood of really touching letters from people to whom *Dr Finlay* means so much, old people, people incapacitated by illness, and others "shut in" for different reasons, to whom the series is eagerly looked forward to as the one big thing of the week, that I really haven't the heart to disappoint them. So I may as well go the whole way and agree to twenty-six new episodes to begin in January 1965. Now, will you please arrange for a press release to this effect so that disappointed viewers can have their minds set at rest and, incidentally, relieve the burden on our local postman...[17]

An article in the *Glasgow Evening Times* claims that it was Graham Stewart's intervention during a BBC-sponsored visit to Cronin in Switzerland that turned the tide, but there is no record in the Corporation's files to that effect. Whatever triggered the volte-face, Cronin's previous accommodating attitude was completely restored. Within a few weeks of agreeing the programme's continuation, he was presented with eight storylines and commented that "the outlines are much more in the genre of my original conception and seem as if they really happened in a small Scottish village such as Tannochbrae. Please stress this with Osborn and express the hope that further stories will continue in this vein, giving also as much outdoor Scottish background as possible..."[18]

Dr Finlay went from strength to strength, and there were no further problems of this kind. The final episode, 'The Burgess Ticket', was screened on 3rd January 1971. Both the BBC and Cronin agreed it had finally run its course.

The relationship between fact and fiction had always been highly complicated in Cronin's work, and this is particularly true where *Dr Finlay* is concerned. Over the years, there has been disagreement as to the identity of the fictional town of Tannochbrae. In its promotional material, the Arden House hotel in the town of Callander stakes its claim to be the television home of Dr Finlay and Dr Cameron. This is also supported by a 2003 online review by Laurence Marcus, which states that Tannochbrae was "in reality the Perthshire village of Callander". The same article offers further insight into the making of the series with references to recollections by David Nisbet:

> My parents bought a small hotel in 1962... the Lake Hotel, which was pretty much a family-run business... The BBC started *Dr Finlay's Casebook* in 1962 and needed a base to work from. Tannochbrae was in fact Callander and the Lake Hotel was isolated and central enough to make it ideal. They used the hotel for many years...[19]

Bill Simpson, who played Dr Finlay, was married there and bought a house, known as Tamavoid, in the area. The other main stars, Andrew Cruickshank and Barbara Mullen, stayed for short periods in the hotel, along with Marius Goring, Alexandra Bastedo, James Ellis, Tracy Reed, Anthony Valentine and many more. David Nisbet, whose parents owned the hotel, was then a young man, and he recalls taking part in some of the episodes:

> One part was running down the hill in front of Bill's house (The Legacy Episode). One other part was running out of the way when Dr Finlay's car came flying along the road… my dad had to do a lot of car driving, but you never saw his face… all the outdoor stuff was shot around the Trossachs and the indoor stuff was in a studio in London…[20]

The fact that Callander was used to film some of the episodes does not qualify the town to claim exclusive ownership of the fictional Tannochbrae. According to a Wikipedia entry, whose accuracy may be doubtful:

> Although it is widely documented that the original series was filmed in the town of Callander in Stirling, the very first six episodes were filmed in Tannoch Drive, Milngavie, where the fictional Arden House was situated on the right-hand side as one approaches Tannoch Loch. It was the ducks on that loch that formed part of the opening sequence of the programme. The preceding shot is of the Red Bridge over the River Teith. In one of the first episodes, Dr Finlay crashed his old Bullnose Morris into the wall of Arden House – and that was not in the script. Another episode, filming at night along Mugdock Road, found the local policeman somewhat inebriated on his bicycle in a scene with Dr Snoddy…[21]

Elizabeth Robertson, in an article entitled 'Dr Finlay of Tannochbrae', which appeared in the *Scots Magazine* in November 1996, vainly attempts to discover a connection between Finlay and Cronin: "Medical directories and medical registers of the time offer no clues." She then tries her hand at identifying the exact location of Tannochbrae: "Tarbet seems the most likely, having the railway station mentioned in Cronin's book, and a former doctor's house and its environs which tally precisely with

Cronin's description of Arden House. But proving the connection is another matter…"

In his very interesting and informative book *On Call with Dr Finlay*, Peter Haining claims that Finlay's and Cronin's experiences were one and the same. He is convinced that Cronin worked for two years as an assistant to the real-life counterpart of Dr Cameron: "It was in 1921 that fate brought him to the West Highlands and the little town (to which he gave the fictitious name of Tannochbrae)… During his two years in the practice, the young Cronin came to realize that Cameron was really a rather sentimental old man…"[22] The truth is that Cronin was never a GP in his native Scotland. As we have seen in an earlier chapter, in 1921 he was in Treherbert, South Wales, his first appointment in general practice, before he moved to Tredegar, where he stayed for only three years.

Possibly the best clue to the real location of Tannochbrae is in the first story of *Adventures in Two Worlds*, in which a patient of Dr Cameron, Lachlan Mackenzie, walks from Inverbeg to Tannochbrae, a distance of seven miles. This helps to pinpoint roughly the area Cronin had in mind when he wrote the stories. Tarbet (Elizabeth Robertson's choice) is north of Inverbeg, which rules it out since, in reaching Inverbeg from Tannochbrae, Dr Finlay recalls seeing the lights of Darrock (Alexandria) on his right and the "amorphous bulk of the Ardfillan [Helensburgh] Hills on his left".[23] This means that Tannochbrae must have been south of Inverbeg, possibly close to the small town of Arden at the southern end of Loch Lomond. Such a location, close to his home town, would be entirely plausible. Indeed, most of the stories that make up *Adventures of a Black Bag* are set in Levenford – the real-life Dumbarton.

The popularity of *Dr Finlay's Casebook*, of course, was not confined to television. On 11th November 1968, well before the end of its television run, the BBC received confirmation from Christopher Mann Ltd, acting on Cronin's behalf, that they were prepared to authorize a radio series of thirteen episodes, each episode not to exceed thirty minutes at a fee of thirty guineas (£31.50) per episode. As with the television series, it grew beyond the initial run into six series and over a hundred episodes, ending in February 1975. In August 1976, a new series began, producing another forty episodes and ending in 1978. BBC Radio 7 broadcast twenty episodes in 2003 and have repeated them since then.

In the 1960s and 1970s it seemed that the BBC could not get enough of Cronin. In November 1969, the Current Affairs Department in Glasgow was anxious to film a series of television interviews about his life. Unfortunately, Cronin was forced to decline because of his wife's illness. Letters flew back and forth, the BBC hoping to catch him during one of his planned visits to Scotland. Whether he ever had any serious intention of visiting Scotland at that time is difficult to say, but he always managed to find a good reason for postponing. On 19th August 1970 he replied to Matthew Spicer, the current-affairs producer:

> It is true that I would be pleased to give you the interview you seek, and at the same time to make a brief tour of Scotland, all this provided a suitable date could be arranged. I had hoped to go to Edinburgh in September but I am afraid this is now definitely out, and instead I shall be going to my house in Bermuda... There is no question of your coming to Switzerland since I wish to couple the interview with a visit to the little west Highland farmhouse attic where I sat up at nights writing *Hatter's Castle* by candle light...[24]

The BBC's determination never wavered until in April 1971 Cronin dealt the project a final blow. Nan wrote, on his behalf:

> Dr Cronin... has asked me to point out quite definitely that anything he would do for Scottish BBC would be in the nature of radio interviews – NOT television. There has obviously been a misunderstanding on this score, and should radio be unacceptable, Dr Cronin would be quite prepared to drop the whole affair...[25]

The initial letters concerning the project stated quite clearly that the BBC wanted television interviews.

Twenty years after the BBC decided to mothball *Dr Finlay's Casebook*, Alistair Moffat, then the Director of Programmes at Scottish Television, acquired the television rights with a view to reviving the series. The team he chose rejected the idea of a rerun and opted in favour of an updated version of the post-war period drama. Far removed from the quaint, almost twee atmosphere of the 1960s production, Major John Finlay returns from the war to an austere Britain and a much-changed medical practice. The aim to create a greater sense of realism was helped by shooting the entire series on location – in Auchtermuchty, the new Tannochbrae – as opposed to studio sets. Technology had also moved on, allowing the use of film, not video, giving actors greater freedom and flexibility in their performances. *Dr Finlay* ran for twenty-seven episodes from March 1993 to December 1996, starring a new trio – David Rintoul, Ian Bannen and Annette Crosbie. It owed much of its success to the Cronin brand. Time and place may have changed, but the humanitarian ethos that was the inspiration for Finlay proved to be as relevant in the 1990s as it had been three decades earlier.

Finlay and Cameron represented, in any period, an aspirational ideal for the medical profession, exhibiting an appealing blend of enthusiasm, dedication and professionalism. *Dr Finlay* occupied a niche at the popular end of television entertainment, creating public awareness of Cronin's name that lives on to this day, although it hardly added anything to his reputation as a writer. It might even have played a part in diminishing the value of his charming stories, which should have been equally commemorated alongside his more famous full-length novels. Nevertheless, Andrew, Cronin's youngest son, affirms that his father always spoke with pride of the *Dr Finlay* programmes, believing that they could satisfy the need for intelligent and serious television. There are few who would deny that he achieved that aim.

Cronin eventually found the inspiration for what turned out to be his last novel, *The Minstrel Boy*, as he was about to leave to spend the winter of 1973–74 in Bermuda with Nan. His first thoughts were for Gollancz, not Heinemann. He wrote to John Bush on 9th November 1973: "For some months past I have been nursing a wonderful idea for my next novel, and if I can only force myself to my desk and away from many other duties and pleasures, I might have something interesting to tell you when we return in the Spring…" On 8th May 1974, he reported to Bush:

> My new novel… is finished. I know always when I have written a good novel and when an indifferent one. *The Minstrel Boy* I regard as probably the best I have ever written… Now, your last letter to me was rather

tepid. Naturally, I will send you a copy of the typescript – these are being duplicated now – but if you are averse, under present circumstances, to promoting the book, please let me know soon and I will have my agents deal with the entire affair.

Then, in a handwritten postscript, he added: "Statements just in by morning post. You do sell me well! So why not again! The new one is smashing!"

Bush was equally enthusiastic, describing the book as "marvellous reading". And so, now nearly eighty years old, Cronin was back with Victor Gollancz Ltd, and happy to be so. Bush paid a visit to Cronin's Swiss retreat to talk about his novel on 12th October 1974. Cronin's state of mind at the time was affected by a recent burglary (or the threat of a burglary) at Champ-Riond, whose precise date cannot be established. The break-in hit Cronin hard – not just the possibility of losing his beloved art collection, but also the concern over his and Nan's safety. Vincent, who was a regular visitor, doubted if his father ever fully recovered from the shock of that event, and recalled an occasion when, some years later, they had become so guarded about visitors that he himself was almost denied entry to the house. Therefore John Bush, who was meeting him for the first time, possibly did not see the real Cronin.

The purpose of Bush's visit was to make changes to the text of *The Minstrel Boy*. Cronin had used his own name in the book, which rendered it unacceptable as a work of fiction. In his article for the *Glasgow Evening Times*, written after Cronin's death, Alasdair Marshall wrote:

John Bush, long-time editor of Cronin's work, had flown to see the Maister ... with some trepidation... Changes were absolutely necessary. But Cronin, as Bush well knew, was a prickly customer, a hard bargainer and a stickler for detail... a difficult man to deal with where books were concerned...

That description was certainly true of Cronin at an earlier time in his career, as is illustrated by his constant wrangles with Victor Gollancz, but by the time John Bush took over the reins Cronin was a declining force and could no longer argue or dictate editorial terms from a position of strength. Also, Cronin was no fool.

He knew well enough that it was not in his interest to rock the boat. His letters to John Bush indicate that not only did he fully accept the new situation, but that he was desperate to return to Gollancz. As head of one of Britain's major publishing houses, whose reputation and future no longer depended on Cronin, Bush was firmly in a position of command.

His letter to Cronin, dated 30th September 1974, less than two weeks before his intended visit, explains his plan:

> What I should very much like to do is to come and see you with my copy of the typescript, bringing with me a page or two of notes where I think a very small amount of rewriting will make the whole book read as continuous fiction... basically one has to change your name and other names of real people (and a couple, I think it is, of your book titles plus one address) and substitute fictional names...

In the same letter, Bush detailed the terms of the agreement between Gollancz and Cronin, which he proposed changing from the last book, *The Judas Tree*. He assured Cronin: "Your total earnings... will be larger on the basis I have outlined." In relation to the textual and contractual changes, Bush was firm and unambiguous. There was no question of negotiation, as there had been in the good old days when Cronin and Victor Gollancz went toe to toe – take it or leave it. Cronin was, therefore, fully briefed as to Bush's intentions well before his visit, and would have had no reason to make trouble. He had great respect for the younger man's reputation in the publishing world and was keen to right the wrong of his earlier transfer to Heinemann.

Several months after Bush's visit, Graham Lord, the literary editor of the *Sunday Express*, tried to interview Cronin in connection with the publication of *The Minstrel Boy*. He used John Bush as an intermediary, but even by April 1975 Champ-Riond had not returned to normality: "The house is still fearfully upset and we still have the workmen doing repair jobs, so I simply can't have reporters coming now." But while he was still nervous for his safety, his famous fighting spirit had returned. Always suspicious of the press, his notorious wariness emerged as he added: "In any case, I think the *Sunday Express* is a bad bet, and I don't even want to be rung up. I could be sensationally misquoted and misrepresented over a phone call. So try and put Mr Lord off, tactfully."[26]

However, Cronin's interfering nature soon emerged again. Once the dust had settled over the break-in, he started badgering John Bush over promotional matters:

> I thought you might like to see the jacket of my novel in the American edition. I like it very much indeed and think it is exactly the right thing, tasteful and distinguished. I don't know why you took me out of the familiar yellow jacket – to my mind it cheapens the book and I am sure it will certainly create a bad impression with the critics…[27]

Cronin will have had his reasons for his enthusiastic appraisal of the book as his best, but these are not apparent to a critical eye. The promise of change offered by the modern style of *A Pocketful of Rye* had not come to fruition. Cronin's last book turned out to be a quaint, old-fashioned, nostalgic romance resembling a curate's egg, not helped by some stilted expressions which would have been passé in the 1930s.

The story is narrated by Alec Shannon. He recounts the life of a former school friend of his – a young, handsome priest with a marvellous singing voice called Desmonde Fitzgerald – who wins the coveted Golden Chalice in a singing contest in Rome while still a seminary student. Desmonde's first clerical posting takes him to rural Ireland, where he is befriended by the worldly Canon Daly. He is soon introduced to the rich, cultured and attractive Geraldine Donovan, the lady of the manor and the munificent benefactress of the local church. A one-time opera singer herself, their relationship blossoms, and she secretly falls in love with him. The arrival of her niece, Claire, spells trouble, as Desmonde falls victim to her charms. She becomes pregnant, and Desmonde is obliged to marry her and relinquish the priesthood. Desmonde and Claire move to Dublin, where she deserts him, taking the child with her. Desmonde starts a new life singing in a pub, where he is spotted by an American impresario who signs him up for a glittering international singing career. He becomes a famous and wealthy singer, but as a result of a spiritual experience in California he is determined to return to a life of service for humanity. Aided by his friend Alec Shannon, he visits Switzerland to see his daughter, who has been brought up by the redoubtable Madame Donovan, and spends some time with Alec Shannon, his wife and secretary, Miss Radleigh, before embarking on a missionary-type career in India.

The Kilbarrack episode, which deals with the newly ordained cleric's introduction to the reality of a lowly parish priest's duties, is arguably the most convincing part of the book. The atmosphere of rural Catholic Ireland in the early part of the twentieth century is absorbing and believable but, like the rest of the book, it founders on a surfeit of cloying pretentiousness. David Moray in *The Judas Tree* unashamedly, though with a certain justification, paraded his wealth, artistic expertise and refined taste on the world stage, but in *The Minstrel Boy* Cronin regales his readers with a gratuitous double dose, well beyond the experience of ordinary mortals, through the activities of Geraldine Donovan and Alec Shannon. They move in an exclusive world of specially imported Ceylon tea, soft-toned Blüthner pianos, Italian marbles, private boxes at La Scala, shopping in Burlington Arcade and Bond Street and lunch at Claridge's – nothing actually germane to the plot. Also, mingled with Cronin's grandiose refinements is a prescriptive measure of familiar Cronin themes and landscapes: the time-worn rags-to-riches story and sectarian strife of his childhood, in a different wrapper admittedly, but recognizable from *The Green Years*, *Adventures in Two Worlds*, *A Song of Sixpence* and *The Judas Tree*.

Revisiting old ground, Cronin takes another swipe at Catholic orthodoxy, on this occasion the hypocrisy of the Church in relation to the celibacy of the priesthood. Canon Daly, the rascally priest, ever the practical, down-to-earth cleric, on first hearing that Desmonde has got Claire pregnant, thunders: "Oh God Almighty. Holy Mary and all the Saints... but what's to do in the parish... if this gets abroad 'twill mak' all the devils in hell dance the fandango!"[28] Then, distraught at the prospect of losing his beloved priest, he rails: "It's the fault of these auld bastards at the Vatican, wrapped in cobwebs, and sae bluidy holy they think it's a sin tae haud their article when they go and make their watter. 'Tis no' only unjust, 'tis bloody unreasonable and agin nature..."[29]

Cronin's lifelong devotion to the Catholic faith, emphatically affirmed by both his sons, made his earlier challenge to orthodoxy in *The Keys of the Kingdom* difficult to explain. But the challenge in *The Minstrel Boy* – celibacy of the priesthood and the practicalities of platonic relations between men and women, whether priests or non-clerics – exists for a different and more personal reason, and is germane, as we now know, to his own life. As far as Cronin's characters are concerned the position is clear. Desmonde makes one mistake, comes to regret it and, given a second chance, lives a life of sexual abstinence, despite temptation. Geraldine Donovan, on the other hand, has a happy, unconsummated five-year marriage – "since my love for him had nothing of sex in it".[30] Whether her purity would have remained intact had Desmonde made advances towards her can only be surmised, but Canon Daly seemed in no doubt that "she was completely gone on you, head over heels".[31]

The discussion of platonic relations in *The Minstrel Boy* is central to Cronin's purpose, since the significance of the book is not its literary merit but its autobiographical content. The book can be regarded as a forerunner of his unfinished, unpublished autobiography, written the following year. Approaching eighty, suddenly Cronin appeared to have no qualms about revealing the most intimate, personal details of his life, scarcely veiled in fiction – remarkable for a man who had gone to such lengths to maintain his privacy. In the American version of the book – *Desmonde* – Cronin's own name even appears in the text.

Critics who had searched for hints of autobiography in Cronin's previous novels, even resorting to invention, were, incredibly, blind to the significance of the fictional relationship between Alec Shannon (Cronin) and Miss Radleigh (Nan). Cronin's position on platonic relationships seems to be that they are possible, provided both parties are of one mind – a position he explores in the novel. The timescale of the book is 1930s Britain, the London flat is Eldon Road and Mellington is Sullington Court in Sussex. The first mention of the Shannon-Radleigh relationship refers to how indispensable she was: "What a splendid girl, so good, so trustworthy and hard working. What on earth would I do without her?"[32] Within a few pages that feeling deepens: "We looked at one another. I knew then that I loved her and that she loved me. I had the overwhelming desire to take her in my arms."[33] Then Alec questions Miss Radleigh on the subject of love, and she replies: "Certainly, I love you and I am happy to think that you love me. But we both have the virtue, the strength, the decency, quite apart from our love of dear Mum, to remain chaste."[34] This is a clear reference to a platonic relationship. At that time in Sussex, Nan was employed as nurse to Andrew.

Time is then suspended as the narrative moves from England to Switzerland, with Alec's wife confined to a home and he and Miss Radleigh living together. Nobody seems to have aged, yet in reality the jump in time is all of forty years. When they are visited by a priest who rather nosily enquires if they are still keeping the faith, Alec's reply is: "Well, Father, the battlements have suffered some crushing attacks, but the portcullis remains unbreached. Often when we have spent a long heavenly day together and at night we must go to our separate rooms, I drool a little."[35] The priest responds: "Yes, it is hard. But you will both be better for it. And love the more..."[36]

Cronin's depression as a result of the break-in at his home did not last long. Within a few months, his letters to John Bush were upbeat again:

> Yours of 10th April, so very full of good news, is most cheering on a beastly wet Swiss day. I am especially pleased that Christina Foyle [owner of the Foyles bookshop on Charing Cross Road in London] has selected *The Minstrel Boy*. And of course the good Tanner [of the New English Library] is absolutely red hot on Cronin. It was particularly clever to get *Adventures in Two Worlds* away from Corgi. When all the excitement over *The Minstrel Boy* fades (and I hope this will be a long time ahead) I wonder if it would be possible for you to recover my two novels, *A Song of Sixpence* and *A Pocketful of Rye*, not only from Heinemann, but from an obscure paperback firm he sold the rights to.[37]

With a keen eye on his own affairs, and to the future, even at the age of eighty, the tone of that letter has a ring of optimism.

The period following the burglary at his Swiss home coincided with a series of unusual requests and assertions made by Cronin regarding money matters and his personal affairs. On 11th March 1975 he wrote to John Bush:

> I've had a word from my friend Mr Tanner of the N.E.L., who briefs me on all my books, that he has paid £11,000 for *The Minstrel Boy*. As

> I am having frightful expense over the damage caused by the break-in could you let me have my share now, under clause 7 of our contract. Sorry to bother you, but I could use the money...

Had this been a one-off request, the result of finding himself temporarily short of ready cash to meet that unexpected bill, it might have been understandable, but it was anything but an isolated incident, as we shall see below.

Two more books appear in Gollancz's lists after *The Minstrel Boy*, but they were reprints of stories that had previously appeared in serialized form. *The Lady with Carnations*, published by Gollancz in 1976, first appeared in print in *Good Housekeeping* in 1935, while *Gracie Lindsay*, serialized in Britain in 1949, was released in book form in 1978. Early in 1976, in a discussion with John Bush over the terms for *Lady with Carnations*, Cronin's response to Bush's offer had an almost pathetic ring to it:

> Finally, I see your point in asking me to take a smaller advance, but I would beg of you to put on another £500 and make it £8,000, still considerably less than your normal advance. After having put my three sons through the best schools and universities I now have four grandsons demanding the same treatment...[38]

It was clear at this stage that he had no further ambitions to write another full-length novel. In a letter he sent to Bush later that year, he mentioned the "vast amount of unpublished material which is not only excellent but probably more saleable than my 'literary' novels'", with a view to reviving it for publication. But he added a cautionary note: "I hope however, John, that you are not looking for something cheap."[39]

Gracie Lindsay, Cronin's final book, came up for publication in 1977. On 5th July, he wrote to John Bush:

> Your letter of 30th June made me feel low! I thought of the good old days when dear Victor received my manuscripts with affection, a word of praise and a cheque for £30,000... well, I accept your terms. I need the money, such as it is, although the day must soon dawn when I shall sell my beautiful house, with all its beautiful contents, and retire to a seaside hotel, or possibly a neighbouring monastery that takes paying

guests... the contract is enclosed herewith. You may alter it to express the terms you have now imposed...

Two weeks later he wrote again: "Now that we have agreed the price on *Gracie* may I have your cheque for £9,000 now. I really need the money."

A month later, he realized that he had sent all he possessed of *Gracie Lindsay* to John Bush and had nothing to offer his American publishers. He wrote to Bush:

This is from the agony column... can you possibly help me!!! Send me a proof or in desperation a fresh typescript of the novel, for which I must of course pay! I have two grandsons going to Georgetown Prep at my behest – this costs the earth and I will have to start getting the fee money quick... don't want to mortgage my house or start selling my antiques...[40]

In November, he accepted John Bush's suggestion to sell *Gracie Lindsay* in Canada on his behalf, and added: "Let me know if you get an advance. I am frightfully hard up... do try and send me some cash soon."[41] His final letter to Bush – undated – ended with some wistfulness and a little humour:

Your cheque was a short time "on the way" but I knew it would arrive, and here it is today, Thank you! And now that you have *Gracie* please give her a good start on publication. I think this a fine novel, absolutely true to the main character, and indeed to all the characters. The end scene between the two old men and the little boy is perfect. So too the background of the little Scottish town... incidentally, your phrase "it is on the way" has been adopted by my household from whom, of course, nothing is sacred... "cheque still on the way, dad?" And when I shout for my morning coffee "It's on the way, dad!"... and again, "Hasn't the bloody postman come?" "He's on the way, dad!" Pacifyingly "I think I hear his motor bike!"... well John, once again, do your best for *Gracie* – I think she deserves it! The book is tender, but never sentimental...

Cronin's erratic behaviour about money had also an effect on his domestic life. In a letter to Andrew and Anne in America in the late Seventies he pleaded poverty, saying that he did "not have a curdy to his name". At the end of his life his income from royalties had naturally reduced, and though the extravagant Cronin lifestyle was running down – he no longer bought paintings – it appears he took it upon himself to educate his grandchildren. There was also the cost of his wife's full-time care in Canada. The extent of his assets and investments was never revealed, but however extensive they were, he would probably have been loath to touch them for the day-to-day running of his affairs.

Cronin made one last attempt at a full-length novel, *The New Governess*, which was half-completed by January 1976. It was a story of a young woman employed to teach "a fat little bastard of seven" in a beautiful old country house. Unfortunately, nothing of it remains. Cronin described his feelings about it in a letter to John Bush of Gollancz:

> The early chapters are very, very good and funny. But then, one after another, they are all more or less "converted" – horrible word – reconciled to the old vicar, and adjusted to their neighbours, who have previously shunned them. This is where I jibbed, as they hymned in the little old country church! I threw the manuscript from me, crying aloud "Cronin, this is not you!" I thought of *The Stars Look Down* and *Hatter's Castle* and said, "Ditch it"… Now I must close, with a heightened heart. Nan, who approves of my assassination of *The New Governess*, is calling me to tea. Here it is a heavenly day; fresh and magnificent sunshine. I am happy for I have been true to myself and to James Brodie – the mad hatter of Levenford…[42]

It is, perhaps, fitting that he should end over forty years of authorship where he started, in the company of, possibly, his most famous character, James Brodie, who launched him on a remarkable literary career.

Cronin's discussions with John Bush over plans to breathe life into some of his unpublished works came to nothing.

Cronin's relationship with Nan was brought into sharp focus again in April 1976 with the making of his will. To his wife he bequeathed the entire fund he had created with Credit Suisse Lucerne for her care and her nursing and medical treatment. Champ-Riond, his

Swiss home, was left to his three children, along with paintings, furniture and other capital assets. In fact, Patrick, the middle son, decided to take over the house and moved his family to Switzerland soon after his father died, and continued to live there until his own death in 2007. But perhaps the most startling clause in the will concerned the provision for Nan. It reads:

> I give, devise and bequeath to my ever most faithful secretary-house-keeper and most dear friend Margaret Jennings who for more than thirty years has devoted herself exclusively to my family and myself with unsparing loyalty and courage in many emergencies and who by devotion, care and tenderness in my later years when, broken by the loss of my beloved wife, quite alone, homeless and afflicted by infirmities, she has been more to me than any daughter, the sum of two million Swiss francs free of tax. Also the following articles from the contents of my villa…

It went on to list various articles of furniture and five paintings. It ended with the following clause:

> If any beneficiary under this will should protest the conditions or provisions therein he or she will forfeit all of his or her benefit therein. I enjoin my sons to love one another, to remember, if they wish, their mother and myself in their prayers and to be grateful not only for their portions of my estate but for the many benefits bestowed upon them during my lifetime: their safe and protected upbringing, costly educa-tion, marriage and other gifts…

Considering there were only five major beneficiaries – one of whom, his wife, was probably in no condition to understand – this clause is interesting. Cronin seemed to be anticipating a reaction from his sons that Nan had been left too much. Cronin, of course, was a formidable man, used to having his way, and so the peremptory clarity of his wishes is, perhaps, not surprising. According to the *Glasgow Evening Times*, Cronin's oldest son, Vincent, said many years later that Nan's share in the will had caused no friction in the family, and that she remained a close friend.[43] The will, amount-ing to £11,082, was finally published in 1984, leading the same newspaper to refer to "The Mystery of the Missing Millions".[44]

Andrew Cruickshank, the actor who played Dr Cameron in *Dr Finlay's Casebook* – whom the paper claimed had become a friend of Cronin – is quoted as saying: "Do not be misled by that will. If you dig deep enough you'll find that he spread his money in many places but not in this country… the man was worth millions from his books, films and *Dr Finlay*."[45]

Tongues may have wagged about the generosity of the settlement on Nan, but the significance of the document reaches far beyond any petty monetary consideration. The public affirmation of his feelings for Nan, especially the words "she has been more to me than any daughter", does not go as far as Alec Shannon's expression of love in *The Minstrel Boy*, but it is clear that Cronin wanted the world to know the depth of his feelings for her.

The drawing of the will seemed to act as a catalyst for further confessions. With his financial affairs in order, Cronin next set about the truth of his life. Only two months after signing the document he embarked on a remarkably candid account of his marriage, and his love for two other women: Nan and Mary, the girl he had met in Treherbert during the early days of his medical career. The unpublished 1976 autobiographical piece is at times brutal in its frankness, calling into question the sentence in the will that he had been "broken by the loss of [his] beloved wife".

It is a highly significant though perplexing document. Because of its brevity and the fact that it reveals only one specific aspect of his life, it cannot be considered a full autobiography. Yet the work is complete. Cronin wrote "THE END" at the point when he and his wife moved back to New Canaan from a holiday spent at their French property La Meluitza in about 1954. As far as his last work was concerned, he had finished what he set out to achieve. He had said all he wanted to say.

The document is not without its inconsistencies, mistakes and lapses of memory, but its importance lies in the fact that Cronin felt compelled to write it. If he never intended to publish it, who was it intended for? Certainly not his family. When they were made aware of its existence, they steadfastly disputed its contents. Nor was it intended for Nan, who at the time was the one person alive who knew the truth. That leaves Cronin himself, possibly looking for a catharsis for his troubled soul in the written word instead of a simple confession to God in accordance with orthodox Catholic practice.

Cronin was eighty when he chose to reveal the intimate details of his life. Knowing the kind of man he was, precise almost to the point of pedantry, it is impossible to regard the document as the half-remembered jottings of a tired old man. Further proof that he was fully compos mentis at the time can be found in letters to John Bush of Gollancz, which contain typical passages of humour and evidence of his native shrewdness in trying circumstances.

Vincent, Cronin's eldest son, a successful writer himself, said of the last years of his father's life:

> I saw him regularly, at least once a year, and I know he got tremendous enjoyment out of life... my mother's illness had a shattering effect on him. If he suffered from a little depression from time to time, it would be entirely natural...

Andrew, his youngest son, said that when he visited his father in 1980 his health was fine, "except once when he pointed out an old woman up a tree holding a baby girl". By that time he was eighty-four and nearing the end of his life, but still he saw the humour in his "senior moments". Andrew would tease him by suggesting that he should go to Sweden and write a book about Finland. At the end of his life, Cronin's thoughts, perhaps naturally, turned to his religious beliefs, and he confided to Andrew, after much contemplation: "I don't know if it's true – I just like to believe what I believe." Many interpretations can be put on that remark, but what cannot be denied is that his mind was still active at that time.

Cronin died on 6th January 1981 in Glion. The funeral took place at the Notre Dame Catholic Church in Vevey, and he is buried, with his wife, at the cemetery of La Tour-de-Peilz in Montreux. On his headstone is the simple inscription "Author of The Keys of the Kingdom". In an obituary of his father, Vincent wrote:

> In old age, when he could no longer go out, the centre of his week was *Le Jour du Seigneur*, televised Mass usually from a French country village which reminded him of his boyhood. And in his last years Providence brought him a friend, an English priest of his own age of exceptional vigour, Canon John Roger Fox of the abbey of Saint Maurice, resident in Switzerland and jocularly referred to as chaplain

to the Anglosaxophones (Montreux has a jazz festival). Soon after being admitted to the Valmont clinic, where Rilke had spent his last days, he received the sacrament of the anointing of the sick from Canon Fox, after which the mental anguish induced by sclerosis yielded to a serenity remarked on by all. He who had done much to bring Christ's message to the nations died peacefully on the feast of the Epiphany. [46]

Many other obituaries hastened to condense his life into a shortened account of part fact and part fiction. The dwindling impact of his books over the previous twenty years or so may explain why the confessional content of his last book went unnoticed. Cronin's name hit the headlines again, at least in Scotland, when the *Glasgow Evening Times* ran a series on famous Scotsmen on 4th, 5th and 6th December 1984. Alasdair Marshall, who wrote the articles, had not missed the significance of the ending of *The Minstrel Boy*. He wrote:

> The key to the relationship between The Lonely Millionaire and his faithful secretary/companion, Margaret Jennings, lies in Cronin's last published novel... Margaret Jennings, the only person alive who could describe their relationship, now lives in the United States...

After his father's death, Andrew and his wife, Anne, invited Nan to share their home and lives together. She went with them, firstly to Potomac and then to their house in Germantown, which had five acres of lawn and woods, perfect for Nan and her three cats. She became part of the family and the community, attending church every Sunday, shopping at the local grocery store and preparing family meals. In 1997, aged eighty-five, though in good health, but by now too frail to travel, she chose to move into a nursing home close to Andrew's home rather than be alone while Andrew and Anne spent their winters in The Bahamas. In the last few years of her life she lost her lucidity, and she died peacefully in her sleep, from old age, on 29th May 2004. At the private ceremony at Monocacy Cemetery in Beallsville, Maryland, Alexandra Cronin read the first two stanzas of Keats's *Endymion*, one of Nan's favourite works. Buried with her was some of the real truth of Cronin's life and character. She told Andrew and Anne that the years she spent with them were the happiest of her life. If only Marshall had pursued the story when memories were relatively fresh, how different our understanding of Cronin might have been.

The paper accorded Cronin three full spreads on successive days. Apart from a few factual errors in the first two articles, the research was conducted meticulously and two of the articles were very good reportage. The final article, however, dealing with Cronin's last period, abused even the most generous interpretation of journalistic licence. Far too sensational, and too liberally strewn with innuendo, it gives a false impression of the man and of his last years. Marshall paints a picture of a "sad", "lonely", "prickly", "difficult", "embittered" old man who had lost interest in life, was out of touch with the world and whose writing power was on the wane. One of those claims is defensible – Cronin was no longer a literary force – but there is not much evidence to support the rest of them. The information contained in Marshall's last article was based on interviews with John Bush and his wife Sheila, who – as mentioned in a previous chapter – worked for Victor Gollancz from 1936 to 1954 and met Cronin in America in 1951 while she was on a book-hunting mission. In fact, in the light of subsequent discoveries, the headlines of the article in question, proclaiming that Cronin was a "prisoner" in his own home and "trapped by success", miss the essential truth of his life. However he appeared to the outside world, it is now clear that for the last ten years of his life Cronin was living happily with Nan, the one person he had always wanted to share his life with. They had loved one another for almost forty years and, after May's admission to a nursing home, they at last found the intimate exclusiveness they had long sought.

After his death in 1981, Cronin's books sold very slowly. Of all the paperback publishers only the New English Library were interested in relaunching the best of his works. Their editorial Director, Nick Webb, commented to Jane Blackstock of Victor Gollancz Ltd on 8th February 1982 that:

> A.J. Cronin alas now sells very slowly. I fear he may be becoming rather gentle and old-fashioned for the current paperback market, but nevertheless we are determined to have another go at reanimating his backlist sales…

They did a magnificent job, continuing to bring out impressions of Cronin's greatest works well into the 1990s. Sadly, soon after the New English Library discontinued publishing, Cronin's books became unavailable in British bookstores. In the last few years, however, several paperback reissues have appeared on the market: *The Keys of the Kingdom* was published by Hodder and Stoughton in 2007 in their "Great Reads" series; *Hatter's Castle* and *The Citadel* were republished by Read Books in 2008 and 2009 respectively; 'Vigil in the Night' and 'The Valorous Years' were republished by A.J. Cornell Publications, New York; and an omnibus edition of *Dr Finlay's Casebook* was published by Birlinn, the Edinburgh publisher, in 2010. Birlinn is also hoping to reissue other famous Cronin titles in the near future, possibly starting with *The Stars Look Down*.

Today Cronin is survived only by his youngest son, Andrew. Andrew moved to America in 1939, where he remained. In 1959, while in the final year of his engineering-management degree at Yale University, he took American citizenship, later working for NASA and becoming head of government programmes for Control Data Corporation. He now lives in Maryland. He married Anne Payne in 1962, and they have three children: Mark, born in 1963, an attorney; Chris, born in 1964, a surgeon; and Alexandra, born in 1973, a writer. Andrew and Anne have four grandchildren.

Patrick, Cronin's second son, passed away in January 2007. He attended Princeton University aged sixteen, but interrupted his studies in 1943 to enlist in the Royal Canadian Air Force, training as a tail gunner, transferring to the British Army between 1945 and 1947. He returned to Princeton after the war, then attended McGill University Medical School, gaining an MD in 1953 and his MRCP in 1955, before becoming Dean of the Faculty of Medicine there from 1972 to 1977. He took Canadian citizenship, and in 1954 married Sis Robinson. The couple had three children: David, Diana and Daphne, who in turn produced five grandchildren. A noted health consultant, Patrick was widely recognized for his work in the developing countries, initiating exchange programmes between McGill and local doctors in Nairobi, Kenya and student-exchange programmes with Kenya, Kuwait, Bahrain, Qatar, Ethiopia, Pakistan and Tunisia. In 1976 he was asked by the Aga Khan to help set up a teaching hospital in Karachi, and worked in an advisory capacity for the next fifteen years in the construction and operation of hospitals in Africa and Pakistan. As mentioned before, he and his family moved into Champ-Riond after the death of his father. Towards the end of his life he suffered, like his mother, from Alzheimer's, and he died of pneumonia in 2007 in Territet, Switzerland.

Vincent, Cronin's oldest son, sadly died in January 2011. He was educated at Ampleforth College in Yorkshire before moving to America, where he attended Harvard at the age of sixteen, and then Trinity College, Oxford. During the Second World War he served as a lieutenant in the Rifle Brigade in the British Army. After the war he moved to Hyde Park Square, London, to begin his career as a full-time writer. He is best known for his biographies of Napoleon, Louis XIV and Catherine the Great, and his books on the Renaissance. Fluent in French, he also translated several works into English, most notably *Towards a New Democracy* by Valéry Giscard d'Estaing. He received the W.H. Heinemann Award in 1955 and a Rockefeller Foundation Award in 1958, and was a Fellow of the Royal Society of Literature. In 1949 he married Chantal de Rolland, who survives him with two sons and three daughters: Sylvelie, James, Dauphine, Luan and Natalie.

They settled in Normandy, in the Manoir de Brion, an ancient Benedictine priory of the abbey of Mont Saint-Michel, founded in the twelfth century. Of Cronin's three sons, only Vincent remained a devout Catholic throughout his life.

Postscript

Cronin was that rare being who succeeded at everything he attempted. He possessed the Midas touch. He was notably silent on the subject of his own standing in the literary world. Of the writers he admired, J.B. Priestley and Robert Louis Stevenson stood out. Vincent, his oldest son, felt that his father, late in life, finally accepted his peers' judgement of him as a middlebrow writer. But however Cronin is viewed, the move to America was certainly a watershed in his life. Rejecting his homeland, he possibly turned his back on greatness. In Britain he tapped a rich vein of literary inspiration that left a legacy of considerable distinction, but was never recaptured.

Was it America itself, the march of time or simply disillusion that transformed his ambition? There was no shortage of problems in the rapid realignment of post-war society. Injustice and inhumanity, once the lifeblood of his work, did not suddenly disappear, only the passion to expose them.

From humble beginnings he became a legend in his own lifetime, selling over twenty million books and illuminating the lives of countless readers worldwide. His global following remained loyal, even after the Second World War when, arguably, he was no longer at his best as a novelist.

Explaining Cronin's appeal is not easy. Did he accidentally or instinctively stumble on a truth, so basic and universal as to serve him faithfully in a career spanning fifty years? His secret was perhaps a conviction that he once shared with his author son, Vincent – that characters were more important than plot in a novel. Despite obvious differences between peoples of the world, the hopes, fears and expectations of human beings everywhere are essentially the same. His stories, therefore – never circumscribed geographically or temporally, to any significant degree – were easily understood at any time and in any corner of the globe, and so had universal appeal. Thus Victorian Dumbarton could just as readily have been a small town in Illinois, Sleescale might have been a mining town in Poland and Drineffy a village in a Pyrenean valley.

Cronin wrote simply. He detested that mentality that considers obscurity a synonym for genius. Novelists, he maintained, should represent life, not as it should be but as it is – and he sought to do that all his life. It was this realism that underpinned his greatness. His inspiration came from the great nineteenth-century novelists whose longevity he hoped to equal.

Cronin's conventional appearance belied a mind riven with regret and uncertainty, and a lifestyle some might consider bizarre. Reconciling his faith and his domestic life demanded a high price, and only his determined self-control guaranteed equilibrium and order. Perversely, it was his faith, Catholicism, that was the root of the problem. While it provided the bedrock of family unity, the circumstances of his marriage threatened its existence. The Catholic position on marriage – a covenant for life that cannot be severed – was probably more strictly applied in 1921, when he married, than today. Even so, his entrapment on the grounds of a bogus pregnancy, if that was the case, might have constituted grounds for an annulment, had he acted immediately. But it is clear that his own sense of guilt and shame rendered such an option unthinkable, and by the time he met Nan, some sixteen years into his marriage, even the remotest possibility had disappeared. His obligation to his wife and his clear duty to his children were by his own admission merely the spiritual values that kept them together, undoubtedly powerful but hardly fulfilling.

If the conclusion reached earlier in this book concerning the platonic relationship with Mary, his first love, followed by Nan, is believed, then essentially Cronin sentenced himself and them to a life of celibacy. Mary's solution to a thwarted love and its implied celibacy was to remove herself from temptation by entering a convent, and so withdraw from life altogether. Nan's feelings on the subject are not known, unless her views were those expressed by Miss Radleigh in *The Minstrel Boy*, who professes that virtue, strength and decency have kept her chaste. Cronin, from 1937 to the end of his life in 1981, faced the temptation of almost daily contact with the second woman he loved, when a simple solution was available. His position is far from clear. There seems to be an implied contradiction between the strict acceptance of one aspect of his faith – his self-enforced denial of a physical relationship with the woman he loved – and his almost peremptory freedom to question other ideological issues. Despite the obvious clarity in Catholic dogma, nothing prevented him developing his own brand of belief. Long before he went public with the irreverent messages in *The Keys of the Kingdom*, he challenged orthodoxy: "Let every man look into his own heart – that is the old, the best presentation of religion – provided that man shudders at what he finds therein!"[1] Even at that point in his life, in 1933, he was already questioning the rigid rules of the self-condemnatory forms of religion such as Catholicism, against the implied benefits of other faiths that allow greater flexibility in personal and emotional interpretation. En route to California on a TWA flight to meet David Selznick to discuss plans for a film, he once observed that "drifting through the clear sky in this great plane, the world beneath seems very small with men like tiny ants. If we look like that to God, it's awfully hard to tell a bishop from a bricklayer."[2]

The obvious question, therefore, is, given his predilection for rebellion, why did he cling so tenaciously to a faith that denied him so much – even happiness itself? There is no obvious source of spiritual strength to explain it: no single religious experience, no near-death revelation, no miracle cure or blinding conversion. He wrote that by accepting discomfort and pain, disappointment and misfortune, we survive the supreme test of submission to the will of God. Materially, for most of his life, he lacked nothing, but his spiritual denial may have been the route to his personal salvation.

Cronin's life defies understanding without reference to religion. As a child of a mixed Protestant-Catholic union it might be argued that his religious awareness started in the womb, transferring to an emotional roller-coaster immediately after birth. The day-to-day effects of sectarianism on his early life and personality have always been grossly exaggerated, but there is no doubt that out of that atmosphere of intolerance there emerged the deep humanitarian convictions that characterized his life and writings.

The unseen hand that moves from one generation to the next left a rich legacy. His immigrant roots were a source of both spiritual strength and inspiration, a reference point in his journey. Significantly, it was that background that gave his life direction.

The Cronin family from Northern Ireland settled in a minority religious community in western Scotland. Their unquestioning adherence to Catholicism, a way of life as necessary as breathing is to survival, was strengthened by the inherent challenge of their exclusion from the host population. Their conviction, nourished by his mother's conversion, was easily and almost unavoidably absorbed by Cronin's fertile mind. His personality, therefore, the man he became, was defined by his past and is understandable only in relation to it. Cronin's forebears married for life, shunned progressive beliefs, clinging to the dignity of family life in the evolution of human culture. Cronin could not escape that inheritance.

It is easy to forget that Cronin was a Victorian, who lived through the reigns of four monarchs, times of immense social change, which saw class barriers swept aside and human rights enshrined in law. Today, technology dominates contemporary society, whereas the first half of the twentieth century was defined by extremes of political philosophy – socialism and fascism – neither enthusiastically religious.

It may be the case that only his priest at the very end of his life will have gained an understanding of the price he paid for his faith, and hence a real insight into his nature, but hopefully some truths of this very remarkable man may also have emerged from this book. The iniquities of an unjust society and Man's inhumanity to Man permeate his writings, while the constant search for reality and the truth behind a man's time on earth led him inevitably to a belief in the fundamental goodness of the human spirit. He believed passionately in the existence of the human soul, the mainspring of truthfulness, accessed through the confessional, either circumscribed by the strict practices of the Catholic Church or privately with an honest conviction drawn from a pure heart. Hopefully, at the end, like his favourite character, Father Francis Chisholm, who said in a quiet voice, "I shall render an account of my life to God", Cronin was ready to face the judgement of a long and varied life.

Categorizing him is impossible. He belonged everywhere and nowhere. He was as much at home in the grim industrialized world of his native Clydeside, or in the fast-food joints of Mid-Western America, as in the hushed portals of the university library or the opulence of European art galleries. Ultimately self-assured, yet never free of doubt, he became a man of the world.

Acknowledgements

I owe most to my publisher for his vision in looking beyond mere commercial gain in publishing this book. Cronin was always too influential a writer not to warrant a biography. Alessandro Gallenzi appreciated that, and his enthusiasm never wavered. Next, I must thank Alex Middleton for his editing prowess.

Cronin's two sons, Vincent and Andrew, endured my persistent questioning with admirable patience and were encouraging from start to finish. Alexandra, Andrew's daughter, produced photographs with a conjuror's skill, and much valuable comment. Without them there would have been no book. I am also grateful to John Donnelly, a very distant relative of the Cronin family, still living in the Vale of Leven, who helped fill in a few gaps in the Cronin family history.

I must express my gratitude to the Orion Publishing Group for allowing me access to the Gollancz files, especially to Frances Wollen, who organized everything for me. Also I would like to thank Paul Stark, her assistant, and Jim Palma of Littlehampton Book Services in Durrington, West Sussex.

I found all librarians and archivists a special breed. Without exception they were interested and helpful and never failed to find time for me: thanks to Michael Davis of Helensburgh, Nerys Tunnicliffe of the Mitchell Library, Glasgow, Keiron Hawkins of Treorchy, Dr Caroline Cradock of the Scottish Catholic Archives – and finally special thanks to Graham Hopner of the Dumbarton Library, whose interest in Cronin has helped many a student and researcher. I wish him a happy retirement.

Mr John Stoer, headmaster of St Aloysius' College, Glasgow, and Mr John McCabe, the Alumni Director, offered me great encouragement in the early days of the project and provided me with valuable information. I cannot thank them enough.

I also owe a debt of gratitude to Robert Michel, a first-rate researcher, who "nosed" out information in weeks that would have taken me months. Also, for their help and encouragement, on my first trip to Scotland, I want to thank three inhabitants of Cardross – Margaret Ferguson, Jeanette Scobie and Mr Phillips – Patricia Drayton of Helensburgh and Miss C.M. Murray of Dumbarton. Also in Dumbarton, two gentlemen deserve my thanks, one an ex-newspaper editor, whose names I have unfortunately lost, but who, if they read this book, will recognize themselves in it.

I must commend the work of Dale Salwak, who trod the path before me, from a different viewpoint perhaps, but with such expertise that his work was and is invaluable to any researcher interested in Cronin.

Finally, I would like to express my gratitude to every person and organization who gave permission to quote in this book. Many thanks to the National Library of Scotland (abbreviated NLS), the BBC Written Archives, and to the Random House Group for the use of the Heinemann files. Special thanks to the Orion Publishing Group for the use of letters between Cronin and Victor Gollancz and John Bush and excerpts from the biographical works of Ruth Dudley Edwards and Sheila Hodges.

As for my own family, my wife, Gwyneth, acted as a sounding board and spell-checker throughout, while my younger son, Jez, researched several aspects of Cronin's life and, together with my elder son Tim, combined to provide computer advice when my technical expertise and temper were on the point of failing.

Notes and References

CUE-TITLES

AB   Foot, Michael, *Aneurin Bevan 1945–1960* (London: Davis-
            Poynter, 1973)

ABIN   Jones, Gareth, *The Aneurin Bevan Inheritance: the story of
            the Nevill Hall and District NHS Trust* (Abertillery: Old
            Bakehouse Press, 1998)

ACP   St John, John, *William Heinemann: A Century of Publishing,
            1890–1990* (London: Heinemann, 1990)

AJC   Salwak, Dale, *AJ Cronin* (Boston: Twayne Publishers, 1985)

AJCRG   Salwak, Dale, *AJ Cronin: A Reference Guide* (Boston: G.K.
            Hall, 1982)

C76   Cronin's 1976 unpublished autobiography. National Library
            of Scotland Archives.

CUD   Cronin's unpublished documents. National Library of Scotland
            Archives.

CWS   Bruce, Maurice, *The Coming of the Welfare State* (London:
            B.T. Batsford, 1971)

EP   Bartley, Paula, *Emmeline Pankhurst* (London: Routledge, 2002)

GOLL   Hodges, Sheila, *Gollancz: The Story of a Publishing House,
            1928–1978* (London: Gollancz, 1978)

HMRS   Blaikie, Andrew, 'Household Mobility in Rural Scotland:
            The Impact of the Poor Law after 1845', *Scottish Tradition /
            International Review of Scottish Studies*, 27 (2002), pp. 23–41

IMS   Handley, J.E., *The Irish in Modern Scotland* (Cork: Cork
            University Press, 1947)

MAWB   Paley, Ruth, *My Ancestor Was a Bastard: A Family His-
            torian's Guide to Sources for Illegitimacy in England and
            Wales* (London: Society of Genealogists Enterprises Ltd,
            2004)

MMMN	Davies, Horton, *A Mirror of the Ministry in Modern Novels* (Oxford: Oxford University Press, 1959)
OCDF	Haining, Peter, *On Call with Doctor Finlay* (London: Boxtree, 1994)
VG	Dudley Edwards, Ruth, *Victor Gollancz: A Biography* (London: Gollancz, 1987)

EDITIONS OF CRONIN'S BOOKS CITED

HC	*Hatter's Castle* (London: New English Library, 1970)
TL	*Three Loves* (London: Gollancz, 1932)
GC	*Grand Canary* (London: New English Library, 1977)
SLD	*The Stars Look Down* (London: New English Library, 1984)
CIT	*The Citadel* (London: New English Library, 1983)
KK	*The Keys of the Kingdom* (London: New English Library, 1988)
GY	*The Green Years* (London: Gollancz, 1949)
SW	*Shannon's Way* (London: New English Library, 1983)
SG	*The Spanish Gardener* (London: Gollancz, 1950)
ATW	*Adventures in Two Worlds* (London: New English Library, 1987)
BTP	*Beyond This Place* (New York: Little, Brown, 1953)
CT	*Crusader's Tomb* (London: New English Library, 1977)
NL	*The Northern Light* (London: Gollancz, 1958)
JT	*The Judas Tree* (New York: Little, Brown, 1961)
SS	*A Song of Sixpence* (London: The Book Club, 1965)
PR	*A Pocketful of Rye* (London: Heinemann, 1969)
MB	*The Minstrel Boy* (London: New English Library, 1977)

INTRODUCTION

1.   *AJCRG*, p. xiv.
2.   *Ibid.*
3.   Reid, Alexander, 'The Story of a Best-Seller', 1953. The Cronin File, Dumbarton Library.
4.   Speech by Mrs Cronin to an unknown American audience in about 1946, courtesy of Vincent Cronin. In it the quotation was wrongly credited to Walt Whitman. In fact it comes from George Borrow's 'Lavengro': "There's the wind on the heath, brother; if I could only feel that, I would gladly live for ever..."
5.   Speech by Cronin to an unknown literary gathering, probably in London pre-1939.
6.   *Ibid.*
7.   http://www.robertburns.org.uk/lochlomond_dumbarton.htm
8.   Matthew, 22:14.

CHAPTER ONE

1.   I am indebted to John Donnelly, a very distant relative of Cronin, for this information.
2.   'Famous People'. Cronin file, Dumbarton Library. I have been unable to verify the date.
3.   *TL*, p. 15.
4.   *IMS*, p. 136. By kind permission of Cork University Press.
5.   *CUD.*
6.   *SS*, p. 23.
7.   *Ibid.* p. 27.
8.   *Ibid.* pp. 23–24.
9.   *MAWB*, pp. 20–21.
10.   *Ibid.*
11.   *Ibid.*
12.   *EP*, p. 3.
13.   *AJC*, p. 3.
14.   *SS*, p. 11.
15.   *AJC*, p. 3.
16.   Again I am indebted to John Donnelly for this information.
17.   *IMS.*
18.   A disparaging term to describe poor Irish immigrants who came over to pick potatoes in western Scotland in the nineteenth and twentieth centuries.
19.   *AJC*, pp. 3–4.
20.   'The Man Behind Dr Finlay'. Cronin file, Dumbarton Library.
21.   'Dr Cronin's Casebook'. www.helensburgh-heritage.co.uk.
22.   *SS*, p. 55.
23.   *Ibid.* p. 56.
24.   *Ibid.* p. 62.
25.   *Ibid.* p. 56.

26. *Ibid.*
27. *Ibid.*
28. From an unidentified newspaper article dated 19th August 1964. Cronin file, Dumbarton Library.
29. *SS*, pp. 111–12.
30. Glasgow City Corporation Archives.
31. 'Dr Cronin's Casebook'. www.helensburgh-heritage.co.uk.
32. Article in Cronin file, Dumbarton Library.
33. *MAWB*, pp. 6–7.
34. 'Alleged Cruelty of Victorian Fathers'. *British Weekly*, 16th July 1931.
35. Extract of a letter to Dumbarton Football Club, 18th April 1972.
36. *AJC*, p. 4.
37. Dumbarton Academy School Prize Lists. Cronin file, Dumbarton Library.
38. From an unidentified newspaper article dated 19th August 1964. Cronin file, Dumbarton Library.
39. *AJC*, p. 3.
40. *HMRS*.
41. *British Labour Statistics 1886–1968* (London: HMSO, 1971).
42. *GY*, p. 34.
43. St Aloysius' College records.

CHAPTER TWO

1. *Helensburgh Advertiser*, 14th August 1964.
2. *CWS*, p. 248.
3. From the obituary of Father Francis Cronin. By kind permission of the Scottish Catholic Archives, Edinburgh.
4. I am indebted to John Donnelly for this information.
5. *CUD*.
6. *Ibid.*
7. From school notebooks, NLS Archives.
8. *Current Biography Yearbook 1942* (New York, H.W. Wilson Company, 1943), p. 167.
9. *CUD*.
10. Cronin's time at the Rotunda Hospital could not be verified from medical directories.
11. *AJC*, p. 10.
12. *AJCRG*, pp. 24–42.
13. *JT*, p. 99.
14. *Ibid*. p. 100.
15. *Ibid*. p. 139.
16. *Ibid*. p. 156.
17. *CIT*, p. 17.
18. *ABIN*, p. 11.
19. From minutes of the Tredegar Medical Aid Society held in the Gwent Record Office, Cwmbran, Wales.
20. *ABIN*, p. 13.
21. *Ibid.*
22. Speech by Mrs Cronin, op. cit.

23. *Ibid.*
24. Speech by Cronin, op. cit.
25. *CUD.*
26. Letter to Victor Gollancz, 11th November 1931. Orion archives.
27. *Ibid.*

CHAPTER THREE

1. *ATW*, p. 222.
2. From an unidentified article entitled 'The Stars Look Down'. Cronin file, Dumbarton Library.
3. *Ibid.*
4. *Ibid.*
5. *GOLL*, p. 70.
6. *ATW*, p. 229.
7. Speech by Cronin, op. cit.
8. Letter to Victor Gollancz, 9th November 1930, Orion archives.
9. *VG*, pp. 142–59.
10. *Ibid.* pp. 172–73.
11. *Ibid.*
12. *Ibid.* p. 190.
13. *GOLL*, p. 69.
14. *Ibid.* p. 57.
15. 'Alleged Cruelty of Victorian Fathers', op. cit.
16. *HC*, p. 135.
17. *Ibid.* p. 134.
18. *Ibid.* p. 142.
19. *Ibid.* p. 136.
20. *Ibid.* p. 168.
21. *Ibid.* p. 163.
22. *Ibid.* pp. 40–41.
23. *Ibid.* pp. 419–20.
24. *Ibid.* p. 295.
25. *JT*, p. 145.
26. *PR*, p. 41.
27. Letter from T.J. Pringle to Victor Gollancz, 20th March 1935. Orion archives.
28. Letter from Victor Gollancz to T.J. Pringle, 21st March 1935. Orion archives.
29. Letter to Victor Gollancz, 22nd July 1931. Orion archives.
30. Speech by Cronin, op. cit.
31. Letter to Victor Gollancz, 26th November 1931. Orion archives.
32. Letter to Victor Gollancz, 11th February 1932. Orion archives.
33. *GOLL*, p. 71.
34. Letter to Victor Gollancz, 22nd July 1931. Orion archives.
35. Letter to Victor Gollancz, 1st January 1931. Orion archives.
36. Letter to Victor Gollancz, 26th November 1931. Orion archives.
37. Letter to Victor Gollancz, 8th December 1931. Orion archives.
38. *Ibid.*
39. Letter to Victor Gollancz, 11th December 1931. Orion archives.

40. *VG*, p. 190.
41. Letter to Victor Gollancz, 11th February 1932. Orion archives.
42. *VG*, p. 190.
43. Letter to Victor Gollancz, 11th February 1932. Orion archives.
44. *VG*, p. 171.
45. *Ibid*. p. 338.
46. *Ibid*. p. 191.
47. Letter to Victor Gollancz, 11th February 1932, Orion archives.
48. *Ibid*.
49. *Ibid*.
50. *GOLL*, p. 72.
51. Davenport, Basil, 'Chasing Balloons'. *Saturday Review of Literature*, April 1933.
52. Letter to Victor Gollancz, 11th November 1931, Orion archives.
53. *Ibid*.
54. *Times Literary Supplement*, 25th February 1932.
55. *GC*, p. 177.
56. *Ibid*. p. 222.
57. Letter to Victor Gollancz, 12th September 1932. Orion archives.
58. *Ibid*.
59. *Ibid*.
60. *Ibid*.
61. *Ibid*.
62. Letter to Victor Gollancz, 11th February 1932. Orion archives.
63. *The Observer*, 7th May 1933.
64. *Ibid*.
65. *Ibid*.
66. Letter to Victor Gollancz, 13th May 1933. Orion archives.
67. *Ibid*.
68. From the article 'The Stars Look Down', op. cit.
69. *VG*, p. 168.
70. *Ibid*.
71. Speech by Mrs Cronin, op. cit.

CHAPTER FOUR

1. From the article 'The Stars Look Down', op. cit.
2. *Ibid*.
3. *Ibid*.
4. *Ibid*.
5. *Ibid*.
6. Letter to Victor Gollancz, 11th November 1933. Orion archives.
7. Letter to Victor Gollancz, 21st February 1934. Orion archives.
8. Letter to Sir John Reith from Alice Head. BBC Written Archives.
9. Letter to Charles Siepmann, 18th October 1934. BBC Written Archives.
10. Internal BBC memo dated 31st October 1934. BBC Written Archives.
11. Letter to Richard Lambert, 13th November 1934. BBC Written Archives.
12. Letter to Victor Gollancz, 28th April 1934. Orion archives.
13. From the article 'The Stars Look Down', op. cit.

14. Letter to Victor Gollancz, 29th May 1934. Orion archives.
15. *GOLL*, p. 71.
16. Letter to Victor Gollancz, 22nd July 1934. Orion archives.
17. Letter to Victor Gollancz, 19th June 1935. Orion archives.
18. *Ibid.*
19. From the article 'The Stars Look Down', op. cit.
20. *SLD*, p. 8.
21. *Ibid.* p. 94.
22. *Ibid.* p. 403.
23. *Ibid.* pp. 559–60.
24. From the article 'The Stars Look Down', op. cit.
25. *SLD*, p. 527.
26. *Ibid.* p. 595.
27. *Ibid.* p. 546.
28. *Ibid.* p. 598.
29. From the article 'The Stars Look Down', op. cit.
30. *Ibid.*
31. *CIT*, p. 17.
32. *Ibid.* p. 30.
33. *Ibid.* p. 22.
34. *Ibid.* p. 31.
35. *Ibid.* p. 231.
36. *Ibid.* p. 260.
37. *Ibid.* pp. 331–32
38. *Times Literary Supplement*, 4th August 1937.
39. *AJC*, p. 64.
40. *AB*, p. 103.
41. *Ibid.* p. 105.
42. Letter to Victor Gollancz, 10th February 1937. Orion archives.
43. Letter to Victor Gollancz, 18th May 1937. Orion archives.
44. *ABIN*, p. 22.
45. *AJC*, p. 68.
46. *Daily Mirror*, 19th November 1937. By kind permission of Mirrorpix.
47. Letter to Victor Gollancz, 1st January 1931. Orion archives.
48. Cronin speech to the Press Association, unknown date. Vincent Cronin papers.
49. Statistics supplied by Treorchy Library.
50. *Ibid.*
51. *CIT*, p. 187.
52. McKibbin, Ross, 'Politics and the Medical Hero: A.J. Cronin's *The Citadel*'. *The English Historical Review*, 2008, CXXIII.
53. *Journal of the Society of Occupational Medicine*, 1982, 32.
54. *Journal of Industrial Hygiene*, July 1926, VIII, 7.
55. *GOLL*, p. 59.
56. *VG*, p. 181.
57. *GOLL*, p. 61.
58. *Ibid.* p. 71.
59. C76.
60. *Ibid.*

CHAPTER FIVE

1. Speech by Mrs Cronin, op. cit. Also quoted in *ATW*.
2. *ATW*, p. 271.
3. *Ibid*.
4. Letter to Ray Everitt of Little, Brown, 12th January 1940. NLS.
5. Letter to Alfred McIntyre of Little, Brown, 21st August 1940. NLS.
6. Cronin, Vincent, 'Recollections of a Writer'. *Tablet*, 21st February 1981.
7. Letter to Ray Everitt of Little, Brown, 12th February 1940. NLS.
8. *Ibid*.
9. Letter to Alfred McIntyre of Little, Brown, 7th November 1939. NLS.
10. From the article 'The Stars Look Down', op. cit.
11. Letter to Ray Everitt of Little, Brown, 21st April 1940. NLS.
12. Letter to Ray Everitt of Little, Brown, 16th August 1940. NLS.
13. Letter to Alfred McIntyre, 16th December 1940. NLS.
14. *Daily Mirror*, 3rd July 1933. By kind permission of Mirrorpix.
15. *Ibid*.
16. *Ibid*.
17. *ATW*, p. 283.
18. *America*, 23rd August 1941, p. 549.
19. Letter to Victor Gollancz, 19th December 1941. Orion archives.
20. *MMMN*.
21. From the article 'The Stars Look Down', op. cit.
22. From notes by Father Meinrad B. Koester of Lacrosse, Wisconsin, January 1942. By kind permission of the Georgetown Library, Washington D.C.
23. *Ibid*.
24. *Ibid*.
25. *Ibid*.
26. Letter to Cronin from Bernard Weaver of St Gabriel's Monastery, Boston, Massachusetts, 29th November 1941. By kind permission of the Georgetown Library, Washington D.C.
27. Letter from Bertrand Weaver to Sister Mary Joseph of The Gallery of Living Catholic Authors, 31st October 1942. By kind permission of the Georgetown Library, Washington D.C.
28. Letter to Victor Gollancz, 19th December 1941. Orion archives.
29. *Ibid*.
30. Conversations with the author.
31. Letter to Victor Gollancz, 19th December 1941. Orion archives.
32. *Ibid*.
33. *Current Biography Yearbook 1942*, op. cit., p. 169.
34. Letter to Alfred McIntyre of Little, Brown, 27th November 1944. NLS.
35. Letter to Alfred McIntyre of Little, Brown, 28th May 1943. NLS.
36. From correspondence with Andrew Cronin.
37. From the article 'The Stars Look Down', op. cit.
38. Letter to Alfred McIntyre of Little, Brown, 15th December 1943. NLS.
39. *Ibid*.
40. Letter to Alfred McIntyre of Little, Brown, 22nd January 1944. NLS.
41. Letter to Alfred McIntyre of Little, Brown, 16th March 1944. NLS.

42. From the article 'The Stars Look Down', op. cit.
43. Letter to Victor Gollancz, 14th April 1953. Orion archives.
44. *AJC*, p. 92.
45. Letter to Alfred McIntyre of Little, Brown, 16th August 1944. NLS.
46. Letter to Alfred McIntyre of Little, Brown, 24th August 1944. NLS.
47. Western Union telegram, July 1945, from Nantucket Island.
48. Letter to Alfred McIntyre of Little, Brown, 14th April 1945. NLS.
49. Letter to Alfred McIntyre of Little, Brown, 14th November 1945. NLS.
50. *ATW*, p. 270.
51. Letter to Victor Gollancz, 29th December 1950. Orion archives.
52. From correspondence with Andrew Cronin.
53. *Book Reviews*, 15th November 1952.
54. *Times Literary Supplement*, 23rd October 1933.
55. Letter to Victor Gollancz, 24th September 1949. Orion archives.
56. *SG*, p. 157.
57. *Ibid.*
58. *Ibid.* p. 168.
59. From a letter to Graham Hopner, 24th September 1986. Cronin file, Dumbarton Library.
60. *AJCRG*, p. 101.
61. Letter to Victor Gollancz, 2nd December 1950. Orion archives.
62. Letter to Victor Gollancz, 29th December 1950. Orion archives.
63. *Ibid.*
64. *ATW*, p. 248.
65. Speech by Mrs Cronin, op. cit.
66. *BTP*, p. 80.
67. *Ibid.* p. 81.
68. *Ibid.* p. 224.
69. Letter to Victor Gollancz, 21st December 1954. Orion archives.
70. *Ibid.*
71. Letter to Victor Gollancz, 22nd April 1955. Orion archives.
72. Letter to Victor Gollancz, 10th May 1955. Orion archives.
73. *ATW*, p. 271.
74. Letter to Victor Gollancz, 31st October 1955. Orion archives.
75. *CUD.*
76. Letter to Victor Gollancz, 10th May 1955. Orion archives.
77. Letter from Victor Gollancz to Cronin, 3rd April 1956. Orion archives.
78. *Ibid.*
79. Letter to Victor Gollancz, 6th May 1956. Orion archives.
80. *GOLL*, p. 26.
81. Letter to Victor Gollancz, 11th May 1956. Orion archives.
82. Speech by Mrs Cronin, op. cit.
83. *Ibid.*
84. *Ibid.*

CHAPTER SIX

1. Letter to Victor Gollancz, 4th October 1957. Orion archives.
2. Letter from Victor Gollancz to Cronin, 7th October 1957. Orion archives.

3. *GOLL*, p. 164.
4. Letter to Victor Gollancz, 4th October 1957. Orion archives.
5. Letter to Victor Gollancz, 1st June 1955. Orion archives.
6. Letter from Victor Gollancz to Cronin, 7th October 1957. Orion archives.
7. Letter to Victor Gollancz, 18th December 1957. Orion archives. The Literary Guild, founded in 1927 in America, was a book club similar to the Book of the Month Club, offering discounted deals to readers who were prepared to commit to buying a set number of books over a predetermined time span. Reader's Digest operated more like a magazine, buying the rights to print from the book's publisher or the author and condensing the text considerably in one or more of their editions.
8. Letter to Victor Gollancz, 6th March 1958. Orion archives.
9. Letter to Victor Gollancz, 9th June 1958. Orion archives.
10. Letter from Victor Gollancz to Cronin, 13th June 1958. Orion archives.
11. *Ibid*.
12. Letter to Victor Gollancz, 14th June 1958. Orion archives.
13. *Ibid*.
14. *Chicago Sunday Tribune*, 1st June 1958.
15. *Times Literary Supplement*, 2nd January 1959.
16. *Manchester Guardian*, 2nd December 1958.
17. *NL*, p. 15.
18. From the article 'The Stars Look Down', op. cit.
19. *AJCRG*, p. 149. Review entitled 'Telegram' by Robert Fulford, 7th June 1958.
20. *JT*, p. 8.
21. *VG*, p. 711.
22. *Ibid*.
23. Letter to Victor Gollancz, 20th March 1961. Orion archives.
24. Letter to Victor Gollancz, 25th March 1961. Orion archives.
25. *Times Literary Supplement*, 27th August 1964.
26. Letter to John Bush, 15th April 1975. Orion archives.
27. *VG*, p. 711.
28. *Ibid*. p. 192.
29. *ACP*, pp. 304–5.
30. Letter to Cronin from Paul Zsolnay. Heinemann archive. By kind permission of Random House Group.
31. Letter from Charles Pick to Cronin, 17th March 1964. Heinemann archive.
32. Letter from Charles Pick to Cronin, 23rd March 1964. Heinemann archive.
33. Letter to Charles Pick, 7th December 1964. Heinemann archive.
34. Letter from A.M. Heath to Charles Pick, 14th April 1965. Heinemann archive.
35. Letter to John Bush, 15th April 1975. Orion archives.
36. Letter to John Bush, 20th January 1968. Orion archives.
37. Letter to Charles Pick, 15th April 1969. Heinemann archive.
38. *AJCRG*, p. 158.
39. *PR*, p. 2 and p. 171.
40. *Ibid*. p. 165.

41. *Ibid.* p. 195.
42. Letter to John Bush, 20th January 1968. Orion archives.
43. Letter to Charles Pick, 12th May 1969. Heinemann archive.
44. Letter to Charles Pick, 5th September 1969. Heinemann archive.
45. Letter to John Bush, 18th August 1968. Orion archives.
46. Letter to John Bush, 18th March 1971. Orion archives.
47. Letter to John Bush, 2nd February 1973. Orion archives.
48. Letter to John Bush, 18th March 1971. Orion archives.

CHAPTER SEVEN

1. *Glasgow Evening Times*, article by Alasdair Marshall, 5th December 1984.
2. Letter to Donald Wilson from Robin Lowe, 9th January 1961. BBC Written Archives.
3. Letter to Cyrus Brooks, 13th March 1961. BBC Written Archives.
4. *Ibid.*
5. Letter to Donald Wilson, 20th March 1961. BBC Written Archives.
6. Letter to Cyrus Brooks, 25th June 1961. BBC Written Archives.
7. Letter to Donald Wilson from Donald Bull, 3rd August 1961. BBC Written Archives.
8. *OCDF*, p. 23.
9. *ATW*, p. 42.
10. Letter to Donald Wilson, 13th October 1962. BBC Written Archives.
11. Letter to Donald Wilson, 12th January 1963. BBC Written Archives.
12. *Ibid.*
13. Letter to Andrew Osborn, 22nd December 1963. BBC Written Archives.
14. Letter to Cyrus Brooks, 11th March 1964. BBC Written Archives.
15. Letter to Cyrus Brooks, 20th March 1964. BBC Written Archives.
16. Letter to Andrew Osborn, 30th March 1964. BBC Written Archives.
17. Letter to Cyrus Brooks, 21st May 1964. BBC Written Archives.
18. Letter to Donald Bull, 16th June 1964. BBC Written Archives.
19. www.televisionheaven.co.uk/finlay.htm
20. *Ibid.*
21. '*Dr Finlay's Casebook* (TV&Radio)', accessed 2nd February 2009, Wikipedia.
22. *OCDF*, pp. 14–15.
23. *ATW*, p. 43.
24. Letter to Matthew Spicer, 19th August 1970. BBC Written Archives.
25. Letter to Matthew Spicer, 16th April 1971. BBC Written Archives.
26. Letter to John Bush, 18th April 1975. Orion archives.
27. Letter to John Bush, 22nd March 1975. Orion archives.
28. *MB*, p. 159.
29. *Ibid.* p. 168.
30. *Ibid.* p. 132.
31. *Ibid.* p. 199.
32. *Ibid.* p. 231.
33. *Ibid.* p. 237.
34. *Ibid.* p. 267.

35. *Ibid*. p. 281.
36. *Ibid*.
37. Letter to John Bush, 15th April 1975. Orion archives.
38. Letter to John Bush, 27th February 1976. Orion archives.
39. Letter to John Bush, 10th April 1976. Orion archives.
40. Letter to John Bush, 8th August 1977. Orion archives.
41. Letter to John Bush, 10th November 1977. Orion archives.
42. Letter to John Bush, 29th January 1976. Orion archives.
43. *Glasgow Evening Times*, article by Alasdair Marshall, 4th December 1984.
44. *Glasgow Evening Times*, article by Alasdair Marshall, 16th October 1984.
45. *Ibid*.
46. Cronin, Vincent, 'Recollections of a Writer'. *Tablet*, 21st February 1981.

POSTSCRIPT

1. *Daily Mirror*, 3rd July 1933.
2. *Life*, 21st October 1941.

Index

CRONIN FAMILY TREE

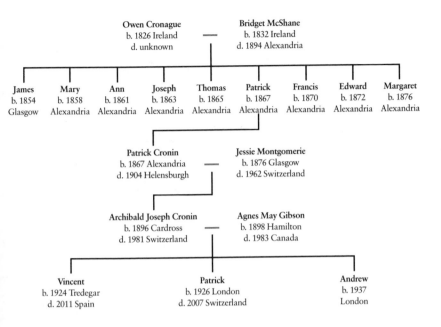

Owen Cronague
b. 1826 Ireland
d. unknown

Bridget McShane
b. 1832 Ireland
d. 1894 Alexandria

James
b. 1854
Glasgow

Mary
b. 1858
Alexandria

Ann
b. 1861
Alexandria

Joseph
b. 1863
Alexandria

Thomas
b. 1865
Alexandria

Patrick
b. 1867
Alexandria

Francis
b. 1870
Alexandria

Edward
b. 1872
Alexandria

Margaret
b. 1876
Alexandria

Patrick Cronin
b. 1867 Alexandria
d. 1904 Helensburgh

Jessie Montgomerie
b. 1876 Glasgow
d. 1962 Switzerland

Archibald Joseph Cronin
b. 1896 Cardross
d. 1981 Switzerland

Agnes May Gibson
b. 1898 Hamilton
d. 1983 Canada

Vincent
b. 1924 Tredegar
d. 2011 Spain

Patrick
b. 1926 London
d. 2007 Switzerland

Andrew
b. 1937
London

MONTGOMERIE FAMILY TREE

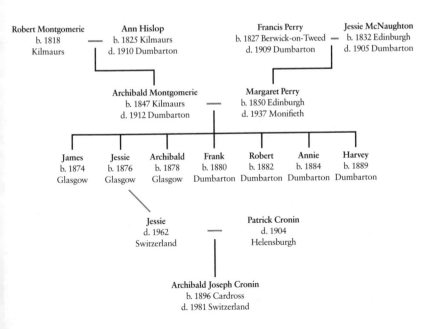

Robert Montgomerie
b. 1818
Kilmaurs

Ann Hislop
b. 1825 Kilmaurs
d. 1910 Dumbarton

Francis Perry
b. 1827 Berwick-on-Tweed
d. 1909 Dumbarton

Jessie McNaughton
b. 1832 Edinburgh
d. 1905 Dumbarton

Archibald Montgomerie
b. 1847 Kilmaurs
d. 1912 Dumbarton

Margaret Perry
b. 1850 Edinburgh
d. 1937 Monifieth

James
b. 1874
Glasgow

Jessie
b. 1876
Glasgow

Archibald
b. 1878
Glasgow

Frank
b. 1880
Dumbarton

Robert
b. 1882
Dumbarton

Annie
b. 1884
Dumbarton

Harvey
b. 1889
Dumbarton

Jessie
d. 1962
Switzerland

Patrick Cronin
d. 1904
Helensburgh

Archibald Joseph Cronin
b. 1896 Cardross
d. 1981 Switzerland